HONG MAI'S
RECORD OF THE LISTENER
AND ITS
SONG DYNASTY CONTEXT

D1520555

SUNY series in Chinese Philosophy and Culture

Roger T. Ames, *editor*

HONG MAI'S
RECORD OF THE LISTENER
AND ITS
SONG DYNASTY CONTEXT

ALISTER DAVID INGLIS

STATE UNIVERSITY OF NEW YORK PRESS

Published by
STATE UNIVERSITY OF NEW YORK PRESS
ALBANY

© 2006 State University of New York

Printed in the United States of America

For information, address
State University of New York Press
194 Washington Avenue, Suite 305, Albany, NY 12210-2384

Production by Kelli Williams
Marketing by Anne M. Valentine

Library of Congress Cataloging-in-Publication Data

Inglis, Alister D., 1963–
  Hong Mai's record of the listener and its Song dynasty context / Alister D. Inglis.
    p. cm. — (SUNY series in Chinese philosophy and culture)
  Includes bibliographical references and index.
  ISBN-13: 978-0-7914-6821-0 (hbk. : alk. paper)
  ISBN-10: 0-7914-6821-6 (hbk. : alk. paper)
  1. Hong, Mai, 1123–1202—Criticism and interpretation   I. Title.   II. Series.
  PL2687.H887Z72 2006
  895.1'308733—dc22   200531413

10 9 8 7 6 5 4 3 2 1

For Emily, Alison, and Myron

Contents

Preface

Although Hong Mai's (1123–1202) *Yijian zhi* 夷堅志 (or *Record of the Listener*, hereafter the *Record*) has stimulated much scholarly interest over the centuries, surprisingly few specialized studies of this work have been undertaken. Apart from the present volume, there has been no other published monograph focusing on the text as a cultural artifact. Yet the work is being increasingly utilized by contemporary scholars as a source of Song Dynasty (960–1279) social and cultural history. This book, therefore, aims to examine some fundamental aspects of the text and its making while rendering significant sections more accessible to English-speaking readers.

Writing at the dawn of the twenty-first century, I am fortunate to have drawn on a more nuanced understanding of Chinese anomaly accounts (*zhiguai* 志怪) and premodern 'fiction' (*xiaoshuo* 小說), to which the *Record* is closely related. I refer in particular to the work of Robert Ford Campany who, in his recent monograph *Strange Writing: Anomaly Accounts in Early Medieval China* (hereafter *Strange Writing*), argued against the hitherto established paradigm which viewed Six Dynasties (222–589) *zhiguai* accounts as the "birth of fiction" in China. The "birth of fiction" hypothesis owes *its* birth to Lu Xun (1881–1936) and, more recently, has been upheld by Western scholars such as DeWoskin. According to this hypothesis, early-twentieth-century Chinese scholars—particularly those active during the May Fourth period, who were keen to establish a lineage of "fiction" in China, identified *zhiguai* writing of the Six Dynasties and earlier as the source for modern Chinese fiction.[1] I, however, fully endorse Campany's strong objection to this, particularly when we think of "fiction" in the Western sense. Indeed, in his monographs *Religious Experience and Lay Society in Tang China*; *A Reading of Dai Fu's Kuang-I chi*, and *The Tale of Li Wa: Study and Critical Edition of a Chinese Story from the Ninth Century*, Glen Dudbridge, rather than approach such texts as works of "fiction," has treated them as historical sources affording insights into matters neglected by official historians. Similarly, in *The Discourse on Foxes and Ghosts: Ji Yun and Eighteenth Century Literati Storytelling*, Leo Tak-hung Chan unapologetically recognizes the widespread belief in gods and ghosts—what he refers to as "supernatural" phenomena—during eighteenth-century China. In this work, Chan contextualizes Ji Yun's 紀昀 (1724–1805) *Random Jottings at the Cottage of Close Scrutiny* (*Yuewei cao-tang biji* 閱微草堂筆記) in the milieu of amateur ghost-storytelling among the "sober-headed, Confucian-trained" literate elite who participated in the debate between skeptics and believers. Rania Huntington also takes a similar approach in her monograph, *Alien Kind: Foxes and Late Imperial Chinese Narrative*, although Huntington stresses that *zhiguai* accounts were not necessarily devoid of "fictitious" tracts. Accordingly, this new approach has implications for works of affiliated genres in other periods, particularly the Tang Dynasty; yet the extent to which a broad gamut of similar works throughout the Tang and post-Tang period defy modern Western notions of "fictionality" must await future research.

In light of such groundbreaking studies, I would argue that the *Record* is far from what contemporary Western-trained scholars conceptualize as "fiction." While it inherited a rich stylistic legacy from *zhiguai* and *chuanqi* 傳奇 writing of the Tang period, epistemologically it seems firmly grounded in the Six Dynasty *zhiguai* tradition as articulated in Campany's monograph. This is not to say that the "paranormal events" reported in many of Hong's accounts were factual in the sense that they actually occurred. But given the widespread "belief" throughout premodern China in what post-Enlightenment Western society would call the "supernatural," I wish to remain sensitive to these contemporary religious ideas. If an erudite, Confucian-trained historian such as Hong Mai, along with his readership, gave credence to the authenticity—or at least the feasibility—of such accounts, then I do not wish to ignore this by imposing a modern Western notion of "fictionality" on the text.

To be sure, the majority of the *Record*'s "supernatural" accounts focus on prophetic dreams, omens, prognostication, destiny, and the like. Certainly the existence of such occurences is prevalent even today in many parts of the world. Yet, to my mind, questions of reception are far more significant than whether or not such events actually occurred. In other words, that someone in Song China experienced a strange dream should not be questioned, but whether the dream is interpreted as the workings of the subconscious mind as opposed to a prophetic revelation from a divine entity is the crucial issue. Apart from dreams, the corpus of *zhiguai* literature abounds with reported sightings of ghosts, dragons, and like phenomena. And while modern Western psychologists might explain these as projections of a psychologically diseased mind in accordance with Jung's theory,[2] the premodern Chinese tended to interpret them as the intrusion of *guai* phenomena into the mundane realm. A fine example has been discussed eloquently by Mark Elvin in regard to the Ming Dynasty (1368–1644) scholar who purportedly saw dragons.[3] Therefore, rather than explain away such religious ideas as protofiction, I prefer to be guided by the premise that the majority of people during Song times believed in the existence of *guai* phenomena.

Of course Robert Hymes has so eruditely identified implied skepticism discernable throughout the *Record*, that is, voices of doubt as to the purported truth of paranormal occurrences which later proved to be the work of charlatans or ghosts masquerading as gods and the like.[4] This certainly highlights Song literati's tendency to historicize even the paranormal. And, at the same time, it points to the long-standing discourse of disbelief stretching back to the Legalist philosopher Xunzi and the arch-skeptic Ruan Zhan 阮 瞻 (281–310). Yet the underlying widespread belief in *guai* phenomena, or at least their plausibility, remains intact.

The present volume comprises five chapters. Drawing from several fine biographical studies,[5] Chapter 1 presents a brief outline of the author's life, particularly where it relates to the *Record*'s compilation. What differentiates this chapter from previous biographies is the several anecdotes I have translated from the *Record* illustrating Hong Mai's personal experience. Chapter 2 examines the thirty-one prefaces which Hong wrote for each installment—since the *Record* is actually a series of books written over the author's lifetime. These prefaces, apart from affording an insight into the text and its making, provide an invaluable theoretical framework *vis-à-vis zhiguai* and *xiaoshuo* writing. Following an annotated translation of each preface, I analyze Hong's comments critically which, in later chapters, fuels further discussion. So as to reconstruct lost prefaces, I have relied on their summarization in Song bibliophile Zhao Yushi's 趙與時 (1175–1231) *Record after the Guests Retire* (*Bintui lu* 賓退錄, hereafter the *Guests Retire*). In the second part of the chapter, I present translations of discourse about the *Record*'s scholarly reception throughout the imperial period up to and including the twentieth century. Given the lack of abundant textual criticism on the *Record*, this is perhaps as close as we can get to a comprehensive textual reception. As with Hong's prefaces, the opinions of these scholars, editors, and bibliophiles will frame our discussion in ensuing chapters. Chapter 3 offers an analysis of selected major themes which underpin the majority of the accounts. In this chapter, I will address some hitherto neglected questions that are important to an overall understanding of the text. In Chapter 4, I examine the *Record*'s generic affiliation, whether it be *zhiguai* (anomaly accounts), *biji* (notebook literature), or *xiaoshuo* ("fiction"). This paves the way for an exploration of truth versus falsity issues in Chapter 5 which, judging from his prefaces, were evidently extremely important to Hong Mai. An understanding of the extent to which the *Record*, as Hong claimed, constitutes a "reliable" record "based on evidence," is crucial to any reading of the text and one which demands attention. This would seem particularly important given the recent mining of the text by Western-trained scholars. A detailed examination of these issues will further enhance our understanding of the informal, oral storytelling among Song literati and the manner in which selected accounts were transformed by Hong into written form. I would hope that the results thus yielded will provide an informed basis for future discussion.

Finally, it should be noted that investigation into the *Record* is, like many other aspects of Song studies, hampered by the limitation of extant material. That is, while we must be grateful for the survival of a great many documents and cultural artifacts, one should remain mindful that a considerable amount of material has been lost—much like a jig-saw with missing pieces. In the case of the *Record,* however, there would seem to be a plethora of missing pieces. The fact that approximately half of the original corpus has not survived, the lack of sufficient material with which to construct a coherent and detailed textual reception, and the loss of state documents which may have illuminated questions about textual factuality and the transmission of certain accounts are just a few examples of the problems faced in this regard. I am, therefore, ever conscious that we will probably never see the entire jig-saw.

Before proceeding further, I would like to express my gratitude to the following friends and acquaintances for their kind assistance over many years. First and foremost to David Holm for starting me off on this project, not to mention his guidance and friendship. Thanks also to Barbara Hendrishke for help and guidance early in the project. Anne MacLaren has consistently offered encouragement and penetrating insight regarding Chinese pre-modern literature. Thanks to James Hargett for his expert guidance about Song history and scholarship. I am grateful to Colin Jeffcott for his suggestions about translation. I am particularly grateful to Robert Campany for his diligent reviewing of my manuscript, and to the other anonymous SUNY reviewer. Thanks also to Wilt Idema for his stimulating discussion about the milieu in which Hong Mai lived and worked.

My family, for whom this volume is dedicated, deserves special mention. My wife, Emily, for her indispensable logistical support and companionship, without which the book would probably never have come into being. Also, my daughter Alison and my son Myron, both of whom have grown too old over the course of writing.

I am particularly grateful to those who gave permission to reproduce some of the very fine translations included in this volume—apart from my own. Thanks to:

Dr Chu Djang for his and Jane Djang's beautiful renditions from *Ding Chuan-jing's Songren yishi huibian* (*A Compilation of Anecdotes of Sung Personalities*).

Katherine Kerr for permission to reproduce some of the many translations that adorn her doctoral dissertation.

The Research Centre for Translation, the Chinese University of Hong Kong for permission to reproduce two of my own translations, Hong Mai, "The Taoists of Jade For" and "Third Daughter Xie" from *Yijian zhi*. Both first published in *Renditions* no. 57 (spring 2002), pp. 30–31 and 32–34.

Princeton University Press for Valerie Hansen's fine translations from the *Record of the Listener* and the *Tiaoxi ji* published in Hansen, Valerie. *Changing Gods in Medieval China, 1127–1276*. © 1990 Princeton University Press. Reprinted by permission of Princeton University Press.

Foreigh Language Press (Beijing) for sections of their book *Record of the Listener*.

The Metropolitan Museum of Art, The Photograph Library for permission to reproduce four artworks from their collection, each depicting a King of Hell from a set of ten hanging scrolls, *The Ten Kings of Hell*. Chin Ch'u-shih (Jin Chushi). Ink and color on silk. The Metropolitan Museum of Art, Rogers Fund, 1929 (30.76.292; 30.76.294; 30.76.290; 30.76.291). All rights reserved. The Metropolitan Museum of Art.

CHAPTER ONE

The Author and His Collection

THE COLLECTION

It is extremely difficult to characterize the *Record* in general terms. We might say that it contains many thousands of narratives, yet nonnarrative modes of writing are also present. While one may recognize Hong Mai as a recorder of oral stories, one cannot overlook his reliance on a significant amount of written material. The *Record* has furthermore often been cited as an example of the *zhiguai* genre, that is, texts that record the "strange" or stories focusing on the "anomalous"—known in Chinese as *guai*—and are similar to what Western-trained scholars would understand as paranormal. Yet many accounts, such as the transmission of medical prescriptions or the recitation of poetry and riddles, are devoid of this *guai* element. This is not to ignore a vast number of accounts whose cosmological focus could easily be characterized as "strange" or "anomalous," but the eclectic nature of the collection undermines attempts to apply all-encompassing labels.

The *Record*'s title is derived from the fourth-century *Book of Liezi* in which the legendary Yijian recorded the deeds of the legendary sage-king Yu—deeds which he did not personally witness. Below is a translation of the relevant section.

> There is a fish there, several thousand miles broad and long in proportion, named the k'un. There is a bird there named the p'eng, with wings like clouds hanging from the sky, and a body big in proportion. "How is the world to know that such things exist?" The Great Yü saw them in his travels, Po-yi knew of them and named them, Yi-chien (Yijian) heard of them and recorded them.[1]

This set the tone for the collecting of anomaly accounts due to Hong Mai's self-professed "love of the strange."[2] It furthermore places the *Record* in an ancient tradition of collection and recording the unusual, while at the same time linking it to the respected sage-king Yu—perhaps apologetically, given orthodox Confucian disdain for speaking of anomalies.

Perhaps one of the most significant facets of Hong Mai's *Record* is his collecting of what he claimed to be "true" stories from thousands of informants of varying socioeconomic backgrounds, rather than fabricating, as would a modern Western writer of fiction. Consider, for example, his comments in the preface of the second installment. After a discussion of selected works traditionally classified as *xiaoshuo*, in addition to aspects of Daoist philosophy, Hong writes:

> My book, however, having come about within a cycle of no more than sixty years, has utilized both my *eyes and ears*—and the stories within are all based on factual sources. If one does not believe me, they may go to Mr. Nobody[3] and ask him.[4] (italics mine)

The utilization of Hong's eyes and ears refers to his reliance on many hundreds of relatives, friends, and acquaintances who supplied him with accounts. While many of these, whom I call informants, were high-ranking scholar-officials and members of the social elite, others were concubines, petty officials, monks, or else itinerant soldiers. Furthermore, a significant proportion of these are demonstrable historical figures.[5] As did many *zhiguai* writers before him, Hong Mai generally referred to his informant at the conclusion of each account or group of accounts told by the one informant; sometimes one person even supplied sufficient information to fill entire chapters.

The *Record* can, therefore, be seen as a compendium of amateur or informal storytelling. Members of the Song educated elite, without recourse to the plethora of easily-accessible entertainment available today, undoubtedly experienced much boredom from time to time and, therefore, were particularly partial to a well-told tale, gossipy snippet, or else news from afar.[6] Many accounts were based on oral retelling, sometimes having passed through at least two or three sources before reaching Hong Mai. Therefore, if one were to view the *Record* as a work of "oral history," these oral story-artifacts would logically reflect the imperfect memories of their informants, variation in detail, as well as the incremental exaggeration that tends to accompany a story's retelling. Accordingly, not unlike oral history traditions in nonliterate cultures, the concept of a single, original text becomes problematic.[7] This would seem to explain the *Record*'s many parallel texts found in other Song literary sources whereby it is impossible to determine the antecedent due to shared plots and uncertain publication dates.[8]

Nevertheless, many others were based on written accounts supplied to Hong which, presumably, he adapted or edited somewhat. For example, in the preface of the seventh installment, Hong writes of receiving written material.

> When I was a magistrate in Dangtu,[9] the locality was remote and there was little with which to occupy myself. Lü Yuqing of Jinan[10] and Wu Dounan of Luoyang[11] once sent me some enough old tales to fill half a book. I have, therefore, edited them into the *Geng zhi* [installment].[12]

Consider also Hong's comments from the preface to the seventeenth installment in which he speaks of receiving old jottings preserved by an acquaintance's father.

> I have again received twenty stories from Lü Deqing. The country gentle-
> man, Wu Liao (courtesy name Wu Boqin), resurrected some notes written
> long ago by his father, the Dweller of Lofty Places.[13] I have borrowed a third
> of these to make up three chapters so as to complete this installment.[14] I
> have, therefore, been able to finish it this quickly.[15]

Luo Ye's 羅燁 (dates uncertain) Song Dynasty notebook work (or miscellaneous notes, *biji* 筆記), *Record of a Drunken Man's Talk* (*Zuiweng tanlu* 醉翁
談錄), is well known for its historical material about storytelling, *xiaoshuo*, and
drama. In this, Luo tells of how there was not a storyteller alive who did not
consult the *Record*.[16] Even allowing for hyperbole, this suggests that Hong's
informal storytelling influenced that of professionals. It furthermore blurs the
boundaries between informal and professional storytelling.

The arrangement of accounts throughout the *Record* seems to reflect
Hong Mai's methods of collecting material, particularly oral material. Unlike
categorically arranged works, such as the *Extensive Records from the Period of
Great Peace* (*Taiping guangji* 太平廣記, *Extensive Records* hereafter), Hong's
arrangement follows no apparent order but that in which he received his
accounts. Often two or three accounts derived from the same informant were
presented together, presumably when he listened to their telling while in the
company of his informant. And, as I noted above, sometimes entire chapters
were derived from the one informant. While such accounts did not necessarily
feature common macromotifs, two or three of similar *topoi* derived from the
same informant were sometimes presented together, presumably due to their
having been told at the same time in the same place.

In other words, the arrangement of accounts did not reflect any topical
considerations. It is, therefore, not surprising that later editors—perhaps dis-
liking the rambling and haphazard organization of the original—produced
topically-arranged editions such as the *New Re-Arranged Edition of the Yijian
zhi* (*Xinbian fenlei Yijian zhi* 新編分類夷堅志), published by Hong Pian 洪
楩 (dates uncertain) in 1546, or Chen Rihua's 陳日華 (official in Chun'an 春
安—modern Chun'an in Zhejiang Province—in 1180) ten-chapter *Topically-
Arranged Yijian zhi* (*Yijian zhi leibian* 夷堅志類編), published after Hong
Mai's death (year of publication unknown).[17]

I have already noted that the *Record* consists of a series of books, or
installments, written throughout the author's lifetime. These installments were
divided into three series of ten books. A fourth series was begun, but only
two installments were completed prior to the author's death in 1202. The first
series originally comprised 20 chapters (or *juan*, chapter hereafter) per installment, while the second and third series contained 10 per installment. In total,
the entire corpus consisted of 420 chapters. Each installment of the first series

was labeled with one of the heavenly stems: *jia* 甲, *yi* 乙, *bing* 丙, *ding* 丁, and so on, to *xin* 辛, *ren* 壬, and *gui* 癸. As the second and third series were subordinate to the first, each heavenly stem was henceforth prefixed with *zhi* 支 (roughly translatable as "branch" in this context). The third installment in both the second and third series was, however, labeled *zhijing* 支景 and *sanjing* 三景 respectively, rather than *zhibing* 支丙 and *sanbing* 三丙 as would normally have been the case. This was to observe the taboo of mentioning the name (or homonym) of a deceased relative: in this case, the author's paternal great-great-grandfather whose given name was Bing 炳. Hong explains why the third installment in the first series did not follow the taboo in the preface to the thirteenth (*zhijia*) installment (see the translation in chapter 2).

Unfortunately, out of these 420 chapters, only 207 survive—approximately half of the original text. Accordingly, as early as the Yuan Dynasty (1279–1368), only a small fraction of the original was readily available. The present corpus, therefore, comprises 80 chapters of the first four installments (notwithstanding several accounts which were supplemented from later installments by Yuan Dynasty editors), 70 chapters from the second series, and 30 from the third. An additional 20 chapters were extracted from Hong Pian's topicalized Ming Dynasty (1368–1644) edition. An additional five chapters comprising accounts recovered from the *Great Encyclopedia of the Yongle Period* (the *Yongle dadian* 永樂大典) of the Ming Dynasty were later compiled, while two more chapters consisting of rediscovered accounts from a range of sources—such as medical compendia and the like—were also assembled. Apart from this, additional accounts have been recently rediscovered, mostly by Barend ter Haar. In his 1993 *Journal of Sung Yuan Studies* article entitled "Newly Recovered Anecdotes from Hong Mai's (1123–1202) *Yijian zhi*," ter Haar discusses the author of the anonymous Yuan Dynasty notebook work, the *Yiwen zonglu* 異聞總錄, who copied *verbatim* large tracts of the *Record* together with at least one other work in what appeared to have been their original sequence. Ter Haar identified accounts which had been derived from the *Record* and those which had not, then pin-pointed the lost ones.[18] Similar rediscoveries have been made in the People's Republic of China by Kang Baocheng (1986), Cheng Hong (1987), Li Yumin (1990), Li Jianguo (1992 and 1997), Zhao Zhangchao (2004), as well as in Taiwan by Wang Hsiu-huei (1989).[19]

The *Record*'s influence on later literature has been considerable. It spawned several copy-cat works, namely Wang Jingwen's 王景文 (1127–1189) *Yijian biezhi* 夷堅別志 (*The Other Record of the Listener*), Yuan Haowen's 元好問 (1190–1257)[20] *Xu Yijian zhi* 續夷堅志 (*Continuation of Record of the Listener*), and the *Yijian xu zhi* 夷堅續志 (*A Sequel to Record of the Listener*), written by an anonymous Yuan Dynasty author. A small number of micromotifs and subplots found in later romance novels such as the *Water Margin*, *Journey to the West* and the *Investiture of the Gods* (*Fengshen yanyi* 封神演義) have been traced to stories in the *Record*. Many accounts from the *Record* served as an inspiration to renowned Ming author of vernacular short stories, Feng Menglong 馮

夢龍 (1368–1644), particularly his *Sanyan er'po* 三言二拍 collection. Similarly, the *Record* has exerted considerable influence over Yuan and later drama. For example, the story entitled "The Resolute Lady from Taiyuan" (*Taiyuan yiniang* 太原意娘) appears as both a vernacular short story as well as a piece of drama. At least one narrative in the famous Qing (1622–1911) *zhiguai* work, the *Liaozhai zhiyi* 聊齋志異, corresponds almost verbatim to one in the *Record*, not to mention several others featuring shared subplots.[21]

As we can see, Hong Mai was a lifelong collector of strange and newsworthy accounts provided by a large number of people in both oral and written forms. This places him in a tradition of informal storytelling, although the reference from the *Record of a Drunken Man's Talk* implies mutual influence between the two. Certainly the *Record* exerted a remarkable degree of influence over Hong Mai's contemporaries, some of whom were inspired to write sequels to the *Record*, others whom reorganized it into topically-arranged editions. To be sure, this influence gathered momentum over time as both Hong's renown and that of his collection fired the imagination of readers for generations hence, perhaps boosted by nostalgia for the lost Song Dynasty.

A BRIEF OUTLINE OF THE AUTHOR'S LIFE

Born in Xiuzhou 秀州 (modern Jiaxing 嘉興, Zhejiang) in 1123 during the final turbulent years of the Northern Song Dynasty (960–1126), Hong Mai was a renowned scholar-official. Hong's style name was Jinglu 景廬; his other name was Yechu 野處, and he was awarded the posthumous title of Wenmin 文敏. His clan had been settled in the Poyang 鄱陽 area of Zhejiang since the late Tang Dynasty (618–907). His great-great-grandfather, Hong Bing 洪炳 (dates uncertain), enjoyed a civil service career and attained the rank of grand guardian (*shaobao*少保) early in the Northern Song. His wife, née He 何, was awarded the title of Lady Jiguo (*Jiguo furen* 紀國夫人). Hong Mai's great-grandfather, Hong Yansheng 洪彥升 (dates uncertain), attained the rank of *jinshi* in 1085, after which he was eventually appointed an imperial censor. Hong Mai's grandfather, Hong Yanxian 洪彥先 (?–1128), also an official, was granted the title Lord of Qin (Qinguo gong 秦國公), while his wife, née Dong, was titled Lady Taiguo (*Taiguo furen* 泰國夫人).

Hong Mai's father, Hong Hao 洪皓 (1088–1155), was an extremely famous official who attained the *jinshi* degree in 1115 during the reign of the artistic, yet politically inept, Huizong emperor (r. 1100–1126). The Xuanhe period (1119–1125) saw Hao serve in Xiuzhou (in modern Jiangsu), where he won respect from the local populace for his timely provision of emergency flood relief, earning him the nickname "Buddha Hong" (*Hong Fozi* 洪佛子). Following the fall of the Northern Song to the Jurchen tartars—ancestors of the Manchus, Hao received a recommendation from Zhang Jun 張浚 (1097–1164)—first grand councilor of the Southern Song—and was dispatched to the Jurchen court as a peace envoy. Unfortunately, the Jurchen emperor detained him for over fourteen years from 1129–1143, during which time he acted as a tutor for one of the Jurchen princes, Wushi 悟室 (dates uncertain).

Hong Mai was the third of nine brothers among whom the two eldest, Zun 遵 (1120–1174) and Gua (or Kuo) 适 (1117–1184), were the most famous. Both enjoyed successful careers in the civil service while Gua served as grand councilor from 1165–1166.

Hong Mai was born in Xiuzhou during his father's incumbency as a provincial official. When his grandfather died in 1128 in Poyang, his father Hao returned to attend the funeral while leaving his family in Xiuzhou. It was during this time that Xiuzhou was ravaged by rebellious troops, yet—miraculously—they refrained from ransacking the Hong residence. This was thought to be due to Hao's fine reputation as a benevolent administrator. Hao departed as an envoy to the Jurchen court the following year where he was to remain until 1143. Hong Mai, therefore, bade his father goodbye at the age of six (seven *sui*) and was not to see him again until he was twenty.

A somewhat lengthier account from the *Record* gives us a picture of Hong Mai's early family life, especially the family's religious practices. The event here recorded was said to have occurred in 1125. As Hong Mai was but three *sui* at the time, he undoubtedly heard it second-hand at a later date. The venue was the record office in Xiuzhou where the family was then domiciled.

The Office of the Record Keeper in Xiuzhou

There were many strange apparitions in the office of the record keeper (*silu*) in Xiuzhou (Jiaxing county, Zhejiang). One always wore a green kerchief and cloth robe, had a short and broad shape, and walked with slow and heavy steps. A woman also went out every night and bewitched and beat the runners.

At the time my father occupied this post, my older brother the future grand councillor was just nine. In broad daylight he opened his eyes and stared just as if he had seen something and said, "Water, water." Only when we moved him did he regain consciousness.

Two days later, my father came home late from the office. A concubine grabbed his robe from behind, suddenly called out, and fell to the ground. My father had heard that ghosts feared leather belts, so he took one to bind the concubine and carried her to bed. After a long while, [the ghost speaking through her] said, "This person has previously insulted ghosts and gods. Just now he is carrying something in his right hand that is frightening [the belt]. I do not dare to come close. Furthermore he does not know I come from the left, I was just captured, and that I have been detained by an official who uses the Zhong Kui [a famous demon queller] method. I will go now without causing mutual inconvenience."

He was asked, "Who are you?"

He did not want to answer.

After several repetitions he said, "I am farmer Stem Nine (Zhi Jiu) from Jiaxing. With my fellow canton resident Water Three (Shui San), we had nine mouths in our two households. During the flood two years ago we all began to wander begging for food. We died just before the officials began famine relief. Now I live on top of the big tree behind your house. Several days ago, the one the little official [your son] saw was Water Three.

My father said, "I worship Zhenwu [a star divinity] because he is very efficacious, and I also have images of the Buddha, and of the earth (*tudi*) and stove god (*zaoshen*). How is it that you come here?"

The ghost said, "The Buddha is a benevolent deity who does not concern himself with such trivial matters; every night Zhenwu unbinds his hair, grasps his sword, and flies from the roof. I carefully avoid him, that's all. The earth god behind your house is not easily aroused. Only at the small temple in front of your house [to the stove god] am I reprimanded every time I'm seen. I just entered the kitchen, and His Lordship asked, 'Where are you going?'

"I answered, 'I'm just looking around.'

"He upbraided me, 'You're not allowed here.'

"I said, 'I do not dare,' and came here."

My father said, "What are the two things that always come out?"

The ghost said, "The one with the kerchief is Shi Jing, who's called Gentleman Shi. He's just under the hedge outside the study window, about three *chi* [90 cm] under the ground. The woman is Qin Erniang. She's lived here a long time."

My father said, "I give paper money to the earth god on the first and fifteenth day of every month. How can he allow ghosts from outside to come in? You go and ask him for me. Tomorrow I shall destroy his shrine."

The ghost said, "Do you mean to say you don't understand? Even though he has money, how can he go without food? When I enter your house, if I get something, I must give him a share to keep him quiet, and that is why he has always permitted me to come." He ate for a while and then spoke again, "Were I to proceed as you admonish and tell the earth god, he'll be angry that I'm so loquacious, and will use a stick to drive me out."

My father said, "Have you seen my family's ancestors or not?"

He said, "Every time there is a holiday and you make offerings, I definitely come to observe. I smell the fragrant food and want to eat it but do not get any. Among the places are a few empty places, but if a yellow-clothed woman sees me, she gets angry."

After looking around, the ghost gasped and became pale. Eventually he spoke, saying, "Just as I reached the door, I was chased by a woman carrying a stick. I quickly ran in the other direction and barely escaped."

The woman he spoke of was my great-grandmother Jiguo.

My father had asked all that he wanted and said, "You're consumed by suffering and hunger. Would you like a meal? Some wine and a fat chicken? I will offer them to everyone. It won't be like usual when I give a skinny chicken."

> When my father had finished speaking, the ghost cocked his ear as if some-
> one had called him and said, "The earth god is very angry and has expelled out
> two households. Now we'll briefly go to the top of the city wall. We have
> nowhere to return to. Please free me quickly. I won't dare to come again."
>
> My father undid his belt. The concubine slept in a daze for several days
> and then woke up.[22]

This account displays a remarkable degree of attention to historical detail. As
Hansen has noted, the stellar deity Zhenwu was often depicted with his hair
loose.[23] Furthermore, the flood and famine mentioned in the account was the
above-mentioned disaster for which Hong Hao earned the nickname "Buddha Hong." It is also a rare example of ghost storytelling within Hong Mai's
own family. Given that several similar stories also appear in the *Record*, it suggests that Hong's role in recording stories heard at social functions was not
purely passive; that is, rather than always being "the listener," he too indulged
in the telling of strange stories. To be sure, it would seem unlikely that he
would sit there doing nothing but listen to the stories of others without swap-
ping some of his own. Therefore, perhaps the translated title of *Record of the
Listener* needs rethinking.

Furthermore, this anecdote affords a valuable glimpse at the range of
deities worshipped in the Hong household during Hong Mai's infancy, as
well as at the types of offerings made by Hong Hao. The story also supports
recent studies which demonstrate how Confucian-trained officials also sub-
scribed to religious ideas not necessarily compatible with orthodox Confucian thought.[24]

The following year, 1130, saw Xiuzhou fall to invading Jurchen troops.
So as to escape the ensuing mayhem, Hong Mai was taken with his family
to their paternal home in Poyang where he and his brothers remained under
the care and tutelage of their mother until her death in 1138. The boys then
moved to their maternal uncle's home in Wuxi 無錫 (modern Wuxi in Jiangsu)
where they continued to prepare for the imperial examinations. In the *cike* 詞
科 examinations of 1142, both his elder brothers passed while Hong Mai,
unfortunately, failed. An anecdote from the *Record* relating to this provides a
glimpse into contemporary superstitions.

PINE CONES

> It was during the winter of the *wuwu* year of the Period of Continued Ascen-
> dancy (1141) when my brothers and I went to attend the funeral of our good
> mother. We stayed in our maternal clan's mourning-hut by the cemetery at
> Big Lake Dike in Wuxi. There were twenty thousand or so enormous pine
> trees all around the shrine. That spring, two of the four or five meter-tall pines
> produced a cone each. The cones grew at the tree's apex and were surrounded
> by a halo of bright green leaves, yet they appeared completely natural.
>
> Shaoming, the monk at the mourning-hut, told us,

"There was a pine beside the grave of a Madame Bian from a nearby village which did the same thing, except its cone was somewhat smaller. And her grandson, Master Anye, passed the imperial exams. Now there are two large ones. Does this mean that Madame Shen[25] has two sons who will pass?"

At the time, my two cousins, Shen Ziqiang and Ziqiu, had just sat for the examinations. Both, however, were unsuccessful. Nevertheless, my eldest brother and second brother passed the *boxue cike* division in the *renxu* year (1142). Since they happened to be staying in the shrine when they were preparing for this division, their subsequent passing of the exam fulfilled the omen of the pine cones.[26]

This is one of several stories which exhibits Hong Mai's belief in what may be understood as *guai* phenomena; although, in this case, rather than dealing with ghosts and other-worldly matters, the story is predicated on the traditional Chinese notion that auspicious and calamitous happenings could be foretold through omens made manifest in the natural world. Indeed, the Confucian idea of the mandate of heaven was part of this tradition. Hong's implied actual belief in prognostication may help explain why he devoted so much of his life to almost obsessive collecting and recording of anomalous accounts.

The year following the eldest and second eldest Hong brother's academic success (1143) saw the return of their father, Hong Hao, from detention in the north. Hao brought with him numerous stories and anecdotes which were later published by Hong Gua as the *Songmo jiwen* 松漠記聞 in 1155 following Hao's death. Significantly, several of these also appear in the first chapter of the *Record*.[27] This strongly suggests that Hong Hao and his anomalous accounts inspired his son, Mai, to begin collecting and recording similar stories.[28] Yet we cannot be certain exactly when he began putting writing brush to paper, given that Hong Mai's stated year of commencement has not survived (at least as far as we know; I will discuss Hong's commencement year below).

A mere month following his return in the ninth lunar month of that year, Hao raised the ire of the then all-powerful grand councilor, Qin Gui 秦 檜 (1090–1155), whose power base at court relied on sustained peace with the Song's powerful northern neighbors, the Jurchen. Hao, contrary to Qin, very likely supported the "war party": that is, officials who opposed the pacifist policies which kept the Song Empire a vassal of the Jurchen. The "war party" wished to annul the disgrace of invasion and subjugation of the central plains by an ethnic group who Song subjects referred to as "barbarians." The fact that Hao received his appointment as ambassador to the Jurchen by the then grand councilor Zhang Jun—head of the "war party"—cannot but support such a possibility. Accordingly, Qin was understandably anxious to have Hao away from court lest he persuade the emperor to adopt a hostile policy toward the Jurchen. If successful, this would have almost certainly resulted in Qin's loss of power. Yet, whether Hao's banishment from court was due to this or due to Qin's having felt threatened by Hao's renown or both, is unclear. Certainly Qin's hostility toward Hao is well documented by the latter's biography in the

History of the Song (*Song shi* 宋 史).[29] As a result, after initially being sent to Raozhou 繞州 (in modern Zhejiang), Hao was eventually banished to remote Yingzhou 英州 (modern Yingde 英德 in Guangdong Province) In the Song Empire's "deep south." This was to be his final post.

Returning to Hong Mai, it was not until 1145 that he passed the *boxue hongci ke* 博學宏詞科 examination, an anecdote about which appears in the *Record*. Hong writes how he and fellow candidates visited a courtesan's house in Lin'an (Hangzhou) just after the completion of the examination but before the results had been announced. The courtesan foretold his success based on a lyric he wrote before the assembled company.[30]

THE CANDLE AND FLOWER LYRIC OF THE SMALL PAVILION

On the fifteenth day of the third month in the fifteenth year of the period of Continued Ascendancy (1145), I emerged from the examination hall after having completed the third round of the *cike* division held in Lin'an. It was still early, and my fellow candidates He Zuoshan, courtesy name Boming, and Xu Bo, courtesy name Shengfu, and I ventured into town. At the time my paternal uncle, Hong Bangzhi, courtesy name Yingxian, and our compatriot Xu Liangyou, courtesy name Shunju, had both completed the provincial exam. So we all went together.

Having reached Embracing the Sword Street, Boming dragged us off to visit the famous courtesan, Sun Xiaojiu, with whom he had enjoyed a long-standing acquaintance. Wine cups were laid out in her small pavilion. The moon that night illuminated the sky as if it were day, and we repaired to the balustrade to partake of its beauty. There were twin candles which formed snuff-flowers, and they sparkled like a string of pearls.[31]

The ever intelligent and perceptive Miss Sun addressed the assembled company.

"The man in the moon is so bright tonight and the snuff-flowers are a lucky omen. You five gentlemen have displayed your talents in the exams. One of you will pass with honors, of that there can be no doubt. I would like each of you to compose a lyric to commemorate this day which will become the stuff of a good yarn in times to come."

She then took out five sheets of Wu paper and placed them on the table. Shengfu, Yingxian and Shunju each made their excuses, while the dapper and talented Boming seized a brush and composed a lyric to the tune of "On the Banks of the Washing Stream." One of the stanzas read:

Cups and dishes quickly spread
We visit the pretty one.
Snuff-flowers bring good tidings,
Our party lends joy to spring.
You would have us find some lines,
which must be fine and rare.

Shallow brow and sparkling eyes,
Brimming with feeling
Clouds are light,
Willows weak,
Yet their intent is genuine.
The breeze and moon
Henceforth belong to the leisurely.

Everyone looked on in admiration, only regretting the slight imperfection in the final line. I followed with a lyric to the tune of "Immortals Facing the River."

Gathered on a brocade mat,
Our company warm and gay.
In the tower tall,
Good tidings come our way.
A hair pin,
An ancient script,
The candle-flowers crimson.
Happy times will soon arrive
And reward their master fine.
The cassia moon is full,
Half of spring has gone.
Time in the Palace of Vast Chill
Passes far too fast.
Heng'e[32]
faces east
beside the winding railing
Knowing the cloud ladder
Is not so far away.
Steadily she steps,
Making obeisance to the east.

"You, sir, will surely pass with flying colors," announced Miss Sun as she filled a cup to the brim. "The omen is probably meant for you."

Not long after that, I actually did pass the exam. The other four had no luck.[33]

Here, then, is another instance of Hong being personally touched by what could be construed as the "paranormal." The dovetailing of lyric poetry in this account is a typical stylistic feature found throughout the *Record*, and demonstrates its formalistic affiliation with *chuanqi* texts of the Tang Dynasty.

Shortly after the examination, Hong was appointed to a post of reviser in the Law Office of the State Affairs Bureau. Unfortunately, it was not long before he was forced to resign this post after having been criticized by the censor, Wang Bo 汪勃 (1088–1171), for lending undue support to his father

who—as noted above—had been banished to the south by Qin Gui. Hong
was subsequently demoted to the position of an education officer in Fuzhou福
州 (modern Fujian), but did not take up the post until 1148. He spent the next
couple of years there.

The large number of *Record* accounts derived from this locality were apparently collected and recorded during this time.[34] One of them reveals a rare
instance of Hong Mai's having personally witnessed a ghostly apparition. This
supposedly occurred in 1147 during a stop-over in Qianzhou 虔州 (modern
Ganzhou 贛州 in Jiangxi).

The Citadel Tower of Qian Prefecture

In the summer of the seventeenth year of the period of Continued Ascendancy (1147), my younger brother and I accompanied our good father when
he moved to the south. We reached Qian Prefecture on the second day of
the eighth month. Mooring our boat under the Floating Bridge, we repaired
to the citadel tower to take our rest. Then the prefect, Zeng Duanbo, came
to see us.

"This is not a place to stay," he warned. "Only the Yugu Terrace will do.
Zhou Kangzhou has gone there first, but he will be leaving on the morrow.
You may therefore stay here for one night."

That night, we made up a bed for our father in the central hall, and my
brother and I slept on some mats to the side. At around two in the morning,
I rose to visit the privy, going out from the north door. There was a person
doing their hair which trailed to the ground. Our two servants, Wang San
and Cheng Qi, were sleeping inside at the time. Thinking that it was one of
these two, I called out but received no response. I then went back inside to
take a look, only to find that both were sleeping soundly as before. Having
suspected that something was amiss all along, I went back outside. It still had
not finished combing its hair. Facing the crenellated wall, its legs were hanging halfway outside and the wind was whipping its hair into waves. Shaken,
I returned to bed.

The following day my father asked me, "Where did you go in the night? I
heard one of the old guards say that there have always been apparitions in the
tower which are sure to appear every night."

I therefore told of what I had seen the previous night. That day we went
with our father to Yugu, yet I could not sleep the whole night.

I also heard that when Zhou Kangzhou was staying there, someone
opened the Three-Fold Door and went out. Thinking it to be a thief, Zhou
had his son follow. Yet he found that the door had never been opened.[35]

It is interesting to note that, much like the ghost and anomaly stories in Xu
Xuan's 徐鉉 (915–991) *Jishen lu* 稽神錄 (*Examining Spirits*), this account
lacks the didactic twist exhibited by numerous others in the *Record*. Hong's
purpose in recording this account was presumably to record an encounter with

the strange, rather than engage in didactic moralizing for which so many of his other accounts were utilized. Indeed, this example demonstrates Hong and his father's belief in the existence of ghosts and further illustrates prevailing religious ideas in Song society.

Hong left Fuzhou in 1150 to visit his father, who was by then in Ying-zhou. The several accounts from Yingzhou which appear in the *Record* must have surely been collected during this sojourn.[36] Five years later, in 1155, Hong took up a posting as controller-general in Yuanzhou 遠州 (modern Yichun 宜春 in Jiangxi), yet his tenure was cut short by the necessity to mourn his father who died in the tenth lunar month of that year. In 1158, at the conclusion of the morning period, he attained a posting as a palace library official at the Southern Song capital, Lin'an (Hangzhou). Other appointments soon followed. Accounts appearing in the *Record* derived from the capital and vicinity, as well as those heard from informants known to have been officials serving in the capital at the time, indicate that Hong was still working on his first installment during this period.

Hong Mai probably completed the first twenty chapter installment of the *Record* around 1160, during his time in the capital. Unfortunately, the preface of this inaugural installment was lost as early as the Yuan Dynasty and, with it, most likely, the date or year of completion. Nevertheless, 1160 as a likely year can be inferred from Hong's other prefaces in which he discusses the time he spent on the *Record*. To explore this thoroughly, we would need to delve into details of textual history which is beyond the scope of the present volume. Briefly, though, if Hong Mai began writing in 1143, 1160 as a year of completion can be inferred from his comments in the preface to the *Geng zhi* (sixth installment) which, although no longer extant, have been summarized in Zhao Yushi's *Record After the Guests Retire* (henceforth *Guests Retire*). In this, Hong wrote that he spent eighteen years working on the initial installment. If one were to include 1143 as the commencement year and count to eighteen, one arrives at 1160. We can be reasonably certain that Hong counted this way since, in another preface for an installment which took only forty-four days to complete, he clearly specified both the commencement and completion day and included each.[37]

Further evidence is found in the preface to the second installment, dated the 18th day of the twelfth lunar month of 1166, in which Hong briefly discusses the initial reception of the *Record*.

> When the first installment of the *Record* was complete, it was circulated among gentlemen and scholar officials. Today it has been published in Fujian, in Sichuan, in Wuzhou as well as in Lin'an. Every household has a copy.[38]

While he does not specify the form in which this initial installment "circulated," it may well have been a manuscript.[39] Significantly, it also suggests a gap between the work's completion and its initial publication. To be sure, it would have been unlikely for a work such as the *Record* to have been published immediately after its completion. And if the second installment was completed in 1166 after five years, as Hong also tells us in the same preface, we would arrive at 1162 as the commencement year for this second installment using the same method of counting. As I will discuss below, given that he returned to his native Poyang in 1162 after having been relieved of official duties, 1162 is the most likely year of commencement for the second installment. The gap hinted at in the preface is, therefore, all the more plausible.

With regard to internal evidence, the latest date in the initial installment is the fourth lunar month of 1159. Nevertheless, Okamoto Fujiaki argues that a round of imperial examinations held in Lin'an in 1160 acted as the venue for at least one account found in the initial installment. During this time, Hong Mai, along with twelve other officials who also provided him with stories appearing in other parts of the *Record*, were locked together for many days in the examination hall where they acted as supervisors. Hong's fellow examiners told him stories relating to previous examinations held at the same venue, one of which appears in chapter 18 of the first installment.[40] If correct, this is evidence that Hong was still working on the first installment in 1160. After 1160, however, Hong would likely have been far too preoccupied with his duties as a war-time official to commit brush to paper, given the outbreak of war with the Jurchen in 1161.

When hostilities began, Hong Mai was given a post in the Bureau of Military Affairs. He soon after drafted the proclamation of hostilities at the behest of the Gaozong emperor. The following year saw him embark on a peace mission to the Jurchen. This, however, did not go well, as a dispute arose about the wording of documentation. At Hong's prior suggestion, the state documents and official letters had been worded in such a way as to accord enemy status to the Jurchen state. Prior to this, the Song Empire acknowledged itself as a vassal of the Jurchen according to the peace treaty of 1141, which had been rigorously enforced by Qin Gui. Hong insisted that the wording remain, while the Jurchen were adamant that it be changed. Hong relented only after having been held under house arrest without food for three days. After his return to Lin'an, he was criticized by the censor, Zhang Zhen 張震 (1151 *jinshi*), for having dishonored the Song. He returned to his native Poyang after being forced to quit his post. Following this incident, one of the national university students composed a satirical lyric poem to the tune of "Southern Landscape" (*Nanxiangzi* 南響子), criticizing Hong for not having shaken his head when he should have, thus poking fun at Hong's occasional involuntary head movement. This was recorded in Luo Dajing's 羅大經 (?–after 1248) *Conversations Carried on at Helin* (*Helin yulu* 鶴林玉露), from which the following passage was translated.

The year of Hsin-ssu of the Shao-hsing period (1161), the Jurchen chief Wan-yen Liang (1122–1161) had been assassinated and Prince Ke (Shih-tsung, 1161–1189) ascended the throne as the ruler of the Chin. He sent an envoy to talk peace with the Sung. In return, Hung Mai was dispatched to the Chin court as an envoy to congratulate the new ruler on his inauguration. As soon as he entered the Chin territory, Hung negotiated on protocol with the Chin minister, who came to meet him at the border. It was agreed that the two states should be accorded equal status. Hence, this was reflected in all documents and credentials, the same as those written in the old Eastern Capital [Pien-liang] days.

Soon, however, all the documents were rejected. Hung was told to change the wording of the documents according to the current form [that is, to address the Chin court from the position of a dependant state]. As Hung refused to do so, the Jurchens locked him and his party up without supplying them any food. The next day, the Chin minister who claimed to have studied with his father Hung Hao (1088–1155) when the latter was an envoy to the Chin court, came to explain the situation to Hung. The visitor advised him not to be too obstinate and warned that unless there was some accommodation on his part, the worst could happen. Fearing to be detained in the enemy country, Hung agreed to change the format of the documents.

Hung was afflicted with a kind of palsy which made his head shake slightly. One of his contemporaries wrote a poem to ridicule his capitulation as follows:

> For nineteen years Su Wu in
> Captivity suffered privation.
> A modern envoy can't endure hunger
> Even for a day's duration.
> Let there be a word of advice
> To the wise
> You should have shaken your
> Head even if it's not your choice.[41]

The poem's reference to the Han Dynasty minister Su Wu can also be read as an oblique reference to Hong Mai's father, Hao. Su Wu's twenty or so year detention during his diplomatic mission to the Xiongnu hordes—a non-Han Chinese enemy of the Han state—was well known at the time. His loyalty to the Han court henceforth became the stuff of legend. Similarly, after his return to the Southern Song court after fourteen years, Hong Hao was compared to Su Wu by none other than the Gaozong emperor; it is no wonder that Hao incurred the enmity of Qin Gui. Therefore, the poet here seems to be ridiculing Hong Mai's inability to live up to his father's determination and courage.

As noted above, judging from the preface to the second installment of the *Record*, work began on this installment around or shortly after Hong's return from his mission, during which period he spent much time in the vicinity of Raozhou and Poyang. This second twenty-chapter installment was completed by 1166 and was named with the second heavenly stem: the *Yi zhi* 乙志.

Hong was recalled to Lin'an in 1166 by the recently-installed Xiaozong 孝宗 emperor (r. 1163–1190) and was appointed a drafter of records for rest and repose (*quju sheren* 起居舍人), that is, the emperor's daily (and nightly) activities. The following year he was appointed to a post of a state (official) historiographer and worked on the *History of the Three Courts* 三朝國史 (*Sanchao guoshi*) as well as the veritable records of the Qinzong 欽宗 emperor (r. 1126). He appeared to enjoy a good relationship with Xiaozong, which was possibly fueled by a mutual love of poetry. It was during this period that he presented an anthology of Tang poems to the emperor. Hence, anomaly accounts were not the only object of Hong Mai the collector. Below is a translation from Song literatus Ye Shaoweng's 葉紹翁 (1175–1230) *Record of Things Heard and Seen in Four Courts* (*Sichao wenjian lu* 四朝聞見錄), which documents Hong's conversation with the emperor regarding these poems.

> Once Hung Mai was in attendance upon the emperor Hsiao-tsung who was enjoying his leisure. The emperor mentioned that he was compiling an anthology of four-lined Tang poems to while away his spare time in the palace and that so far he had collected some 600 poems.
>
> "To your servant's recollection, there are a good deal more than that," Hung said.
>
> "How many are there?" the emperor asked.
>
> "I would say about 5000," Hung replied.
>
> "If that's so, I think I'd ask you to compile it," the emperor commanded.
>
> Hung spent over a year searching for Tang poems. He collected about twenty to thirty percent of what he was to collect, supplemented with those contained in novels and supernatural stories as well as poems by women. He presented the finished compilation to the emperor. The emperor knew it was far short of target, but commended the effort nevertheless.[42]

Hong's relationship with Xiaozong, however, evidently gave rise to jealousy and he was forced to leave the capital in 1168 after having been accused of flattery by the vice councilor, Chen Junqing 陳俊卿 (1113–1186).[43] Hong returned to Poyang where he tended his garden and, undoubtedly, devoted more time to the *Record*.

The year 1170 saw Hong take up a position as prefect of Ganzhou 贛州 (Ganzhou in modern Jiangxi). The third installment of the *Record* was completed the following year and published there. While it is unclear whether this edition comprised a single installment or multiple installments, given that there is a listing in the *Bibliographic Treatise* (*Yiwen zhi* 藝文志) of the *History of the Song* for an edition comprising the first three installments, this is a likely reference to the Ganzhou edition. There is not, however, the scope to discuss textual history here.

Hong received a promotion to the large metropolis of Jianning 建寧 (modern Fujian) in 1177, where he remained until 1180. The fourth installment of the *Record* was completed in the seventh month of 1180 and was published together with the first three. We can be sure of this thanks to the oldest extant copy of the *Record* which was reprinted in the Yuan Dynasty using original Song wood blocks. Some time during the Yuan, the blocks used to print the original Song edition were found in Jianning's prefectural school. Missing blocks were then supplemented so as to produce a new edition.

The first installment of Hong's other major work, the philological *Rong-zhai suibi* 容齋隨筆, was also completed in 1180 and, as can be seen from the anecdote below, was well received by the Xiaozong emperor.

> In the fourteenth year of the *Ch'un-hsi* period (1188), Hung Mai had a private audience with the emperor Hsiao-tsung one day. "I recently came across a notebook by someone from a certain studio," said the emperor. "I wonder who the author was."
> "It is called *Jung-chai sui-pi*, written by your servant," Hung replied. "There is nothing worth reading."
> "But there are quite a few good comments therein," the emperor said.
> Hung made obeisance to thank to emperor for his kindness.[44]

Hong returned to Poyang after leaving Jianning. He did not take up another post until 1183 when he was sent to govern Wuzhou 婺州 (in modern Jiangxi). He was recalled to the capital in 1185 to serve as an official historiographer and was appointed a Hanlin academician the following year. Unfortunately, he was forced to resign this post in 1188 after being criticized over his proposed temple name for the late Gaozong emperor, in addition to other controversies surrounding Gaozong's memorial. The ensuing years saw him undertake two further provincial postings: Taipingzhou 太平州 (modern Dangtu 當塗 in Jiangsu) from 1188 to 1190, and Shaoxing 紹興 (modern Zhejiang) in 1190. At the end of 1190, he was granted an honorary position with an accompanying emolument and remained in Shaoxing until around 1195 or 1196. The fifth and sixth installments of the *Record* were completed in 1190. By the time Hong left Shaoxing, he had completed ten twenty-chapter installments (two hundred chapters) and had begun work on the second series. In other words, approximately half was completed before Hong's effective retirement. This dispels Lu Xun's misconception that the *Record* is a product of Hong's late years.[45] While Lu undoubtedly made this mistake based on the erroneous biography of Hong Mai in the *History of the Song*, it has unfortunately been parroted by subsequent scholars and editors who have written brief introductions to the work in literary encyclopedias and the like. While there is no extant information on the publication of installments other than what I have mentioned above, we do know that the tenth was published in the Fukienese printing village of Masha 麻沙, which was notorious for its poor quality imprints.[46] Yet whether this was a single installment or a multiple-installment edition is unclear.

The years following 1196 saw Hong devote most of his retirement to the writing of both the *Record* as well as the *Rongzhai suibi*. Judging from remarks made in his prefaces from this period, it is clear that he derived great pride from his writing speed. In the preface to the *Zhijia zhi* (the eleventh installment), completed in 1194, he discussed the length of time required to complete various installments up until that time. In the preface to the *Zhiyi zhi* (the twelfth installment), dated the twenty-eighth day of the second [lunar] month of 1195, Hong writes that three installments were completed the previous summer and boasts how this twelfth installment was completed in a mere month. In the preface of the *Zhijing zhi* (the thirteenth), also completed in 1195, he tells us that this installment took but ten months to complete. In the preface to the *Zhigeng zhi* (the seventeenth), completed in 1196, he not only brags that it was completed in forty-four days, but—as mentioned above—he even gives us the commencement and completion days: the *gengwu* day of the tenth month to the *guichou* day of the twelfth month.[47] The *Zhigui* installment (the twentieth) was completed in thirty days in 1197. In the preface of the *Sanzhi jia* (the twenty-first) installment, completed between 1197 and 1198, Hong expresses his pride in having completed the installment in a mere fifty days.

Given the frequency of reference, one cannot help wonder if this seeming obsession with writing speed was somehow linked to Hong's ego. An anecdote from Zhou Mi's *Words of a Retired Scholar from the East of Qi* (*Qidong yeyu* 齊 東 野 語) affords a precious glimpse into Hong's life as a Hanlin academician. His preoccupation with writing speed is clearly discernible.

> Hung Mai was assigned to the Hanlin Academy as a drafter of proclamations. On one occasion, he drafted no less than twenty documents in a single day. Having finished them, he took a stroll in the courtyard. He met an old man sunning himself in the garden. Upon inquiry, the old man, in his eighties, told Hung that he was a native of the capital and that for several generations his family had been the caretakers of the premise of the Hanlin Academy. Now that his sons and grandsons were continuing his job, he explained, he was spending his last days in retirement. He further mentioned the fact that as a boy, he had met many academicians of the *Yüan-yu* period (1086–1093) at the academy. "I heard that many documents need to be drafted today," the old man added. "Your honor must be rather tired now."
>
> Pleased with what he heard, Hung Mai told the old man that he had drafted over twenty documents that day. "The academician is talented and fast thinking. Few people can be your peers," the old man praised him.
>
> "I would imagine that Su Shih in his days was no better than me," Hung said proudly.
>
> The old man nodded. But after a pause, he said, "Su Shih, indeed, was just as fast as your honor. Only he did not have to look up information from books."
>
> Blushing, Hung Mai hated himself for being so easily carried away.[48]

Hong's self-comparison to a widely recognized genius—Su Shi 蘇軾 (1036– 1101)—in regard to writing speed suggests that, to him, speed was somehow related to self-esteem. Well may we ask, therefore, if he viewed high production speed as a mark of intelligence? This anecdote suggests that he did and, if so, it helps explain Hong's frequent references to such speed.

Another recurrent idea expressed in these later prefaces was Hong's professed attempts to cease the collecting and writing of strange stories, yet being unable to do so due to force of habit. Consider his words from the preface to the *Zhiren zhi* installment (the twenty-ninth) completed between 1196 and 1197, as paraphrased in Zhao Yushi's *Guests Retire*.

> The [preface to the] *Zhiren* states: Male relatives tell me that my devotion to writing and my ceaseless collecting of strange stories is not the kind of rest and relaxation fit for an elderly gentleman, and that I should desist. I took their advice, and within a day I had lost my palate for wine. I felt too constrained for strolling. My heart had lost its repose and my spirit had become dull. Those who had advised me to stop did not know what had come over me. And so, self-satisfied, I laughed at them.
>
> Could this be my destiny? Like a stallion charging down an endless hill, wanting to stop but unable to do so. I am, therefore, giving rein to my urges, and will follow them to the end of this life. Later on, if I become unable to recognize the world around me, I will surrender myself without any outside pressure.[49]

Hong also discusses his ceaseless collecting and recording in the preface of the *Sanzhi ding* installment (the thirty-fourth).

> The [preface to the] *Sanzhi Ding* states: When a man reaches seventy or eighty, and should he have the good fortune to enjoy good health and well being, he should [be able to] retire to his retreat, be early to bed and early to rise, mull over books and pledge himself eternally to his good lady.[50]
>
> Otherwise he could entertain seasoned travelers from the four corners of the earth, or else he could meditate and train his body with the climbing bear and gazing owl method.[51] As for the writing of books, this comes from the basest of motives. Yet I cannot release myself from this folly. Regretting it, I once hastily cleared away all my material, not looking at it again. But it was like forbidding a toddler from falling down. Before long, I was once again involved, more so than ever. I will not listen [to the advice of others] again, even should the mountains collapse and the rivers run dry.[52]

Judging from these prefaces, the collecting and recording of anomalous accounts occupied much of Hong's life in retirement. To be sure, the completion dates of each preface bear witness to his rapid rate of production. As can be seen from the table below, even though the completion year for some installments is unknown, we may infer that in the three years of 1196, 1197, and 1198, some sixteen installments were completed. Since each of the later installments comprised ten chapters, we can determine that a massive 160 chapters were completed within three years. In other words, approximately twenty-six percent of the entire corpus was completed in this space of time.

Compared to this, the four years required to write the remaining three installments completed between 1198 and Hong's death in 1202 seem an unusually
long time. Given the phenomenal speed maintained in the three years prior to
1198, it is unlikely that Hong would have spent the next four to produce just
three installments. Therefore, it seems highly likely that he was too ill to write
in the last years of his life. If correct, it is likely that the final installment of the
largest single collection of its kind ever to have been written by one person was
completed in 1199.

When Hong died in 1202, he was buried at the foot of Roaring Dragon
Mountain (*Longhou shan* 龍 吼 山) in his ancestral Poyang.

TABLE I: COMPLETION DATES OF
THE INSTALLMENTS FROM THE *RECORD*.

INSTALLMENT	NO. OF CHAPTERS	COMPLETION DATE	REMARKS
Jia zhi	20	1160?	
Yi zhi	20	1166	
Bing zhi	20	1171	
Ding zhi	20	1180	
Wu zhi	20	1190	lost
Ji zhi	20	1190	lost
Geng zhi	20	unknown	lost
Xin zhi	20	1194	lost
Ren zhi	20	1194	lost
Gui zhi	20	1194	lost
Zhijia zhi	10	1194	
Zhiyi zhi	10	1195	
Zhijing zhi	10	1195	
Zhiding zhi	10	1196	
Zhiwu zhi	10	1196	
Zhiji zhi	10	unknown	lost
Zhigeng zhi	10	1196	
Zhixin zhi	10	unknown	lost
Zhiren zhi	10	unknown	lost
Zhigui zhi	10	1197	
Sanjia zhi	10	unknown	lost
Sanyi zhi	10	unknown	lost
Sanjing zhi	10	unknown	lost
Sanding zhi	10	unknown	lost
Sanwu zhi	10	unknown	lost
Sanji zhi	10	1198	

INSTALLMENT	NO. OF CHAPTERS	COMPLETION DATE	REMARKS
Sangeng zhi	10	unknown	lost
Sanxin zhi	10	1198	
Sanren zhi	10	1198	
Sangui zhi	10	unknown	lost
Sijia zhi	10	unknown	lost
Siyi zhi	10	unknown	lost

Source: The information for the above table has been extracted from all extant prefaces, in addition to Chen Zhensun's 陳振孫 *Zhizhai shulu jieti* 直齋書錄解題, ch.11, and Ma Duanlin's 馬端臨*Wenxian Tongkao jingji kao* 文獻通考經籍考, 217.

CHAPTER TWO

Authorial Voice and Textual Reception

As mentioned in chapter 1, Hong Mai wrote a preface for each installment except for the last. I have already observed that, although only thirteen are extant, lost ones are summarized in Zhao Yushi's *Guests Retire*. Zhao was a member of the Song imperial clan who attained the *jinshi* degree during the Baoqing era 寶慶 (1225–27). He was an author of some renown and compiled the *Notes from the jiawu Year* (*Jiawu cungao* 甲午存稿), an anthology of poetry which, however, is no longer extant. His *Guests Retire* is a collection of miscellaneous notes published during the Song which contains valuable material on literary history. Chapter 8 focuses solely on the *Record*.

Not only are Hong's prefaces valuable for their information about the compilation of the *Record*, a variety of other important topics are also addressed, such as literary and textual criticism, the purported historical veracity of the collection, publication details, facets of the author's personal life, genre-related issues, and so on. Furthermore, they contribute to the discourse on premodern notebook literature in general, that is, collections of short accounts written in classical prose on a wide variety of *topoi*. As Liu Langming has noted, these prefaces represent an unprecedented accomplishment in the field of literary criticism.[1] The prefaces are of particular importance to the present inquiry as many of the pertinent questions surrounding the text and its making can be answered by reference to them. And, should one be hesitant to take Hong's words at face value, many of his assertions—as we shall see—are supported by both internal and external evidence.

In this chapter, I will first present an annotated translation of all the prefaces followed by critical analysis where appropriate. Some prefaces, especially those redacted from the *Guests Retire*, are extremely brief and yield little information worthy of comment. I therefore leave these to speak for themselves, even though I draw on them in later chapters. After having dealt with the prefaces, I will turn attention to past scholarly writing on the *Record*, which is, perhaps, the nearest thing we have to a reception of the text. As is the case with the prefaces, the opinions of these scholars, editors, and bibliophiles are also pertinent to issues addressed in later chapters.

23

THE PREFACES

As mentioned in chapter 1, the preface to the *Jiu zhi* has, unfortunately, been lost and its summary in the *Guests Retire* is extremely brief. All it tells us is that this preface outlined the author's intentions—whatever they may have been. I therefore begin with the preface to the second installment—the *Yi zhi*.

PREFACE TO THE *YI ZHI*

When the first installment of the *Record* was complete, it was circulated among gentlemen and scholar officials. Today it has been published in Fujian,[2] Sichuan, Wuzhou[3] as well as Lin'an.[4] Every household has a copy.

Due to my interest in the extraordinary and veneration of the strange, people from far and wide send me details whenever they hear of such a story. Therefore, the amount of material I have received these last five years is comparable to what I had previously collected. And so I compiled it all under the name of *Yi zhi*. In total, both the two books of *Jia* and *Yi* comprise of six hundred stories and all manner of strange and uncanny stories found throughout the world have been included therein.

As for the anomalies of Qi Xie[5] and the reciprocity of Zhuangzi,[6] they are but illusive and insubstantial and cannot be questioned. Moreover, Gan Bao's *Record of the Search for Spirits*,[7] Niu Sengru's *Anomalies of the Recondite*,[8] Gu Shenzi's *Broad Expanse of the Extraordinary*,[9] the *East of the River*,[10] the *Record of the Dark Chamber*,[11] the *Examining Spirits*[12]—these works cannot all be without some allegorical content.[13] My book, however, having come about within a cycle of no more than sixty years, has utilized both my eyes and ears—and the stories within are all based on factual sources. If one does not believe me, they may go to Mr. Nobody[14] and ask him.

Hong Mai Jinglu of Poyang.

18th day of the twelfth month of the second year of the Qiandao period (1166).

The fifth month, summer, of the eighth year of the Qiandao period (1172): The Kuaiji edition has been republished in Ganzhou. Five stories have been omitted, two have been replaced and there has been a significant degree of editing throughout. Another edition was published in Jian'an[15] in the seventh month of the seventh year of the Chunxi period (1180).

The first section of the preface, as does the last, provides valuable information about the reception and initial publication of the work. Hong appears to be drawing a comparison between when the text was first completed and when it was published in several places including the capital. The pride which he took from such wide circulation is readily discernible.

Next he mentions his interest in the strange (*haoqi shangyi* 好奇尚異). This was evidently no secret, as people throughout the country sent him stories. Here, then, is the first of several references to Hong's method of collecting material and also to the collaborative nature of the undertaking. The eagerness of others to help Hong Mai also bears witness not only to Hong's enthusiasm for the "strange," but also to that of literati society at large.

Hong then mentions texts and authors associated with the earliest references to the term "*zhiguai*," that is, Zhuangzi and Qi Xie. From there he cites other *zhiguai* texts: the *Record of the Search for Spirits* from the Six Dynasties—generally considered an archetypal work of the "*zhiguai* genre." The next four are from the Tang and the last from the early Song. Hong regards the first two as "illusive and insubstantial" (*xuwu huanmang* 虛無幻茫), while the others, he alleges, contain allegory (*yuyan* 寓言). He then contrasts his own work with these supposedly allegorical works by claiming that his is not allegorical. It is, however, uncertain what Hong meant by "*yuyan*." As Charles Hartman has observed, while this approximates the Western concept of "allegory," the correlation is not exact.[16] I have opted to translate it as "allegory," mindful of the crucial difference between allegory in the Western literary tradition and in that of premodern China.

At the risk of oversimplification, the fundamental difference may be delineated as follows: although the concept of allegory changed over time in the West, what remained fundamental was the importance placed on the "other" level of meaning over and above the words on the page. In other words, the surface meaning of a text was disregarded and replaced by a "higher" level of meaning. This notion of allegory was, of course, predicated on the duality of Western cosmology and fitted well with the Judeo-Christian tradition's bifurcation between flesh and spirit. Such ideas were well articulated by Quintilian when he wrote that: "[allegory] presents one thing in words and another in meaning" (*aluid verbis aluid sensu ostendit* [VIII.6.44]).[17] Hence, in the twentieth century, theorists such as Angus Fletcher could postulate that allegory is where the surface meaning of a text is effaced and replaced by an "other" level of meaning.[18]

The premodern Chinese concept of the universe, on the contrary, did not allow for such ontological dualism, but rather conceived the world as an integral "whole." It did not differentiate between the phenomenal world and a metaphysical "other." In traditional Chinese cosmology, all reality existed on the same plane. Chinese allegorical devices, therefore, operated along a horizontal axis and, according to Plaks, were closer to the Western concept of synecdoche.[19]

This brings us to a crucial difference between the two: allegory as conceived according to the Western notion was necessarily lodged in fictional texts, while nonfictional ones could not logically support allegory. Yet Chinese allegorical devices allowed for the preservation of the text's historical integrity as when an historical figure was imbued with allegorical content. This was by no means limited to literary production. Chinese painting also drew upon this form of allegorical device. Examples most contemporaneous to Hong are some of the paintings Gaozong commissioned early in his reign, such as *Duke Wen of Jin Regaining his State*, attributed to Li Tang 李唐 (ca. 1070s–ca. 1150s).[20] Datable to the 1140s, this painting recalls the famous story from Sima Qian's *Record of the Grand Historian* (the *Shiji*) in which Prince Chung'er, the future Duke Wen of Jin (modern Shaanxi Province), was forced into exile over a dispute regarding his succession in 656 B.C.E. After many years, he finally returned to become Duke Wen in 636 B.C.E. The story of Duke Wen and its resonance with the plight of Gaozong early in his reign is all too apparent: after uncertain beginnings which—at one point—saw him flee to the ocean, Gaozong established the Southern Song, which ensured the survival of the Dynasty for almost 150 years. Here, therefore, one historical event was used to allude to another historical event. The anonymous painting from the same period, entitled *Eighteen Songs of a Nomad Flute: the Story of Lady Wenji*, is another apt example.[21] It recalls the story of Lady Wenji, who was abducted in 195 by Xiongnu hordes. After spending twelve years in Mongolia as wife of a Xiongnu chieftan, during which time she bore two sons, she was ransomed and returned home.[22] There are obvious parallels between this story and that of Gaozong's mother, the Empress Dowager Wei, who was captured along with the rest of the imperial clan and held hostage in the north. She was not released until a peace treaty was concluded between the Song and the Jurchen in 1142. This type of allegorical device was even used as recently as the Cultural Revolution (1966–75) when the virtuous Ming official Hai Rui (1514–1587) was used as a figure for Mao Zedong (1893–1976). Hence, Chinese allegorical devices do not necessarily rely on a fictitious text, as do those in the Western tradition.

In this respect, Chinese allegorical devices appear closer to the medieval European concept of *figura*. Auerbach defines this as: "something real and historical which announces something else that is also real and historical. The relation between the two events is revealed by an accord or similarity."[23] This idea was often used to interpret passages in the Bible. For example, Isaac's sacrifice in the Old Testament was regarded as a figure, or type, for that of Jesus' sacrifice.[24] This, however, undermines the logical link between allegory and fiction in the Western tradition.

Returning to Hong Mai's preface, he distinguishes between the possible existence of *yuyan* (however we choose to interpret it) in the previous works and his own accounts, which he claimed "are all based on factual sources" (*jie biaobiao you juyi zhe* 皆表表有據依者), or more literally, "all are based on something." Both *yuyan* and *juyi zhe* are somewhat ambiguous terms. Given, as we shall see in other prefaces, Hong's obsession with achieving an historically accurate record, his attempts to veto unreliable material, as well as the further research he carried out in regard dubious accounts, I would argue that Hong was referring to "factual or reliable sources" when he wrote "*juyi zhe*;" that is, his accounts are based on events which were thought to have actually occurred. This strongly suggests that *yuyan*, when contrasted to something that is factual, should be read as "allegory," given that writing which is allegorical—even according to traditional Chinese notions—points to something beyond the meaning of the words on the page, as in *yan zai ci er yi zai bi* 言 在 此 而 意 在 彼 (the words are here but the meaning is there). The plausibility of this interpretation will become apparent as we read more of Hong's prefaces. To be sure, in the preface of the *Zhiding* installment, Hong constructs a similar binary opposition: while asserting that selected tracts from the *Zhuangzi* and the *Annals of Spring and Autumn* are "allegorical" (*yuyan*), he argues that "all of the books of *Yi Jian* come entirely from tales passed on." In other words, they had a (more or less) factual basis. In short, Hong seems to be drawing a contrast between truth and falsity here.

Alternatively, *yuyan* might refer to a genre of didactic tales prevalent throughout the corpus of *zhiguai* literature. This would still fit the "truth versus falsity" paradigm. Yet Hong would likely not have claimed his collection devoid of didactic tales given that perhaps a fifth or a quarter of the extant text comprises such accounts, ranging from stories of karmic retribution for murder to execution-style death-by-lightning for unfilial acts. We may, therefore, be confident that he was referring to allegory. Hong's comments thus give us a valuable guide as to how he wished the *Record* to be interpreted: that is, not in an allegorical manner.

The *Record*, furthermore, as I observed in chapter 1, contains a powerful, didactic element discernible in an enormous number of extant narratives. This didacticism is predicated on Chinese traditional concepts of retribution as articulated in early works such as the *Master who Embraces the Simple* (*Bao puzi* 抱 樸 子) and the *Compendium of Supreme Retribution* (*Taishang ganying pian* 太 上 感 應 篇). The didactic message of such stories would logically rely on a nonallegorical interpretation of events. Should they be accorded an allegorical interpretation, this didacticism would not only be robbed of its persuasive power, the accounts themselves would be rendered meaningless, given that they were designed to act as warnings to others. That is, were contemporary readers to believe that so-and-so's unfilial daughter-in-law's death-by-lightning was not due to retribution for immoral behavior, then the whole didacticism so prevalent throughout the text would be undermined. In other words, it was the possibility that given accounts may have actually occurred which made the *Record* such a powerfully persuasive vehicle for the propagation of orthodox morality. Indeed, Leo Tak-hung Chan has made similar observations regarding the didactic nature of Ji Yun's accounts in his *Random Jottings at the Cottage of Close Scrutiny*.

> For Ju Yun, only when events are "true" can one draw moral lessons from them. His "didactics of the strange" is of a different order than, say, the didactics of Bunyan's *Pilgrims Progress*, in which moral exhortations are voiced in the context of a fictionalized narrative.[25]

Consequently, applying allegorical interpretations to the *Record*, against Hong Mai's expressed wishes, would seem inappropriate.

In a final comment to this preface, Hong directs any doubt about sources or reliability to Mr. Nobody, a character from Sima Xiangru's Han Dynasty rhapsody "Sir Fantasy" (*zixu fu* 子虛賦). On one level of interpretation, Hong appears to be saying "believe it or not." On another level, however, it could be viewed as an ambiguous disclaimer to his stated factuality. Since he asks the skeptic to verify the stories from someone who does not exist, he seems to observe that there can be no satisfactory verification—at least, presumably, in regard "paranormal" events. Hence, this implicit acknowledgment that the veracity of the stories might come into question would appear to be an exercise in preemptive apologetics. The "Sir Fantasy" rhapsody, in which Mr. Nobody first appears as a literary construct, was written in three parts and centers around an argument between three parties as to which hunting park (in the states of Qi and Chu) was best. In it, Mr. Nobody rebuffs the first speaker and is, in turn, himself rebuffed. Perhaps, then, the fact that Mr. Nobody was himself dismissed points to the idea that there is no supreme authority in regard to the veracity of the accounts.

Preface to the *Bing Zhi*

> When I first began compiling the *Record*, I was solely concerned with the extraordinary and the adoration of the strange. I originally had no intention of discussing the works of men or exposing their wickedness.[26] However, perhaps because it was easy to collect material, or due to my eagerness to fill chapters and complete the work, I more or less went against this initial intention. For example, the were-birds in the *Jia zhi*,[27] "Huang of Jianchang's Injustice,"[28] "Feng Dangke,"[29] "The Matters of Jiang Mao's Heart" from the *Yi zhi*[30] are all largely unlike [the facts] and even border on the slander of good people. Furthermore, the story of "Madame Dong—the Female Knight-Errant,"[31] is also not in accord with what was actually said. This is probably partly due to the fault of the tellers, and partly due to my listening and not having verified the details—for this I am deeply ashamed.
>
> I have engaged in a process of correcting and editing the superfluous stories which I have collected, and they are enough to make up a third book. Disheartened by previous misdemeanors, I wished to desist. However, having become intoxicated by habit, I cannot stop despite myself. Some inquisitive gentlemen[32] again led me astray. And so I privately absolve myself with the words "simply relating stories of ghosts and deities is sufficient; there is no need to touch upon anything else."
>
> I have, therefore, turned these stories into the *Bing zhi*, which also comprises of twenty chapters totaling 267 stories.
>
> Hong Mai Jinglu.
> 18th day of the fifth month of the seventh year of the Qiandao period (1171). [33]

In light of Hong's claims in the preface to the *Yi zhi* that his stories were reliable and based on fact, the revelations here that some of them were inaccurate is quite a contrast and qualify his claims of factual reliability. In later prefaces Hong gave further examples whereby subsequent investigations disproved reported events. Hence, while the reader was not apparently supposed to apply an allegorical interpretation and can accept that the narratives display a high degree of historicity, historical accuracy could not always, it seems, be assured.

Hong's scrupulous citing of sources, in addition to known antecedents, is well known. Yet a closer look at the frequency of such citations according to each installment reveals an interesting phenomenon: Hong initially rarely cited precursor texts. It is only from the *Bing* installment onwards that he begins to give a significant number of such references. In the third column of Appendix 1, I show precursor texts for which Hong gave a reference and those for which he did not. From this we can see that throughout the twenty-chapter *Jia zhi*, he only cited two precursor texts, while a mere three were cited in the *Yi zhi*. Yet in the *Bing* installment, no fewer than fifteen are given. In the *Ding* installment, thirteen are given. The remaining installments from the first series are, as previously noted, no longer extant, so it is not possible to ascertain the frequency for these. The next extant installment, the *Zhijia zhi*, contains three citations: fewer than those in the *Bing* and *Ding* installments, yet—as previously noted—installments from the *Zhijia* onward contain only ten chapters. Hence, allowing for the fewer number of chapters, the lower frequency of citation in this installment is still higher than that of the first two. The *Zhiyi zhi* contains four citations, the *Zhijing* eight, and so on.

As can be seen from an installment by installment comparison, the *Bing zhi* appears to have been somewhat of a "watershed" as far as Hong's citing of precursor texts is concerned. What caused this change? If accounts which he previously claimed were historically reliable later came to be proven unreliable, it would have been little wonder that he wished to desist. Yet he continued. After this turning point, the tone of his prefaces became gradually less conceited and he frequently referred to the degree of "accuracy" (or lack of) displayed by his accounts as well as his efforts to verify details. Although we cannot be certain, I would argue that the criticism referred to in this preface was genuine and that it affected his future approach to collecting and recording.

Furthermore, we know that the *Bing* installment was completed in 1171, given the date of its preface. Yet, in the concluding colophon to the extant preface to the *Yi* installment, Hong tells of how the 1172 Kuaiji edition was a reprint with significant editing and replacement of certain accounts. The timing of this revised edition and the completion of the *Bing zhi*—in whose preface Hong makes this apology—closely coincides. This strongly suggests that Hong's motivation for revising the Kuaiji edition was to replace accounts whose historical reliability had been subsequently discredited. Here, perhaps, is further evidence of behavioral change. Therefore, the possibility that the criticism he responded to in the preface of the *Bing zhi* was indeed factual becomes all the more likely.

The account entitled "Madam Dong—the Female Knight-Errant," told by eminent Song man of letters Fan Chengda 范 成 大 (1126–1193), is of particular interest. In 1997, PRC scholar Zhang Zhuping demonstrated that the conclusion of this account as it appears in the 1981 Beijing edition—the most expanded one to date—was missing. Zhang then reproduced the hitherto unknown section based on a manuscript kept in the Shanghai library.[34] This copy was made by eminent calligrapher and scholar, Zhu Yunming 祝 允 明 (1460–1526) and seems to have been based on an earlier edition of the *Record* than that on which the 1981 edition was based. The account tells of a Song Dynasty official, Dong Guoqing 董 國 慶, who was stranded in the north after the Jurchen invasion. He was, however, assisted by a clever concubine who was given to him during his stay in the north. The concubine enlisted her brother's help to return Dong to his home. After his return, he was swiftly honored with an official appointment by the then grand councilor, Qin Gui, given their close personal connections. The account concludes with Dong's death shortly after his return.

According to Zhu Yunming's manuscript, however, Dong's given name should be Guodu 國 度, rather than Guoqing, an error possibly committed by careless block-carvers. Toward the end of the story, the concubine eventually ran away after having been mistreated by Dong's wife. The metatextual information about Qin Gui is the same, but the reader is told how Dong died in a bizarre and unnatural manner. The reason given was retribution for his ingratitude toward the loyal concubine who had been instrumental in his survival and subsequent return. Hence, this shares the strong didactic theme discernible throughout the *Record*. Zhang Zhuping convincingly concludes that Hong later reedited the account after having discovered that the circumstances surrounding Dong's death were untrue.[35] This, therefore, is further evidence of Hong's sincerity concerning achieving a factually reliable record.

It also sheds light on the nature of any unreliable material that undoubtedly found its way into the *Record* in addition to what Hong considered to be "reliable." In this case, Hong did not erase the entire account, only the details about Dong's death and the events following his concubine's arrival. Given that these events supposedly did not occur, Hong is clearly aiming to record material that is factually correct, that is, events that actually occurred (or in the case of paranormal events, those which were thought to have occurred).

While it is unclear if Fan Chengda was aware of the unreliable details, or if he deliberately fabricated them to Dong Guoqing's (or Guodu's) detriment, Hong gives this as an example of how unreliable accounts amounted to "slander"—or more precisely, in modern Western legalistic terms, libel. As there may well have been other similar accounts that libeled their protagonists—as Hong implied, perhaps some of Hong's informants knowingly told him unreliable tales with the intention of borrowing his brush to vilify their adversaries.

Scholars who use the *Record* as a source of Song social history would do well to bear this possibility in mind.

I do not intend to dwell on why Hong continued to strive for historical accuracy when he realized that spurious content would be included, or that the existence of precursor texts would compromise the professed contemporaneous nature of his spatio-temporal setting. In the preface of the *Ding zhi*, however, he mentioned how he would supply a comment at the conclusion of an account should he have harbored doubts about authenticity. Here he cited "love of the strange" as his reason for persevering.[36] Perhaps Gardner's observation about the Chinese historiographical tradition offers us a tool by which to further understand Hong's method of collecting and recording stories, in addition to the degree of historicity they exhibited; that is, statements not contradicted were entitled to be accepted.[37] Hence, Hong's self-professed love of the unusual was so great that dubious stories were, to a greater or lesser degree, included. Paradoxically, admission of partial inaccuracy reveals Hong's sincere wish to provide an accurate record. This preface, therefore, alerts us to a variation in Hong's authorial intention during the 1160s and early 1170s, during which the production of the *Yi* and *Bing* installments was undertaken.

The preface also reveals the possible contents of the missing *Jia zhi* preface. That is, Hong's professed interest in the strange and his avowed intention to write about nothing but the "paranormal." Lastly, we gain an insight into his eagerness to complete further installments—something which became more apparent in later years when he sometimes took but a few months to complete one installment, albeit one smaller than the *Bing zhi*.

PREFACE TO THE *DING ZHI*

The four books from the *Jia* to the *Ding zhi* contain 1150 stories of no fewer than 30,000 words.[38] There was one who read them and laughed, saying:

"The *Book of Odes*, the *Book of Documents*, the *Book of Change* and the *Annals of Spring and Autumn* did not exceed 10,000 words altogether. Sima's [Qian's] *Records of the Grand Historian*, from beginning to end, contained several thousand entries and was no more than 80,000 words. Unable to concentrate on the classics, you open your doors and spend thirty years taxing your heart, mouth, ears and eyes on bits and pieces about extraordinary gods and fanciful anomalies. You search for ink and waste paper, yet the end result amounts to about half of the historical work by the Grand Historian.[39] Rambling and disorganized, it is not what the sages[40] would have said and is not what Yang Ziyun would have read.[41] Having this book brings not one bit of good, and of what loss would it be should the world be without it? Given that it is already quite laughable, you still search for proof. Heeding not what comes from wise men and scholar officials, you all too eagerly accept whatever strange story is to be had from the down and out, wild monks, mountain travelers, Taoists, blind shamans, common women, minor officials, itinerant soldiers—and there are never any questions asked. Why is it necessary for people to seek truth in these tales—is that not even more ridiculous?"

I, too, laughed and said: "The Six Classics come to us from the hands of the sages, so who am I to contest them? As for the Grand Historian's stories, let me expand a little on what you have said. He recorded matters relating to Duke Mu of Qin and Zhao Jianzi; are these not tales of extraordinary gods?[42] The spirit gentleman of Changling and the yellow stone beneath the bridge;[43] are these not fantastic? When writing about the deeds of Jing Ke[44], were not the events verified by an imperial doctor, Xia Wuju?[45] When writing about the appearance of the Marquis of Liu,[46] was it not verified by an artisan? Imperial doctors and artisans; what is the difference between them and the down and out, the shamans and the minor officials to whom you have referred above? As for one who knows how to learn from the Grand Historian, there is probably no one like myself. You should take your tongue and go back from whence you came—cease your laughter."

On another day, the *Wu zhi* was completed.

Annotation from the Yan (Yuanzhao 嚴元照 [1773–1817]) edition: This preface is not complete. The Yuan Dynasty edition supplemented it with a page of a chapter's ending from the *Ding zhi*; absurd! Today there is a blank page.

Also, this preface seems to be the preface from the *Wu zhi*.[47]

Hong uses the exchange between himself and the anonymous interlocutor to problematize the fluid boundary between what modern readers intuitively understand as *zhiguai* writing (here referred to as the extraordinary and the fantastic) and that of official historiography. Ouyang Xiu 歐陽修 (1007–1072) was the first to expunge the *zhiguai* from the history section of the *Bibliographic Treatise* (*yiwen zhi*) when he edited the *New History of the Tang*, and this set a precedent thereafter. Up until then, works now considered *zhiguai* were classified as a sub-branch of history. After Ouyang Xiu, they were mostly relegated to the *xiaoshuo* section under the rubric of "philosophers" in the four-fold classification system. Part of the earlier confusion between the *zhiguai* and official history writing, it would seem, was due to the overlap between the two in terms of motif and form—particularly motif. Official histories included much astrological and divinatory material, as well as paranormal events such as those Hong Mai referred to in this preface; indeed, many examples exist throughout the *Records of the Grand Historian* (*Shiji* 史記). Also, the *Biography of King Mu* (*Mu Tianzi zhuan* 穆天子傳), while containing mythological elements and paranormal events, in addition to exhibiting a clear cosmological focus, was classified as a record of rest and repose in the history section of the *Bibliographic Treatises* up until the compilation of the *Four Libraries'* (*Siku quanshu* 四庫全書) collection. This was presumably due to the narrative, which is built around a royal tour of inspection focusing on the king's daily routine. Even as late as the Yuan Dynasty, many paranormal events were recorded in the *History of the Song*. Therefore, by pointing out that respected literature such as the *Records of the Grand Historian* included many paranormal events, Hong Mai attempted to deflect adverse criticism of the *Record*'s questionable nature and, at the same time, legitimize *zhiguai* accounts by association with orthodox literature. Seen from this light, the whole preface is an exercise in apologetics. Nevertheless, it remains a unique discussion about the nature of *zhiguai* texts and provides useful material for those wishing to understand what Chinese authors and critics conceptualized as *zhiguai*. Hong's recognition of the liquid boundary between what was regarded as official history and *zhiguai* reveals his perspicacity.

Interestingly enough, his words find an echo in Robert Scholes's ideas about what he regards as a spectrum between history and fiction.

> Now only a recording angel, taking note of all the deeds of men without distorting or omitting anything, could be called a 'pure' historian. And only a kind of deity, creating a world out of his own imagination, could be called a 'pure' fantasist. Both ends of the spectrum are invisible to mortal eyes. All history recorded by men becomes fictional. All human fantasy involves some resemblance—however far-fetched—to life."[48]

The same idea appears in Scholes and Kellogg's *The Nature of Narrative* whereby it is argued that "Aristotle's distinction between history and fiction was one of degree, not of kind."[49] Hong's commentary, furthermore, strikes a chord with Sinfield when he wrote, ". . . the social order cannot but produce faultlines through which its own criteria of plausibility fall into contest and disarray."[50] Such an observation could aptly describe the existence of *zhiguai* motifs in Chinese canonical texts. Hong Mai, over eight hundred years ago, was one who recognized this. The issue of where *zhiguai* writing ends and where official history begins merits further exploration, especially given the catholic nature of the *Record*'s content. I will discuss this further in chapter 4.

Preface to the *Wu Zhi* According to the *Bintui lu*

The [preface of the] *Wu zhi* states:

> While I was in Fujian, Ye Huishu[51] undertook a considerable amount of searching for strange tales so as to assist with my recording. He once told me, "recently there were some merchants who were sailing on the ocean and, before they knew it, they were swallowed up into the stomach of a giant fish. It was sufficiently spacious inside and so they didn't die, not even after a day. Now there also happened to be some carpenters present who cut open the fish's belly with their axes. In pain, the fish splashed back into the great ocean. And everyone aboard the ship—including the fish—died." Teasingly, I

said to him, "If everyone on the boat died, then who was alive to tell the tale?" He laughed heartily, not knowing what to say. I am, therefore, always afraid that this sort of thing will be unavoidable.

This preface affords an insight into Hong's filtering process. Anxious to remain faithful to historical fact, he was understandably unwilling to include stories he considered spurious. Judging by other sources, too, it is clear that Hong pondered long and hard over historicity and plausibility. In his *Rongzhai suibi*, he raises doubt about the truthfulness of one of the *Ji zhi* accounts and expresses his regret at having included it.[52] In the case of the above story, as Hong realized, it could not have possibly occurred. Perhaps most significantly, his final comment reveals awareness of possible unreliable content—contrary to his bold claims from the *Yi zhi* preface.

Hong's informant, Ye Huishu, seems to have attempted a joke here, that is, passing off fictitious material as historical for no particular reason other than to test Hong's gullibility. Other seemingly spurious *Record* accounts may well have been told to Hong for the same purpose.

Preface to the *Ji Zhi* According to the Guests Retire

The [preface to the] *Ji zhi* states:

> I used *Yi Jian* to name my book, thinking that it did not emulate previous works. Later I obtained a copy of Zhang Shensu's (Magistrate of Huayuan during the Tang) *Record of Yi Jian*[53] who also took the story from the *Book of Liezi*. I was pleased that he had the same idea.

The mention of Liezi refers to the above-quoted passage from the fourth century B.C.E. *Book of Liezi* in which Yijian, a legendary figure, heard and recorded the acts of the legendary King Yu.

Preface to the *Geng Zhi* According to the Guests Retire

The [preface of the] *Geng zhi* states:

> When I was a magistrate in Dangtu,[54] the locality was remote and there was little with which to occupy myself. Lü Yuqing of Jinan[55] and Wu Dou-nan of Luoyang,[56] once sent me enough old tales to fill half a book. I have, therefore, edited them into the *Geng zhi*. The completion of the *Jia zhi* took eighteen years.
>
> Installments from the *Yi* to the *Ji zhi* required sometimes seven years, sometimes five or six. Now it has taken but a few months—how leisure time has helped. I have had much leisure time in my life, so how could I not be interested in writing? Yet it (the *Record*) still would have been easier to circulate without its enormous size. Toward the end I wrote about Zhang Deyu's (Zhang Sen) embassy to the Jurchen.

Readers have asked: "Will there be any more after *Yijian's Ding zhi* installment?" And so I used the stories of Letian[57] and Dongpo[58] to illustrate my point.

This preface speaks of the increasingly collaborative nature of the work. Hong, prior to this installment, was known to have collected several stories from the one informant and arranged them together. But here two informants send him a large amount of material which formed a major part of this installment. Since the installment is no longer extant, it is not possible to determine exactly how much. Unfortunately, no biographical details are known about these two informants.

PREFACE TO THE *XIN ZHI* ACCORDING TO THE *BINTUI LU*

The [preface of the] *Xin zhi* records:

> When I first began writing my book, I wished to emulate Duan Chengshi's *Nuogao ji* by calling mine the *Rongzhai nuogao.*[59] I later disliked such imitation. In any case, I would not have been able to tolerate readers constantly querying it. So I changed it to the present title. I gave the questions and answers of Xiang Juyuan as my reason.[60]

The last section of Duan Chengshi's 段程式 (c. 800–863) *Miscellaneous Morsels from Youyang* (*Youyang zazu* 酉陽雜俎) was entitled the *Nuogao ji* 諾皋集.[61] This is the first time Hong mentions this famous Tang Dynasty *zhiguai* work, which he obviously regarded highly. The *nuogao* section is extremely similar to the *Record*'s format in regard to references made by its author. The arrangement of material is also similar.

PREFACE TO THE *REN ZHI* ACCORDING TO THE *BINTUI LU*

The *Ren zhi* is entirely comprised of quotations from the preface of Wang Jingwen's *Other Record of the Listener.*

Wang Jingwen's *Other Record of the Listener* (*Yijian biezhi* 夷堅別志) was the first imitation of the *Record*. It is, unfortunately, no longer extant. Part of the preface, however, was summarized in renowned Ming (1368–1644) bibliophile Hu Yinglin's 胡應麟 (1551–1602) *Collected Essays from the Shaoshi Shanfang Studio* (*Shaoshi shanfang bicong* 少室山房筆叢, hereafter *Essays*). As Wang lavishly praises Hong Mai and the *Record*, I will return to it later in this chapter when I discuss textual reception.

PREFACE TO THE *GUI ZHI* ACCORDING TO THE *BINTUI LU*

The [preface of the] *Gui zhi* states:

> I was 71[62] by the time nine installments were complete. When I began work on the *Gui zhi* my youngest son, Huaifu,[63] said to me, "You need to continue

the book using the twelve earthly branches, from *zi* to *hai*. Only then will it be complete."

I said to him: "Heaven would have to grant twice the years allotted me before this is possible. Life is, however, unpredictable. Who knows whether I can do this?"

This is the first we hear of Hong's youngest son. Although little is known about him, we do know that Hong conferred official status on him in 1179 under his *yin* privilege: this appears to have been the year of his birth.[64]

PREFACE TO THE *ZHIJIA ZHI*

The book of *Yijian* is complete. There are ten installments totaling two hundred chapters which contain 2,709 stories. This has taken about 52 years from start to finish. It took approximately four cycles [of twelve years] from the [beginning of the] first (*Jia zhi*) to the [completion of the] fifth record (*Wu zhi*), yet only five years were expended from the sixth (*Ji zhi*) to the tenth (*Gui zhi*). The speed of production has been thus irregular. Although some have told me that quantity can not be uniform, this has not been a problem.

Some have suspected my recordings of having similar parts to those before me. There have even been busybodies who have gone as far as accusing me of stealing in order to fuel my stories. This is incorrect. From ancient times until now, there has always been the inexhaustible, and there has always been the never ending[65]—the vast and the illusive, the myriad of different things. If one analyses them closely, one finds that there are no two things alike. To quote Zhuangzi:

"[Things are what they are called.] What are they? They are what they are. What are they not? They are not what they are not."

He also says: "Right is also not right, and 'so' is also 'not so.' If right were necessarily right, then with regard to the difference between right and not right there should be no dispute. If 'so' were necessarily 'so,' then with regard to the difference between 'so' and 'not so' there should also be no dispute."[66]

Those able to understand this precept will be able to read my book.

Initially, I intended to adopt my youngest son's suggestion of using the twelve earthly branches to name future installments. Duan Kegu,[67] however, named the four follow-on installments of his work, *Miscellaneous Morsels from Youyang*,[68] with the character *zhi* 支: that is, the *Zhi Nuogao, Zhidong, Zhizhi*. This was new and innovative. I therefore named the present installment the *Zhijia*. Since it is an add-on to the previous ones, I have shortened it to ten chapters.

Old Man of the Wilderness.

The first day of the sixth month in the fifth year of the Shaoxi period (1194).

As shown in Appendix 1, a significant proportion of Hong's stories are taken from previous literary works, some for which Hong cited references, others for which he did not. This practice of borrowing from the works of others was, nevertheless, not uncommon throughout the Song and was especially prevalent during the Yuan. Appendix 1 affords some indication of Hong Mai's borrowing—although it is by no means an exhaustive list. Conversely, the borrowing of Hong's stories by others enabled the survival of narratives which would have otherwise been lost.[69] Moreover, borrowing and replicating the accounts of others was part of the traditional Chinese historiographical tradition.

Hong quotes from the *Zhuangzi* in an attempt to deflect adverse criticism that he stole material. The lines to which he refers are taken from chapter 3. The title of this chapter—the "Qiwu lun" 齊物論—is the invention of later scholars, and English translations vary greatly depending on the philosophical predilection of the translator. For example, Wing-tsit Chan renders it as "The Equality of Things and Opinions," in *Sources of Chinese Tradition*.[70] A. C. Graham translates it as "The Sorting Which Evens Things Out."[71] Fung Yu Lan, in his *History of Chinese Philosophy*, has opted for "The Equality of Things and Opinions."[72] Watson renders it as the "Discussion on Making All Things Equal,"[73] while Legge prefers "The Adjustment of Controversies."[74] These differing titles reflect a fundamental divergence in the interpretation of the title (and by extension, the chapter), which is inherently ambiguous. One could read it to mean "all things are equal" and thereby impose a relativistic interpretation on the content. Alternatively, one could view the chapter as a discourse among others and one which is not indicative of authorial standpoint. The first three translators adhere to the relativistic interpretation, while the latter two opt for ambiguity, which relies on the discourse itself to unlock the text's meaning.

According to a relativistic interpretation, Hong seems to be referring to the relative nature of things. His preamble about things being inexhaustible and neverending would appear to refer to the unique aspects of all things, including the subtle variations between different "versions" of the same "story," whether the mode of transmission was oral or written. Given that much of the material reproduced in the *Record* was told orally, Hong's comments are reminiscent of what Jack Goody has observed about the transmission of oral texts in oral cultures, particularly in relation to the telling of the Bagre myth by the Lo Dagaa of northern Ghana. Goody observes that the concept of a one, fixed "original" version is inappropriate when discussing oral cultures. A lack of written texts, which could otherwise be compared by setting them "side by side" (as is the case with literate cultures), makes it impossible to determine which of several variations is the "original." Therefore, versions proliferate.[75] While Song China was far from an oral culture, Goody's remarks would seem applicable to the informal storytelling, of which Hong's collecting and recording formed a significant part, that proliferated during this period.

Hong uses Zhuangzi to illustrate the relativistic nature of these oral texts and urges the reader to not be overly concerned with their likeness. Hence, as with his utilization of orthodox history to lend *zhiguai* texts authority, he enlists the venerated Taoist classic to apologize for including "contemporary" accounts which may be traced to older ones. His statement, "[t]hose able to understand this precept will be able to read my book," amounts to an emotional appeal aimed at subduing his detractors. By linking a reader's ability to understand the *Zhuangzi* with an understanding of his methodology, Hong subtly engages the readers' approval through their intellectual vanity. His implicit message seems to be: if you can't understand my precept, then neither can you understand the *Zhuangzi*.

Nevertheless, the adverse reaction by those "busybodies" to whom Hong refers demonstrates that at least some contemporaries held expectations of an original account, perhaps fuelled by the growing importance placed on written texts at the time, given advances in printing. Similarly, in the preface below, Hong himself expresses fear that material he collected would be "stolen" (*wei wai duo* 為外奪) by outsiders. Therefore, perhaps we should not be overly lenient to Hong Mai when uncited antecedents are discovered. These comments also lead to the question of originality and authenticity. This, however, will be addressed in chapter 5.

Hong's discussion of Duan Chengshi's work further demonstrates his high regard for this Tang text which, as I discussed above, shares much intertextual commonality with the *Record*.

Preface to the *Zhiyi Zhi*

During the month of the *La* Festival[76] in the *gengxu* year of the Shaoxi period (1190), I returned west from Kuaiji (modern-day Shaoxing in Jiangsu).[77] There had been a heavy snowfall and snow was clogging the roads. I had come from afar and both tiredness and cold were vying with each other. So I rested for over a month, restoring my soul and organizing my manuscripts. I am old. Neither do I pay attention to reading books anymore, nor have I any taste for writing; only my love for the strange is still very strong. The ears heaven bestowed me have not failed and I can still appreciate the stories of guests. My mind has not deteriorated and I remember all I have heard without forgetting anything. The power of my writing brush has not dissipated and, for the most part, I can still narrate the stories I come across.

When my many relatives travel to Hunan, Sichuan, Hubei, or Guangxi they always inform me when they hear of an unusual tale. So as to prevent the material being stolen by outsiders, in the summer of the *jiayin* year (1194), the three additional installments to the *Record* of *Xin*, *Ren*, and *Gui* were completed,[78] totaling sixty chapters along with ten chapters of the *Zhijia*. A mere eight months later, the *Zhiyi* was also completed.

I have, therefore, been pleased with my seventy-three years of recording events and have thus marked the passing of time.

Old Man of the Wilderness.

The 28th day of the second month in the inaugural year of the Qingyuan period (1195).

This preface was written soon after Hong Mai's permanent return to his birthplace once he had received an honorary emolument. It would seem that the three installments of *Xin*, *Ren*, and *Gui* were all possibly published in the same year—1194. In any case, not only did he complete three, twenty-chapter install-ments in one year, the ten-chapter *Zhijia zhi* was also brought to a conclusion the same year. Were they, then, published together as an integral set? Was publication a catalyst for such speed? Unfortunately, unlike the preface of the *Yi zhi*, in which Hong brags about wide circulation, he is silent on publication details here.

Although these installments are no longer extant, we are able to deter-mine their completion year from this preface, hence the dates given in Table 1. Since each comprises twenty chapters, it would seem unlikely that Hong could have gathered the stories, adapted, and transcribed them all in the same year. It is, therefore, likely that the material had already been collected and partially worked on prior to 1194. Hong's statement that he wished to prevent the material from being stolen, as well as organizing his manuscripts, would appear to support this. Furthermore, the four-year gap between their comple-tion and that of the last installment for which we know the completion year— the *Ji zhi* finished in 1190—also points to this.

Hong's reference to his relatives providing material from far-away Sichuan is also of interest, given that a significant number of accounts about Sichuan can be found throughout the extant corpus of the *Record* despite Hong's never hav-ing stayed there for any extended period of time—as far as we know. Even had he made a trip which did not survive in extant historical records, the volume of material about Sichuan suggests numerous informants over an extended period.

PREFACE TO THE *ZHIJING ZHI*

The *Zhiyi* installment was completed in one year and two months; the *Zhi-jing* was completed in ten months. The speed of production has surpassed my previous efforts.

The given name of my great-great-grandfather, who was a junior guard-ian,[79] coincided with the heavenly stem which follows that of *yi*, except that it had the fire radical to its left. Therefore, since I am writing another series, I have used that which I borrowed from the Tang Dynasty gentleman[80] and have named this installment the *Zhijing zhi*.

When the third book of *Yi Jian* came out, someone who saw it remarked in astonishment, "[i]t is not lacking in propriety to mention a private taboo name should it already be in the public domain. You are just wasting words."

And so I directly referred to it. Yet the book is sprouting off-shoots, and so my youngest son beseeched me, "[w]hat you are writing is unofficial history, which is different from the official documents which he referred to. It is, therefore, not inappropriate to adhere to private taboos. You *should* refrain from mentioning [the name]."

I therefore entitle it *Zhijing*. As I am afraid that like-minded [gentlemen] who see it will be confused should they have read the first series, I take this opportunity to explain what I have done.

The 13th day of the tenth month in the inaugural year of the Qingyuan period (1195).

As I discussed earlier, Hong Mai followed the traditional taboo whereby names of deceased relatives were not directly invoked. He discusses the merit of this with an interlocutor whereby—through recourse to his youngest son—he distinguishes between the writing of official documents and discursive essays and of unofficial historiography. Because of his self-proclaimed affiliation with the latter, he apparently felt it appropriate to adhere to the taboo. Hong's reference to himself as a writer of unofficial history is significant when we consider the *Record*'s genre, which I explore further in chapter 4.

Also of significance is the correspondence between Hong's behavioral change—the alteration of the title—and the contents of his preface. Were one to view Hong's prefaces as mere literary constructions aimed to pique reader's interest, rather than serious discussions "based on something," the content would not necessarily be corroborated by tangible evidence such as a title change.

Preface to the *Zhiding Zhi*

As for the yarns of minor officials,[81] their words cannot be relied upon; this has always been so. Reliability begets reliability and suspicion begets suspicion. This has been the case ever since the three commentaries to the *Annals of Spring and Autumn*, let alone stories of resisting pirates and those of Hui Shi,[82] the works of Zhuangzi and his disciple, Gengsang Chu, and the commentaries of all his followers;[83] they are all profound and allegorical!

All of the books of *Yi Jian* come entirely from tales passed on. If I receive a story from somewhere, I keep it; that is all. If it was difficult to read or parts were mis-transcribed, I would correct it myself.

When the *Zhiding* installment was complete, I took several stories in order to test their strangeness, such as "Wu Geng of Hezhou Passes the Examinations of 1137,"[84] or "Liu Guo of Xiangyang Passes the Examinations of 1175;"[85] I checked them in the *Record of Successful Examination Candidates*[86] and found them to be untrue. Zhang Yuan of Yongde obtained a giant bamboo from a coastal mountain and a foreign merchant gave him five thousand strings of cash [for it].[87] Someone named Zhu from Shangrao obtained a rock crystal, and a landscape gardener gave nine thousand strings of cash [for it].[88] Wang the scholar from Mingzhou proved the phenomena of Karma Temple, which was reminiscent of the business at the Cheng County mountain convent. Brother Enlightened, the monk of Sichuan, died in the stead of Zhao Anhua; how on earth can one die in another's stead?[89] The stone tablet of the Four Ancestor's Pagoda in Qizhou[90] was written by Guo Jingchun,[91] yet Jingchun died in the early Eastern Jin period (317–420)—over two hundred years from the time of the tablet. Anything like these stories is truly controversial. When I write of such things, I will make a note beneath the story. This is the curse of loving the strange. I would wish the reader to simply enjoy them and not be over-critical.

The 19th day of the third month of the second year of the Qingyuan period (1196).

Here Hong discusses the historical factuality of *Record* accounts and his attempts to verify their accuracy. He also gives us an insight into one of his methods—recourse to (official) historical records. And from the results of the investigation he conducted here, we can understand something of the gap between his professed reliability (particularly discernable in earlier prefaces) and the demands of collecting, whereby the inclusion of misleading or inaccurate reports became inevitable given the breadth and nature of his undertaking, something which he expressed fear of in the preface to the *Wu zhi*. Yet, as was standard procedure for traditional Chinese historians, stories not contradicted deserved inclusion[92]—whether they were contradicted due to internal inconsistencies, by comparison with other sources, or through later investigation. Discourse like this would seem, nevertheless, indicative of Hong's desire to achieve historical reliability while simultaneously warning us about placing unwarranted credence in any given account without support from other sources.

PREFACE TO THE *ZHIWU ZHI*

There are a hundred or so stories about dreams in every installment of the *Record*. With eerie and sinister overtones, they tell of omens which have proven correct. Yet none surpasses those of the *Annals of Lü Buwei*[93] for their abnormality. According to this, Duke Zhuang of Qi[94] had a minister called Bin Beizhong. He once dreamed of a warrior type who wore a hat of thin, white silk with a crimson chin-strap and tails. Dressed in fine cotton, he was shod in new sandals and carried a black scabbard. Following the dreamer, he bellowed out at him and then spat in his face. Bin promptly woke up, but sat despondent for the remainder of the night. On the following day he called his friend over and told him, "I have admired courage since I was young and have never suffered any slight from people in my sixty years. Now that I have been humiliated by this person in the night, I will go and seek him out. If I find him within a given period, then well and good. If I do not, then my life will be forfeit." And so he and his friend encamped for three days at an appointed hour on the main road without coming across him. He returned to commit suicide.

Now I believe that, although people throughout the ages have harbored differing ideals, there have probably been those who have conducted themselves with straightforward directness. But a story such as this in no way displays emotions which human beings should harbor. I suspect Mr. Lü has fabricated it for the purpose of composition. Otherwise, how could there be one who, after being insulted in the night, goes to seek the aggressor on the highroad, which then brings about his own death devoid of any regrets? His so-called friend is also an imbecile. He did not utter one word with which to console him—this is folly indeed! I cannot help but laugh whenever I read this book. Thus, on completion of the *Zhiwu zhi* installment, I have presented the story here for the amusement of the curious.

The fifth day of the seventh month of the second year of the Qingyuan period (1196).

Hong's attitude toward his own writing in relation to what he saw as similar works can be seen clearly from this preface. It is significant to note that he does not apply an allegorical interpretation to this narrative. His criticism that the narrative is "fabricated" (*jia she* 假設), or fictitious, appears to be based on its apparent lack of verisimilitude, illogical plot development, and unrealistic portrayal of human emotion. By implication, it reveals the importance Hong places on these considerations. Furthermore, Hong's criticism that the above narrative was "fabricated" stands in contrast to the purported historical accuracy and high degree of verisimilitude exhibited in his own narratives. This binary opposition, therefore, is further evidence of his faithfulness to factuality, as well as the disdain he seemed to reserve for "fabricated" texts.

Hong's comments about the *Annals of Lü Buwei* aptly illustrate Rania Huntington's point about truth versus falsity in *zhiguai* accounts. When discussing how premodern authors problematized questions of belief, Huntington observes that, "[b]elief in some level of supernatural interaction with the human world was the mainstream view throughout the history of pre-modern China, but at the same time it was acknowledged that these were particularly fertile grounds for fabrication and delusion."[95] Hong, nonetheless, appeared to carefully assess the factuality of accounts he recorded. Given its importance to him, the exploration of truth versus falsity issues I undertake in chapter 5 is all the more pertinent to our understanding of the text.

Preface to the *Zhiji Zhi* According to the *Bintui lu*

The [preface to the] *Zhiji* states that:

> There has never been a time without stories of the marvelous and strange. Therefore all the books of *Yijian* examine such stories; from journies to the towering firmament made through tranquil dreams, excursions to Penglai,[96] meetings

with the vastness [of the universe], dying, dying and returning to life, seeing the center of the earth and the Oceans of Ming and Zhang; to island ghosts and spirits of the abyss, serpentine spirits and bovine demons—tens of thousands of such things [are recorded therein]. Such phenomena has been seen by more than one person; what one hears reported is more than one account; and the dimensions traversed are more than one, yet none are the same.

PREFACE TO THE *ZHIGENG ZHI*

The *Zhigeng* installment of the *Record* was completed in forty-four days, from the *gengwu* day of the tenth month to the *guichou* day of the twelfth month.[97] It includes 135 stories in all. My youngest son beheld it and jumped as though enraptured [by it]—even I am astounded by his cleverness.

I record the stories of guests whenever I hear them. If we are busy drinking and there is insufficient time, I will write them down the following day and show the teller as soon as I can. I do not cease until there are no discrepancies therein. Hence I do not lose what I have heard and its truthfulness may be passed on.

I have again received twenty stories from Lü Deqing. The country gentleman, Wu Liao (courtesy name Wu Boqin), resurrected some notes written long ago by his father, the Dweller of Lofty Places.[98] I have borrowed a third of these to make up three chapters so as to complete this installment.[99] I have, therefore, been able to finish it this quickly.

The 8th day of the twelfth month of the second year of the Qingyuan period (1196).

This preface, as with those of the *Geng* and *Zhiding zhi*, not only alludes to Hong's methods of collecting stories for later installments, but also refers to one of his verification methods and his editing procedure—that is, his claim of minimal editing. It is interesting to note that he included only a third of the borrowed manuscript rather than accepting it entirely. Here then is further evidence of filtering, although his criteria is unclear. Was he only extracting tales of the strange among accounts of a miscellaneous nature, or was he concerned with issues of factuality, or both? Yet his terminology—to steal (*piaoqu* 剽取)—contradicts his rebuttal from previous prefaces that he did not borrow on a large scale from other works. Perhaps he makes an unspoken distinction between material borrowed from living informants and that taken from previous literary works?

Again there are references to the speed of production—presumably due to the collaborative nature of information gathering, which was particularly apparent in the later installments.

PREFACE TO THE *ZHIXIN ZHI* ACCORDING TO THE *BINTUI LU*

The [preface to the] *Zhixin* states:

Four or five works, such as the *Dongpo zhilin*,[100] Li Fangshu's *Record of Conversations Between the Master and His Friends*,[101] Qian Pi's *Miscellaneous Notes Over the Years*,[102] are all peppered with strange events yet amount to no less than Yu Chu's nine hundred chapters.[103] I have borrowed about a third of these since there may be gentlemen who are unaware of them.

Again this preface is testament to Hong's borrowing from other literary sources, as traditional historiographers were wont to do. Here he supplies a reason: the preservation of material which might have been otherwise lost. Hong occasionally expresses a similar intent throughout the corpus of the *Record*. For example, in a metatextual comment to a story from the *Zhiding* installment, he states that the reason for his replicating an account found in Guo Tuan's *A Cartload of Ghosts* (*Kuiche zhi*)[104] was his desire to increase its circulation.[105]

This desire for preservation and dissemination also affords an insight into the publication and circulation of books during the Southern Song. That is, even though printing on an unprecedented scale facilitated a wider circulation of sutras, stories, classics, and the like, Hong's desire for preservation—and by implication his fear that tracts from already-published literary works could fall into obscurity—suggests limitations to the diffusion of printed material. The amount of material written during this era that has since fallen into oblivion certainly vindicates Hong's fear.

Preface to the *Zhiren Zhi* According to the *Bintui lu*

The [preface to the] *Zhiren* states:

> Male relatives tell me that my devotion to writing and my ceaseless collecting of strange stories is not the kind of relaxation fit for an elderly gentleman, and that I should desist. I took their advice, and within a day I had lost my palate for wine. I felt too constrained for strolling. My heart had lost its repose and my spirit had become dull. Those who had advised me to stop did not know what had come over me. And so, self-satisfied, I laughed at them.
>
> Could this be my destiny? Like a stallion charging down an endless slope, wishing to stop but unable to do so. I am, therefore, giving rein to my urges and will follow them to the end of this life. Later on, if I become unable to recognize the world around me, I will surrender myself without outside pressure.

Hong's self-professed, almost obsessive collecting and recording of stories did not escape Valerie Hansen's attention and is vividly portrayed here in metaphoric language.[106] How reliable, however, are these claims? Did Hong really lose his taste for wine and suffer from insomnia because of attempts to cease writing? Allowing for hyperbole, there would seem little cause to doubt him: the massive size of the *Record* is evidence enough. And, as I discussed in chapter 1, the temporal gap between the last known year of completion for the

Sanren zhi (the 39th installment, completed in 1198) and Hong's death in 1202 strongly suggests that his remarks here were not without a factual basis. His words are also echoed in the preface to the *Sanding zhi*, which I discuss below.

PREFACE TO THE *ZHIGUI ZHI*

The *Qilüe*[107] is a joint treatise by Liu Xiang[108] and son, and was used by Ban Mengjian[109] for his *Bibliographic Treatise (Yiwen zhi)*.[110] Its *xiaoshuo* section includes the work of fifteen authors. The *Sayings of the Yellow Emperor*, the *Tianyi*, the *Sayings of Yi Yin*, the *Sayings of Yuzi*, the *Green-clad Official*, the *Wu Chengzi* are all there.[111] These works were disregarded, probably because they were considered illogical and superficial, fabricating myths about the sages. Later came Yu's [Chu] *Stories of Zhou* in 945 chapters,[112] derived from accounts of minor officials and hearsay from the lanes and alleyways.[113] During the time of [Han] Wudi, justiciars of the domain and attendant gentlemen were termed envoys of the yellow carriage[114] and were truthfully recorded by Zhang Ziping in his *Rhapsody of the Western Capital*.[115] Alas, it has been lost!

If we were to rank the hundred or so authors listed in the [*xiaoshuo* section of the] *History of the Tang*, the only ones worth reading are: Li Fuyan's *A Continuation of Anomalies of the Recondite*,[116] Chen Han's *A Collection of Strange Tales*,[117] Hu Qu's *Talking Guests*,[118] Wen Tingyun's *Qian Sun*,[119] Duan Chengshi's *Miscellaneous Morsels from Mount Yu*, Zhang Du's *Record of the Dark Chamber*, Lu Zi's *The Leftover History*,[120] Xue Yusi's *Tales of Hedong*— the remainder are not worthy to be read. Yet, when delving into the dark and inexplicable, the *Extensive Records from the Era of Great Peace* discarded nothing. Only Liu Xiang's *Record of the Xiao Xiang Region*[121] is shoddy and a wasted effort; an affront to one's eyes and ears. Li Yin's *Fantastic Stories of the Great Tang Dynasty* is one and the same as this work, although they have erroneously been thought of as different works by two separate authors.[122] *The Records of the Tang*[123] lists them as separate works, but it has been lost.

When I completed ten installments of the *Record*, I expanded it and have produced three hundred chapters containing four thousand accounts of which a mere one in ten cannot be filled; this is half of what is recorded in the *Records of the Tang*. The *Zhigui* installment was completed in a period of thirty days. I would hazard a guess that, what the world considers foolish speed, nothing has surpassed this. The work itself would not seem too foolish, though. I have continued to hear other stories and will include them in a third series which will again begin from the first heavenly stem.

The 14th day of the fifth month in the third year of the Qingyuan period (1197).

Throughout this preface, one can detect a dichotomy between historically accurate and inaccurate stories found in *xiaoshuo* works. At one end of this fictional/historical spectrum, there are works which Hong asserts were "considered illogical and superficial, fabricating myths about the sages." We are, however, unable to evaluate these comments fully since many of the works cited are no longer extant. Nevertheless, a common thread seems to run through several of the extant Tang and Song *xiaoshuo* works that Hong mentions. *A Continuation of Anomalies of the Recondite* was based on Niu Sengru's *Anomalies of the Recondite*. This was an influential work which inspired several imitations, among them the *Tales of Hedong*. While the former contains many *zhiguai* motifs and themes, a significant number of historical figures are also dealt with. Duan Chengshi's historical accuracy in his *Miscellaneous Morsels from Youyang* has already been noted. To be sure, Duan included the names of his informants, as well as spatial and temporal markers in the *nuogao* chapters, just like those found throughout the *Record*.[124] The *Leftover History* also featured many historical figures. *A Collection of Strange Tales* contained an element of scientific inquiry. Finally, *Talking Guests* included discussion on poetry, painting, and calligraphy among its anecdotes. The variety of motifs, as well as the element of purported historical accuracy found in these texts, is also found throughout the *Record*. This preface is, therefore, further evidence of Hong's desire to achieve historical reliability; he certainly eschews works that are not.

PREFACE TO THE *SANZHI JIA* ACCORDING TO THE *BINTUI LU*

The [preface to the] *Sanzhi Jia* states:

> My son Huai and my grandson Yan[125] came and laid before me works of unofficial history written by the previous generation of authors. Works such as Xu Dingchen's[126] *Examining Spirits*, Master Zhang Wending's *Old Stories of Luoyang*,[127] Qian Xibai's *Record of Dongwei*,[128] Zhang Junfang's *Examining Anomalies*,[129] Lü Guanyuan's *Plumbing the Recondite*, Zhang Shizheng's *Recording Anomalies*,[130] Bi Zhongxun's *Mufu yanxian lu*; seven works. Many of them took twenty years in the making, yet they do not contain many chapters. The *Sanzhi Jia* took but fifty days. One cannot but say that this has been fast.

Hong's labeling of these other literary works as "unofficial history" (*baiguan* 稗官) is significant. While the term *baiguan* originally denoted minor officials, when later coupled with "*xiaoshuo*" it became a synonym for unofficial history (also known as *yeshi xiaoshuo* 野史小說). This was because the earliest unofficial historical accounts (referred to with the metaphor "hearsay from the lanes and alleyways") were gathered by minor officials—the "gentlemen of the yellow carriage" to which Hong referred in the preface of the *Zhigui* installment. Campany translates *baiguan* as the "fine grain office" and quotes a passage from the *History of the Han* (*Han shu*) in which its author, Ban Gu (32–92 C.E.), discussed *baiguan* as a subgenre of *xiaoshuo* writing. In this, Ban

Gu linked the collecting of *baiguan* accounts with the duties of minor officials.[131] Below is Campany's translation.

> The *xiaoshuo* tradition probably originated from the "Fine Grain" Office. Its works were created from the "hearing in the highroad and retelling in the lane" of street-conversations and alley-stories. As Confucius said, "Even the minor arts are sure to have their worthwhile aspects. But if pursued too far they tend to prove a hindrance, for which reason the superior man does not practice them." Although that is so, neither are they destroyed. Even things touched on by villagers of some little knowledge were collected together and not forgotten, lest they contain just one saying that could be selected out—even though they were [but] the discussions of woodcutters and madmen.

After due reference to Confucius's warning, Ban Gu cites preservation of potentially precious material to justify *xiaoshuo*. This reason was to become one of the main justifications offered for not only this genre, but also *zhiguai* texts for centuries henceforth.

Gardner defines unofficial history (*yeshi* 野史) as follows:

> Chinese historians seldom expose themselves to the charge of recording matters beyond the scope of their documents and observations. Secret matters and personalia of all kinds that may be classified as dubious are relegated to the category of "old tales" which enjoy hardly more repute as history than do the historical novels of the West.
>
> . . . 故事 *gu shir*, or *yeh shir*, "unconventional histories." Collections of these are far more entertaining than sober history, but the author of them is not subject to the usual restraints of responsibility.[132]

As we have seen, "recording matters beyond the scope of their documents and observations" is precisely what Hong Mai did. And, as mentioned above, while many stories came from written documents sent to him, numerous others were derived from oral sources. As I have already observed, the work's title, the *Record*—literally the *Record of Yi Jian*—was formulated because Hong Mai, like the legendary Yi Jian who recorded the deeds of the legendary King Yu, was collecting and recording stories from second-hand sources, which he generally did not personally witness.[133]

Hong Mai himself gives us an insight into what he and, presumably, other members of the Southern Song literati regarded as unofficial history. Below is an excerpt from Hong's *Rongzhai suibi*:

> Unofficial history and miscellaneous sayings—much of it is derived from hearsay that is embellished by the curious (*haoshi zhe* 好事者). It often lacks factuality for this reason. Even our forebears could not avoid it, yet members of the literati (*shidafu* 士大夫) believe in its truthfulness.[134]

He then goes on to give three examples of unofficial history accounts dealing with events from the reign of the Zhenzong emperor 真宗 (r. 998–1022) which proved unreliable when verified by official accounts. Hong's quasi-definition here concurs with Gardner's in regard to unreliability. Hong furthermore identifies another feature of this genre—the presence of embellishment.

His use of the term "the curious" is significant since it had also been used to refer to lovers of *zhiguai* literature since Gan Bao first mentioned it in his preface to the *Record of the Search for Spirits* (*Soushen ji*), which is generally considered an archetypal work of the *zhiguai* genre. Accordingly, it would seem to refer to the readership of unofficial history as well. Nevertheless, I will discuss these issues further in chapter 4 when I examine the question of the *Record* and its relationship to literary genres. What is important to note here is Hong's implicit comparison between the *Record* and these other Song works—all exhibiting many *zhiguai* motifs—which he labeled as "*baiguan.*" This seems to reflect the way he saw his own creation.

PREFACE TO THE *SANZHI YI* ACCORDING TO THE *BINTUI LU*

The preface to the *Sanzhi Yi* states:

> This entire installment was obtained from Xu Qian, the diviner.[135] Xu is blind in both eyes, but he can listen intently and has an excellent memory. Those who patronize his shop tell him stories, all of which he remembers and forgets not. Then he has a third person record them to show others. In previous times, Xu Zhongju[136] was deaf, yet there was not a single thing throughout the world which he did not know. Could it be that Xu is his descendant? Wisdom and foolishness cannot be concurrently spoken of yet, in their difference, so also lies their commonality.

This preface reveals one of the venues in which the *Record* accounts were told; a diviner's shop. The proprietor's method of recording the stories was not unlike that of Hong Mai. Nevertheless, retelling to a third person is proof of how these stories passed through several mouths before finding their way to Hong Mai. To be sure, the accounts from Xu were at least fourth-hand by the time Hong recorded them. It is little wonder that Hong worried about inaccuracy.

PREFACE TO THE *SANZHI JING* ACCORDING TO THE *BINTUI LU*

The [preface to the] *Sanzhi Jing* states:

> Districts and locales must have local gazetteers, yet Poyang is the only one without. The strange events included throughout the *Record*, from the *Jia* to the *Sanjing*, record some 550 strange stories from the prefecture. There will come a time when more than half of these will be used by the curious for inclusion in gazetteers.

Again Hong expresses faith in the historicity of his narratives, specifically those from Poyang and surrounds—reflecting his connection to Poyang as his native district. How prophetic this statement is when we consider the numerous accounts that were included in later gazetteers, as demonstrated by Wang Hsiu-huei's recovery of lost accounts.[137] Rather than viewing these narratives as *xiaoshuo*, Hong treats them as historical. And, as we shall see below, such sentiments were echoed by Qing scholar, Shen Qizhan 沈屺瞻 (dates uncertain). In his preface to the Qing Dynasty edition of the *Record*, Shen inferred that its historicity was superior to that of unofficial historiography.[138] This forges another link between the *Record* and unofficial history.

Preface to the *Sanzhi Ding* According to the *Bintui lu*

The [preface to the] *Sanzhi Ding* states:

> When a man reaches seventy or eighty, and if he has the happy fortune to enjoy good health and well being, he should [be able to] retire to his retreat, be early to bed and early to rise, mull over books and pledge himself eternally to his good lady.[139] Otherwise he could entertain seasoned travelers from the four corners of the earth, or else meditate and train his body with the climbing bear and gazing owl method.[140] As for the writing of books, this comes from the basest of motives. Yet I cannot release myself from this folly. Regretting it, I once hastily cleared away all my material, not looking at it again. But it was like forbidding a toddler from falling down. Before long, I was once again involved, more so than ever. I will not listen [to the advice of others] again, even should the mountains collapse and the rivers run dry.

Again Hong discusses his attempts to cease writing, given outside pressure. The completion year of this installment is not known. We do know, however, that the *Zhigui* installment was completed in 1197, and those of *Sanji, Sanxin,* and *Sanren* were finished in 1198. This installment, therefore, was probably completed in either 1197 or 1198. As I discussed in chapter 1, given that habit compelled him to continue writing and collecting, this preface suggests that he became bed-ridden in the last two years of his life, particularly when we consider that only three more installments were undertaken after the *Sanren*.

Preface to the *Sanzhi Wu* According to the *Bintui lu*

The [preface to the] *Sanzhi Wu* states:

> The Master spoke of neither anomalies nor restless spirits.[141] Although he did not refute them, he refrained from inquiring about them. When the sages spread their teaching throughout the world, they did not allow talk of gods or anomalies to enter their discourse. Yet such things can be found in the *Annals of Spring and Autumn*, the *Book of Changes* and the *Book of Documents*. They are

particularly prevalent in both the inner and outer chapters of the *Zuo Commentary*.[142] We cannot discard all these as lies and exaggeration.

As in previous prefaces, Hong Mai explores the fluid boundary between official history writing and the writing of *xiaoshuo*, particularly the *zhiguai*. Hong implies that, since respected works of official history and the classics contain *zhiguai* motifs, *zhiguai* and *xiaoshuo* works have a place in respectable literature. He attempts to defend such works when other members of the literati held them in scorn. Hong's defense of the *zhiguai* follows the same argument found in the preface to the *Ding zhi*, in which he cited the *Zhuangzi* and Sima Qian's *Records of the Grand Historian* to refute criticism of the *Record*'s historicity. His defense here is also relevant to Ouyang Xiu's bibliographical reclassification of the *zhiguai*. I will, however, discuss these issues further in chapters 4 and 5.

PREFACE TO THE *SANZHI JI*

Whenever a story or a poem comes to my attention, I always record it—there is no end to it. In this way I continue to record stories and poems and forget none, as though my hands were made for it. There have, however, always been times when I missed out on material due to tardiness.

When Teng Yanzhi[143] was in charge of my prefecture (Poyang), he once casually talked of an uncle, Lu Dangke,[144] who had attained [Taoist] methods but was almost defeated by [the case of] Fang's daughter.[145] So as to assist me, he said:

"I have heard of two more stories and will tell you at a later date."

He died, however, before he could relate them.

When Huang Yongfu was my protegé,[146] he spoke of the strange business of how Guo from Dongyang hosted the Purple Maiden,[147] but I did not write of it immediately. Then later he came to serve in my prefecture. We renewed our association and I inquired about the old story. He said that he had already made enquiries, and the names and dates were all accurate with only minor inconsistencies. I then made [further] inquiries.

Day after day, I spurn my past regrets and remain unable to desist in my dealings [with people]. The *Sanzhi ji* is complete and I have written to vent bottled-up frustration, conscious of the fact that the two gentlemen will not be able to retell their stories.

The 1st day of the fourth month of the fourth year of the Qingyuan period (1198).

This preface echoes the idea expressed in previous ones, that is, Hong's motivation for collecting and recording was—among other factors—the preservation of material which would have otherwise been lost. This, as I have already pointed out, supports Gardner's ideas about the motives of traditional

Chinese historians. The names of the two officials Hong mentions point to the milieu from which his accounts originated, as well as to their readership.

PREFACE TO THE *SANZHI GENG* ACCORDING TO THE *BINTUI LU*

The preface to the *Sanzhi Geng* uses Xu Xuan's *Examining Spirits* to argue that the story of Kuai Liang,[148] as told in Yang Wengong's *Garden of Conversations*,[149] is incorrect.

Well may we particularly lament the loss of this preface as the original may have revealed Hong Mai's attitude to Xu Xuan and his collecting of *zhiguai* accounts. This is all the more significant in view of the charge leveled at Hong by Southern Song literary critic and book collector, Chen Zhensun 陳振孫 (1183–?, known to have been an official in Zhejiang between 1234–1236). As I will discuss in the second part of this chapter, Chen drew a comparison between Hong and Xu, arguing that Xu's informants deliberately passed off fictitious stories as contemporary and original. Chen argued that the same was true in Hong's case. Below is a part translation of his comments on the *Record* found in Chen's *The Straight-forward Studio's Bibliography and Commentary* (*Zhizhai shulu jieti* 直齋書錄解題).

Tradition has it that Xu Xuan enjoyed talking about anomalies.[150] And so those who were unable to make a name for themselves, or those who were out of favor, invented stories to tell him so as to curry favor. This is also the case with Hong Mai. Anxious to complete the book in his later years, he indiscriminately took old stories from the *Extensive Records*. These he changed somewhat, gave another name and included in his work—even to the extent that several chapters contain stories that were published without amendment.[151]

We have seen Hong Mai's dismissal of accusations, in the preface to the *Zhijia* installment, that he relied on precursor texts. And while we cannot be certain that his comments are not simply a self-contained exercise in apologetics with no reference to actual critics, the comments refuted therein nevertheless reflect those of Chen Zhensun. This suggests that the criticism Hong outlines represents actual criticism. What is significant here is that Kuai Liang, who was Xu Xuan's servant, reportedly fabricated strange stories so as to regain his master's favor following an alleged falling out. In light of this, a negation of Kuai Liang's role may well indicate that this preface was another exercise in apologetics. The anecdote below, from Jiang Shaoyu's 江少虞 (ca. 1115–after 1145) *Collection of Famous Words and Deeds in the Northern Song Dynasty* (*Shishi leiyuan* 事實類苑), illustrates Kuai Liang's relationship with Xu Xuan.

Hsü Hsüan, though not a Buddhist, had a penchant for ghost and supernatural stories. He gathered this kind of lore and compiled it into a volume which he called *Chi-shen-lu*, or "Investigation of spirits." Once he served as an examiner. Many candidates without any real talent who had learned of Hsü's gullibility requested individual interviews, claiming that they had strange stories to tell. Hsü would fall for their schemes and granted them special favors.

A commoner from Chiangtung by the name of K'uai Liang, over ninety years old, was good at spinning yarns, for which reason Hsü kept him as a retainer. Most of the stories in the "Investigation of spirits" were Kuai Liang's inventions. Once, offended by K'uai, Hsü refused to speak to him. One early morning, when Hsü was about to leave for the court, K'uai confronted him, exclaiming, "Strange! A man has just flown away on two wings from the hall." Intrigued, Hsü ordered to have it recorded on paper. From then on, he treated K'uai as before.[152]

Jiang's skeptical tone is unmistakable, and his inference that only Buddhists believed in strange accounts is a rare comment on the social conditions under which anomaly accounts circulated during the early Southern Song.

Preface to the *Sanzhi Xin*

I have always said that, among stories of deities and strange happenings—past and present—there are none the same. Could it be that there are no similar ones? Although their intent differs, I now realize that [the variations] are not [all that] extensive.

In a previous series I wrote about the Sichuan gentleman, Sun Siwen, and of how he visited the Temple of King Lingxian where he became attracted to the effigy of the king's lady.[153] He then dreamed of one who brought a saw and, with it, cut off his head while replacing it with another. Sun awoke and was extremely alarmed, so he called his wife to check with a candle; and she died of fright. I once saw his face in Lin'an.

Allow me to compare this to the [tract from the] *Records of the Living and the Dead*[154] as it appears in the *Imperial Digest of the Era of Great Peace*:[155]

"Jia Bi of Hedong, whose other name was Yi'er, was an adjutant in Langya Prefecture. During the night he dreamed of a person with a scar-covered face, a huge nose and monstrous eyes who entreated him, 'I am enamored with your lordship's features. Are you willing to exchange heads?' And, in his dream, he agreed to swap. When he rose the following morning, although he knew not the reason, everyone evaded him in fear. The King of Langya summoned him and, when he espied him from afar, rose and retired. Bi took up a mirror and looked at himself, and it was then that he realized the abnormality. He therefore returned home where his wife and daughters hid themselves. Bi [then] sat and explained himself. After a long time, [the prefectural office] sent people to make inquiries at his home before they would believe. Later he was able to cry with one half of his face and laugh with the other half. And he could write with a brush in each hand simultaneously."

Hence, are not these two stories very much the same? One cannot say that there have not been similar examples in the days of yore. The *Records of the Living and the Dead* is not extant today. I have, therefore, used it for my preface to this *Zhixin* installment.

The 8th day of the sixth month of the fourth year of the Qingyuan period (1198).

The tone of this preface is noticeably different compared to that of the *Zhijia*, in which Hong Mai defended himself against allegations of borrowing from past works, arguing that "there are no two things the same." Here, however, the question "are not these two stories very much the same" comes as close to admitting defeat as he could possibly admit.

Nevertheless, could Hong's "apology" reflect contemporary criticism on which Chen Zhensun may have based his accusation? That is, Hong borrowed so heavily from the *Extensive Records* that he included many narratives without significant editing. Might Hong, therefore, have bowed to "public" opinion and used this preface as an opportunity to change his stance on this issue, given heightened awareness among his readership of precursor texts? If so, his question about there being "similar examples in the days of yore" hints to the possible existence of other antecedents. Although I will discuss accounts derived from uncited precursor texts in chapter 5, it is not possible to fully investigate Chen's assertion, given that over half of the *Record*'s original corpus has long been lost. Nor would it seem possible to prove conclusively that this was the case given the scant surviving material on textual reception which might have corroborated Chen's argument.[156] More, however, will be said about this in chapter 5.

PREFACE TO THE *SANZHI REN*

Master Changli's[157] work entitled *The Origin of Ghosts*, seeks to explain the divergence of the path taken by the living and that of the dead. He first forwards three arguments to prove his hypothesis. He asserts that, "[g]hosts are without sound or form. Were we to shine a candle on them when they screech between the rafters, we would see nothing. Were we to go and see one that was standing in the hall, we would see nothing. Were we to grasp one which touched our body, we would grasp it not."[158]

This is not so. The world has always had "anomalies co-existing with people and things."[159] They go against heaven, disregard the populace, are not in accordance with matter, are at odds with morality, yet they can have a presence among the vital energies. Hence, on occasions, they take on borrowed form to speak through the living and respond to questions. [Master Changli's] theory is lofty and all-encompassing—there is no obstacle to it. He also quotes phrases such as 'present offerings as though they were alive' and 'make offerings to the gods as though the gods were among us,'[160] and

uses arguments from Mozi's "Illuminating Ghosts."[161] Yet this is at odds
with his initial argument, for as far as illuminating the existence of gods and
ghosts, this (Mozi) is a supreme authority.

All the ghost stories in the *Record*, which comprise over twenty percent
of the total, are extremely varied and diverse. They cannot support the three
errors that Mr. Li submits as evidence. I myself subscribe to Mozi, unable to
escape Mencius' argument against the laying to rest of heresies and banishing
extreme views.[162] He [however] is truly laughable.

The preface of the 6th day of the ninth month in the fourth year of the Qingyuan period (1198).

Hong Mai succinctly summarizes Han Yu's (768–824) argument in this
preface. In his essay, Han Yu argued that ghosts cannot be perceived by mortal
sensory organs. He furthermore argued that many anomalies (*guai*) were con-
trived by humans. It is interesting to note, nevertheless, that he did not refute the
existence of ghosts per se. Nevertheless, as the locus of his argument contradicted
the type of anomalies featured throughout the *Record*, Hong was understandably
anxious to refute it, given his claim of historical factuality. Hong also gave us an
insight into what he conceived of as *guai* and I will return to this in chapter 4
when I discuss possible constructs of *guai* in relation to literary genres.

Preface to the *Sanzhi Gui* According to the *Bintui lu*

The preface to the *Sangui* discusses mistakes found in the *Extensive Records
from the Period of Supreme Peace*[163] and the *Topicalized Compendium*.[164]

Preface to the *Sizhi Jia* According to the *Bintui lu*

The [preface to the] *Sijia* argues that Yi Jian is another name for Gao Yao.[165]

This preface would seem to have been another example of Hong's penchant for textual criticism (*kaozheng xue* 考證學) of the kind found in his
Rongzhai suibi.

As previously noted, the *Record*'s prefaces provide a wealth of information on unofficial history and *xiaoshuo* literature from the hand of an erudite,
Confucian-trained historian. Just as Six Dynasty *zhiguai* writers often used
their prefaces to apologize for the nature of their motifs, so too did Hong
Mai engage in exercises of apologetics. This became increasingly apparent after
the first two installments. Yet, unlike the humble, self-effacing tone discernible
in *xiaoshuo* prefaces throughout the imperial period, Hong's seem somewhat
brash—particularly toward the beginning.[166] This air of confidence, however,
becomes less and less assured with the passing of time. And finally, with the
preface to the *Sanzhi xin*, a major change is discernible.

We have seen his desire to achieve what he considered a "reliable" record in several prefaces, and since this forms an important question regarding the *Record*, I will examine the degree to which selected accounts display historical factuality in chapter 5.

Hong's discussions of what postmodern scholars might understand as *zhiguai* texts and their authors are all the more valuable given the lack of any systematic discourse on this genre throughout the imperial period, although Hong refrains from explicitly using the term *zhiguai*. His preference for the term *baiguan* points to a possible intertextual affiliation between the two, although it further blurs the boundary between *zhiguai* texts and those of other genres. Unfortunately, his discussion of orthodox history in relation to the *zhiguai*, while pertinent, is not particularly penetrating, nor does it help us delineate the two. Yet considering a hitherto lack of commentary on the subject, his observations reveal much erudition.

Throughout the prefaces, Hong often built his arguments around conversations between himself and anonymous—or possibly fictitious—interlocutors, his youngest son in several instances. This certainly reveals what he perceived as his readership. Yet, as I have argued, he may have been responding to actual criticism. To be sure, Hong's revelations of what he considered dubious in the preface to the *Bing zhi* coincided with a change in behavior: that is, his henceforth scrupulous citation of known precursor texts. Furthermore, Hong's denial that he borrowed large amounts of material in the prefaces to the *Zhijia zhi* and the *Ding zhi* reflected Chen Zhensun's criticism of the same issue. As Chen flourished after the period in which these prefaces were written, if the criticism was real, it was likely that Chen owed his idea to another, unknown critic. Unfortunately, insufficient evidence exists which would allow us to arbitrate conclusively on this matter.

SCHOLARLY RECEPTION OF THE *RECORD*

Judging from the preface to the second installment, in which Hong spoke of every household possessing a copy, the text certainly seems to have enjoyed considerable popularity following the initial publication of the first installment. What he meant by the hyperbolic phrase "every household" is, however, unclear. There is, nevertheless, anecdotal evidence suggesting that none other than the Empress Dowager Wu, empress of the Gaozong emperor, counted among its readership.[167] And while it is tempting to postulate a wider readership—possibly among literate women—given imperial patronage, no further evidence exists but this fragment. As I observed above, Hong's remark that the first installment was initially circulated among "gentlemen and scholar officials" (*shidafu* 士大夫) suggested that the literati were, perhaps not surprisingly, among its intended readership. Certainly if most of the accounts were provided by scholar-officials in both oral and written forms—as can be seen from even a cursory survey of his list of informants, the collaborative nature of the undertaking is ample evidence that scholar-officials were among Hong's most avid readers. Significantly, Chen Chun 陳淳 (1159–1223), Neo-Confucian philosopher and disciple of Zhu Xi 朱熹 (1130–1200), discusses a story about human sacrifice in his *Neo-Confucian Terms Explained* (*Beixi ziyi* 北溪字義, hereafter *Neo-Confucian Terms*) which is clearly the same as one found in the *Record*.[168] Although Chen questions details of verisimilitude, he refrains from rejecting the account as a fabrication. While it is unclear whether the *Record* account was Chen's direct source, or whether he heard the story elsewhere, it demonstrates that the type of narratives found throughout Hong's collection were taken seriously by even Neo-Confucian scholars of the Southern Song. I will discuss this account in the following chapter when I turn attention to themes.

The earliest known literary critique of the *Record* is found in a *biji* work, the *Plum Creek Collected Works* (*Meixi wenji* 梅溪文集) by Wang Shipeng 王十朋 (1112–1171), a close associate of Hong Mai. Not only was Wang one of Hong's significant informants, he also features as a protagonist. In his *Plum Creek Collected Works*, he praises the *Record* as follows:

> The expanse of Yechu's[169] renowned garden is extensive, and the diversity of Yijian's phenomena (博物) is reminiscent of Zhang Hua.[170]

The comparison with Zhang Hua 張華 (232–300) affords a glimpse at the way Wang viewed the *Record*. Zhang was an exorcist, diviner, and avid book collector—especially books of an esoteric nature. Campany notes that Zhang's biography in the *History of the Jin* (*Jin shu* 晉書) depicts him as a *fangshi* 方士, or—to invoke Campany's term—a master of esoterica. Zhang's *Bowu zhi* 博物志 (Record of Broad Phenomena) primarily comprises nonnarrative descriptions of anomalies arranged under thirty-nine topical headings. Campany considers it a *zhiguai* work.[171] How Wang viewed the *Bowu zhi*, however, is unclear. We certainly cannot assume that he regarded it in the same way as Campany. Nevertheless, Wang's comparison of the *Record* with a work containing anomalous accounts drawn from extensive sources would seem apt and suggests that the *Record*—at least to Wang—had inherited something of its legacy.

As I previously noted, the *Other Record of the Listener* (*Yijian biezhi*, hereafter the *Other Record*) by Wang Jingwen was the first imitation of the *Record*, published even before Hong's last installments were completed. Indeed, we saw above how, according to the *Guests Retire*, Hong quoted extensively from the *Other Record* in the preface to his ninth (*ren*) installment, completed in 1194. The *Other Record* is, however, no longer extant. And while its publication date remains uncertain, it would have been before the author's death in 1189. In its preface, part of which was summarized by Hu Yinglin, Wang praised the *Record* and, going a step further than Wang Shipeng, placed it within a literary tradition of anomaly accounts. Below is my translation of the beginning.

> *Zhiguai* works are extremely numerous. When the *Yijian zhi* from Poyang came into being, it surpassed them all.[172]

Although positive, it does not, unfortunately, offer any clue as to how Hong Mai's work surpassed other *zhiguai* works. Nor does it define what the writer meant by "*zhiguai* works" (*zhiguai zhi shu* 志 怪 之 書). Did he limit himself to Song *zhiguai*, or did he refer to the corpus of *zhiguai* writing since its conception? What constituted *zhiguai* works in Wang's mind? Does his reference to *shu* (works) imply a generic category, or should it merely be understood in an informal sense as "jottings" or "writing"? This labeling of the *Record* as "*zhiguai*" would, nevertheless, seem significant and I will return to it in later chapters. Unfortunately, as the preface to Hong's ninth installment is no longer extant, we can no longer know what Hong's response was to Wang's evocation of *zhiguai*, if any.

Lu You 陸游 (1125–1209), renowned poet and author, was an acquaintance of Hong Mai who praised the *Record* in a poem. It is perhaps significant to remember that Lu fervently desired the recovery of the northern territories lost to the Jurchen and opposed the pacifist policies instigated by Qin Gui; Hong Mai, as I shall discuss in chapter 3, may well have shared those sentiments. Below is a partial translation of Lu's colophon.

> The writing is the antithesis of the *Li Sao* (*Encountering Sorrow*). The work is unrelated to the *Nuogao*.[173] How can it be merely adjunct to history?[174] It is worthy of a place as a literary masterpiece. A fleet steed makes ordinary horses of no account. A relaxed manner sets up the turtle's domain.[175] How can you hold discussions with a pretentious scholar? You lot also toil in vain.[176]

What Lu means as the antithesis of *Encountering Sorrow* is, however, unclear. Perhaps he refers to the *Record*'s historicity. Given that *Encountering Sorrow* is thought to describe renowned Warring States period (403–221 B.C.E.) poet Qu Yuan's (340?–278 B.C.E.) fantastic journey to visit a deity, Lu seems to imply that Hong's self-professed historically accurate *Record* is the opposite to Qu's obviously fictitious trek. If so, this corroborates Hongs claims of historical factuality by a contemporary reader.

The comparison with historical works is also significant and echoes Hong's own comments throughout his prefaces. Lu's care to distinguish between the *Record* and the *Nuogao ji* supports Hong Mai's own delineation outlined in the preface to the eighth installment. In all, Lu You's observations certainly reveal an intimate knowledge of the text.

Zhao Yushi, author of the *Guests Retire*, also praises Hong's work. In his introduction, Zhao states that "Hong Mai's *Record* comprises thirty-two installments and thirty-one prefaces. Rather than being repetitious, all of them are unique. No one before has achieved this."[177] Unfortunately Zhao does not give further details. His notion that Hong Mai's accomplishment was unique appears to refer to the prefaces rather than to the work itself.

One of the harshest criticisms of the *Record*, however, came from well-known Song bibliophile, Chen Zhensun. In his above-mentioned private bibliographical catalogue, the *Zhizhai shulu jieti*, he attacked Hong's work on the grounds of—among other things—its improbable and unhistorical content.

The *Yijian zhi* comprises 200 chapters from the first (*Jia zhi*) to the tenth installment (*Gui zhi*). From the eleventh (*Zhijia zhi* 支甲志) to the twentieth installment (*Zhigui zhi* 支癸志) there are 100 chapters. From the twenty-first (*Sanjia zhi* 三甲志) to the thirtieth installment (*Sangui zhi* 三癸志) there are 100 chapters. The thirty-first (*Sijia zhi* 四甲志) and the thirty-second installment (*Siyi zhi* 四乙志) contain 20 chapters. In total there are 420 chapters. It has been written by Hong Mai, courtesy name Jinglu, the (former) Hanlin academician from Poyang.

There has always been the petty talk (*xiaoshuo*) of minor officials (*baiguan*). Playing literary games in order to aid their conversation is quite permissible. Yet there has not been one containing as many chapters as this to date. And what a waste of spirit it is!

We consider strange that which is not in accordance with the norm and at odds with nature due to its rarity. If such phenomena were so numerous as to be [virtually] impossible to record, then we would not consider them strange.

Tradition has it that Xu Xuan enjoyed talking about anomalies. And so those who were unable to make a name for themselves, or those who were out of favor, invented stories to tell him so as to curry favor. This is also the case with Hong Mai. Anxious to complete the book in his later years, he indiscriminately took old stories from the *Extensive Records*. These he changed somewhat, gave another name and included in his work—even to the extent whereby several chapters contain stories that were published without amendment. The confused narrative and the vulgar slang usage do not help either.[178]

Chen, although not opposed to the writing of *zhiguai* accounts per se, objected to the work's enormous size and pointed to the irony that such a huge compendium of strange events—by their very frequency—undermined their strangeness. Expressing doubt as to the originality of many stories, he also compared Hong Mai with Xu Xuan. Yet, by doing so, he implicitly linked the *Record* with the *zhiguai*.

The pejorative nature of Chen's accusation that Hong indiscriminately took old stories from the *Extensive Records* should perhaps be viewed in the context of what was a common practice for writers in medieval China. Indeed, William Nienhauser Junior's 1998 article entitled *Creativity and Storytelling in the Ch'uan-ch'i: Shen Ya-chih's T'ang Tales*, is but one of many which illustrates how *chuanqi* and *zhiguai* narratives were adapted from earlier works.[179] Moreover, the large-scale replication of earlier narratives to fill the chapters of Yuan Dynasty *biji* works was quite prevalent. Certainly the mutual copying of material from other literary works was common throughout the Song. Furthermore, as I have already observed, the oral transmission of much of Hong's material would tend to negate the notion of an incorruptible, original text. Therefore, even if Chen's accusation is correct, Hong's borrowing accounts verbatim from other literary works would not seem such an extraordinary thing. Nevertheless, at least one Song *literatus* placed importance on the idea of an "original."

Chen's comments that Hong's quantity detracted from his quality are echoed by those of *biji* author and unofficial historian, Zhou Mi 周密 (1232–1308). Among other works, Zhou authored the *Miscellanies from Guixin* (*Guixin zashi* 癸辛雜識), a six-chapter compilation of miscellaneous notes containing biographical as well as historical material. Its records range throughout the Southern Song period and extend as far as the early Yuan Dynasty—up until 1285. Below is a translation from the relevant section of Zhou's preface.

> When Hong Jinglu wrote the book of *Yijian*, he could not avoid including unreliable stories given his desire for quantity. This was [all] due to an over-zealous curiosity about the paranormal.[180]

As does Chen Zhensun, Zhou condemns Hong's aim for quantity which supposedly affected the historical reliability of his stories. Zhou's criticism about the inclusion of "unreliable" material, interestingly enough, implicitly reveals an expectation of historical factuality. While those such as Wang Jingwen admired the *Record* for its *zhiguai* content, Zhou Mi seems to evaluate it as an historical work, albeit a noncanonical one. This is a precious insight regarding the *Record*'s generic affiliation, which I will explore further in later chapters.

Zhao Xibian 趙希弁 (d. after 1250), author of the Yuan edition of *Memoirs of My Readings in the Jun Studio by Master Zhao De* (*Zhaode xiansheng junzhai dushu zhi* 昭德先生郡齋讀書志) published in 1250 (based on the same title published the previous year by Chao Gongwu 晁公武 [d. 1171]—courtesy name Zhaode—in Quzhou 衢州), refers to the *Record* as *zhiguai*. Below is a translation of the relevant commentary (emphasis and translation mine):

Yijian zhi, 48 chapters:

> This is a book which reports the strange and *records the anomalous* 記異志怪 [written] by Master Hong Minwen (Hong Mai). Its name is derived from the story of [the Book of] Liezi; "the Great Yu saw them in his travels, Boyi knew of them and named them, Yijian heard of them and recorded them." This would suggest that Yijian was an ancient collector of curiosities (*gu zhi bowu zhe* 古之博物者).

While the author would not appear to employ the term *zhiguai* as a reference to a literary genre, his linking it with the *Record*'s content—albeit general—echoes Wang Jingwen. The reference to Yijian as a collector of curiosities is furthermore reminiscent of Wang Shipeng's reference to Zhang Hua.

Respected Yuan scholar and poet, Chen Li 陳櫟 (1252–1334), discussed the merits of the *Record* in his bibliographical *Qinyou tang suilu* 勤有堂隨錄 (c. 1323).[181] I quote him in part below:

The *Yijian zhi* was written by Hong Jinglu. It is clear that he recorded fictitious trickery with the pen of an historian. Yet, can we today disregard the *Zhuangzi* and *Liezi* due to their fictitious content? . . . [T]here is much to benefit people as not all of it (the *Record*) is preposterous. Unfortunately we do not have the original.[182]

An exercise in apologetics, Chen Li considers both the supposedly "fictitious" nature of the work, as well as what he saw as its beneficial aspect—although he did not specify what the latter might be. Did he mean the didactic themes involving divine retribution for wrongdoers and reward of the righteous? Chen also recognized the commonality between the *Record* and philosophical classics such as the *Zhuangzi* and the *Liezi*, a defense often used by Hong Mai himself, as we saw above. Despite its apologetic tone, this is a remarkably favorable critique.

Hu Yinglin, celebrated Ming bibliophile and literary critic, wrote at length about the *Record* in his *Notes from the Shaoshi Shanfang Studio* (*Shaoshi shanfang leigao* 少室山房類稿, hereafter *Notes*) and in his aforementioned *Essays*. In these works, he discussed various aspects of the *Record*, including textual history, veracity, content, and style. In the section entitled "Reading the *Record*" (*Du Yijian zhi* 讀夷堅志) from his *Notes*, he compared the *Record*'s size to the *Extensive Records*. He furthermore echoed the views of Chen Zhensun and Zhou Mi, that is, that the great volume of stories inevitably led to historical inaccuracy. While he expressed his appreciation of the book, as well as his wish for the recovery of its entire corpus, he accused Hong of misleading the "world" in terms of preposterous content. He also pointed out how not all of the *Record*'s narratives contained *zhiguai* motifs, in addition to the fact that jokes, poems, and lyrics did not constitute "coherent" writing (*mi bu cheng shu* 靡不成書). Finally, he expressed a desire to edit the non-*zhiguai* narratives and publish them separately. In the same chapter, he discussed the dichotomy between "factuality" versus "fiction."[183] His criticism of the *Record*'s "fictitious" content echoes that of Chen Li and, like Chen, implicitly reveals an expectation of historical reliability even as late as the Ming.

The Qing scholars Shen Qizhan and He Qi 何琪 (dates uncertain) both wrote separate prefaces for the Zhou edition of the *Record* published in 1778.[184] Both these scholars addressed the work's literary merit.

> . . . [T]he *Classic of Mountains and Seas*[185] seeks the extraordinary, and the *Qi Xie* records anomalies (*zhi guai*). It is not that these did not plumb the depths of what is esoteric, nor did they fail in their diversity or incredibility. It is just that for one book which does not broach the unbelievable as well as being readable, there is nothing like the *Record of the Listener*. . . . it does not subscribe to dry discussion. Picking up this book, one finds it free and uninhibited, singular and original. One can be glad or be astounded; one can have faith and yet be edified. It is sufficient to fill the gap in our narrow

experience of life. Yet scholars and men of letters who seek forgotten records would speak of it in the same vein as unofficial history.[186]

Some ideas expressed by Shen Qizhan echo those of other critics. Reference to the work's originality lends support to the praise offered by Zhao Yushi, Lu You, and Wang Jingwen. Yet his claim that the content was not ridiculous stands in contrast to that of Chen Zhensun and to Zhou Mi. Shen's comment on the work's readability, in conjunction with the remark that it contains no dry philological discussion or theorizing, indicates that he possibly saw it as something akin to popular literature ("popular literature" conceptualized in a very broad sense). Does this, then, point to the *Record*'s intended readership at the time of this edition's publication? The comparison with unofficial history is interesting in light of Chen Li's critique, yet here Shen asserts that the work transcends this genre. The relatively low regard of traditional scholars for unofficial history is clearly discernible here. Let us turn to He Qi's preface.

> [after a reference to previous Song *zhiguai* works] . . . As far as recording unusual events as soon as it reached him, there was none like Hong Wenmin and his *Record of the Listener*. . . . Mr. Chen Zhensun considered it confused and vulgar—what a ridiculous accusation this was! When compared with the *Extensive Records* compiled under imperial decree by Li Fang and his team of editorial officials, the *Record* does not contain nearly as much un-canonical and questionable material. It only includes that which is pleasing to the eyes and ears.[187]

As with Shen's comments, a comparison was made with previous *zhiguai* works (such as the *Extensive Records*) which He considered the *Record* to have surpassed. This is high praise indeed, perhaps reflecting the author's bias toward this particular edition which would have, no doubt, enhanced its circulation. Yet, as I pointed out above, such a comment is supported by previous critics. Again, the unreliable and illogical nature of the content is played down. Perhaps the ambiguous comment about pleasing the eyes and ears points to the seemingly popular nature of the content.

Prefaces written by editors of subsequent editions also claim a place in Chinese literary history for the *Record*. Lu Xinyuan (1836–1894) published an edition in 1879. Lu, whose courtesy names were Gangfu 港甫 and Qianyuan 潛園, was a native of Wuxing in Zhejiang. He was a distinguished collector of Song and Yuan books, in addition to those of the Ming and Qing. His bibliographical catalogue, the *Collected Works of Lu Xinyuan* (*Qianyuan zongji* 潛園總集), included titles such as the *Records of Collecting in the House of a Hundred Song Works* (*Bi Song lou cangshu zhi* 皕宋樓藏書志) and the *Yigutang Collection* (*Yigutang ji* 儀顧堂集). Although brief, his comments on the *Record* are significant. Below is a partial translation from the preface to his 1879 edition.

[After reference to previous *zhiguai* works since the *Classic of Mountains and Seas*] . . . there has never been one as large as this book [the *Record*]. As for the similarities its stories share with other records, and embellishments and borrowings for the sake of storytelling, this is dealt with in the preface to the *Zhijia zhi*. In so far as the literary themes are haunting and thought-provoking (*wensi juanyong* 文思雋永), and its multiple levels of meaning (*cengchu buqiong* 層出不窮), it is truly unsurpassed by later authors.[188]

When assessing the work's stature in literary history, other commentators claimed it to have surpassed previous *zhiguai* works. Lu Xinyuan, however, claims that it was unsurpassed by later works, extravagant indeed considering the literary merit of such works as the *Liaozhai zhiyi*. Yet while past critics tended not to state their reasons for claiming its superiority, Lu Xinyuan goes a step further and, while not perfectly lucid, is somewhat more specific.

The editors of the *Combined Catalogue of the Complete Works from the Four Libraries* (*Siku quanshu zongmu* 四庫全書總目, hereafter the *Four Libraries' Catalogue*) evaluate the work's literary merit along with textual transmission and other considerations.

Chen Zhensun ridiculed Hong Mai for wasting his spirit. His assessment would seem quite correct. Chen Li, in his *Qinyou tang suilu*, mused that Hong, wishing to undertake official historiography, used this for practice.[189] This would seem somewhat extravagant. Yet material such as the poetry and lyrics preserved in its pages are often worth replicating, while most of his anecdotes and forgotten gleanings are sufficient to edify us. It is, therefore, not entirely lacking in value. Throughout [literary] history, works of *xiaoshuo* have been classified and recorded. Where, then, is the need to relegate it to a corner? Is Hong's work the only one befitting such treatment?[190]

It appears that the anonymous *Four Libraries* editor is attempting to rescue the *Record* from the predictable Confucian backlash against *zhiguai* works. The opening homage to Chen Zhensun belies the positive appraisal of the work's didactic themes and its preservation of valuable material. Perhaps the editor-in-chief of the *Four Libraries*, Ji Yun, wrote this entry himself, given his interest in *zhiguai*. Ji was, after all, author of the famous Qing *zhiguai* work, *Close Scrutiny*. Therefore, it is perhaps not surprising that the *Four Libraries* appraisal of the *Record* would be so positive. The value placed on the *Record*'s edifying content certainly reflects Ji's enthusiasm for the didactic role of *zhiguai* literature.[191]

In his *Brief History of Chinese Fiction* (*Zhongguo xiaoshuo shilüe* 中國小說史略), Lu Xun (1881–1936) discussed the work at some length and assessed its literary value. I quote him in part below:

. . . The work lays stress on the narrative form with little descriptive embellishment, and is much the same as the *Examining Spirits* (*Jishen lu*). For this reason, the *Record* relies purely on the fame of the author and the size of its tomes to recommend itself. . . . The *Record* was, however, a product of his (Hong Mai's) later years. . . . Strange stories should be exceptional. Yet, from his own prefaces, the author seems to have taken a certain pride in the magnitude of his undertaking. And he was in such haste to complete it that he sometimes finished ten chapters within fifty days. Without taking the time for appropriate editing, he would include old stories which people had sent him after only minimal alterations—to the extent that several chapters were filled in this way (Chen Zhensun, *Zhizhai shulu jieti*, ch. 11). Since he aimed for quantity, he could not achieve what I have discussed above about 'plumbing the depths of the world of ghosts and gods.' Only the thirty-one prefaces—nine out of ten—are not "repetitious; all of them are unique." Zhao Yushi once summarized these in his *Guests Retire* (ch. 8), remarking that "no one before has achieved this." Thus here is someone who appreciated the book's worth.[192]

Lu Xun's account, however, reveals certain inaccuracies. He gave a brief resume of Hong Mai's biography, not quoted here, based on the erroneous version in the *History of the Song* (*Songshi*) whereby the years given for Hong's birth and death are 1094 and 1175 respectively.[193] This was accepted until the Qing scholar, Qian Daxin 錢大昕 (1728–1804), proved otherwise with his biographical study of Hong Mai.[194] This error, therefore, reveals that Lu Xun was not intimately familiar with the text. Otherwise he would have realized that entries dating from or after the third year of the Chunxi period 淳熙 (1174–1189) indicated that Hong was still living after his supposed death according to the *History of the Song*—assuming that these numerous entries were not all forgeries. Lu Xun's reliance on the erroneous dates led him to other inaccuracies, such as his assertion that the work was written in the latter part of Hong Mai's life. As I have previously pointed out, approximately half was complete by 1192, the year in which Hong would have turned 59 (60 *sui*). In another part of his critique, Lu asserts that Hong was fifty when he passed the imperial examinations; this false assertion is almost certainly based on misleading biographical information.

Lu's comparison of the *Record* with *Examining Spirits* (*Jishen lu*) is hardly justifiable given that narratives in *Examining Spirits* overwhelmingly focus on anomalous occurrences themselves and are devoid of any didactic element. This certainly stands in contrast to the strong didactic undercurrent discernible throughout the *Record*. This ill-considered comparison demonstrates Lu Xun's superficial understanding of the *Record*, although perhaps this is not surprising since he was writing a general history of "fiction."

Twentieth-century scholarship on the *Record* was almost nonexistent until the late 1960s and early 1970s when Chang Fu-jui 張復蕊 published several articles about the text. His "Les themes dans le *Yi-kien Tche*" (Themes of *Record of the Listener*) which appeared in *Cina* (1964),[195] briefly discussed major underlying themes and motifs. His "Le *Yi-kien Tche* et la Societé des Song" (*Record of the Listener* and Song Society), which appeared in the *Journal Asiatique* (1968), discussed the work's reflection of Song society in socioeconomic terms as well as in relation to a handful of well-known personalities found throughout the corpus.[196] In his "L'influence du *Yi-kien Tche* sur les oeuvres littéraires" (The Influence of *Record of the Listener* on Literary Works) from *Etudes d'histoire et de literature Chinoises offertes au Professeur Jaroslav Prusek* (*Studies in Chinese History and Literature Offered to Professor Jaroslav Prusek*, 1976), Chang outlined the *Record*'s influence on later literary works, most notably on Ming Dynasty vernacular fiction.[197] Given that narratives from the *Record* can be found in later literary works up until Pu Songling's *Liazhai zhiyi*, this is a particularly valuable study on an otherwise neglected aspect of the text. His *I Chien Chih T'ung chien* 夷堅志通檢 (*Index to* Record of the Listener,1976) was the first index of the *Record* and included personal and place names mentioned in the text, as well as literary works cited by Hong Mai.[198] Chang's unpublished doctoral dissertation entitled *La vie et l'oeuvre de Hung Mai (1123–1202)* from the University of Paris VII (1971) is, unfortunately, unobtainable—presumably lost. Chang is, to my knowledge, the first scholar to have published biographical information on Hong Mai and his close relatives in a Western language. An entry written by Chang about the *Record* appears in Hervouet's *A Sung Bibliography* (1978), as does the biographical chapters on Hong Mai, Hong Hao, and Hong Gua in *Sung Biographies* (1976).[199] In "'93 *Zhongguo gudai xiaoshuo guoji yantao hui lunwen ji*" 93 中國古代小說國際研討會論文集 (*Collected Works from the 1993 International Symposium on Pre-Modern Chinese Literature*), Chang described general features of the text as well as biographical information about Hong Mai.

Wang Hsiu-huei 王秀惠 published several articles on the *Record*. Her "Vingt-sept recits retrouvé du *Yijian zhi*" (Twenty-seven Accounts Recovered for *Record of the Listener*) from *T'oung Pao* (1989a) revealed the existence of hitherto lost accounts, which were also the subject of her *Hanxue yanjiu* 漢學研究 article (June 1989) entitled "Yijian Zhi yishi jibu" 夷堅志佚事輯補 (Supplementing Lost Accounts from *Record of the Listener*).[200] Her "Guji yu dian'nao fenxi yunyong—yi *Yijian zhi* wei li" 古籍與電腦分析運用—以"夷堅志"爲例 (Electronic Use and Analysis of Pre-Modern Sources: Taking the *Record of the Listener* as an Example) in *Hanxue yanjiu tongxun* 漢學研究通訊 (June 1995), discussed the benefits of electronic databases for Sinological research and used her work with the *Yijian zhi* as an example.[201]

As I discussed above, work on recovery of lost accounts from the *Record* continued with Barend ter Haar's 1993 *Journal of Sung Yuan Studies* article, in addition to discoveries made by Kang Baocheng (1986), Cheng Hong (1987), Li Yumin (1990), Li Jianguo (1992 and 1997), and Zhao Zhangchao (2004).

In 1988, Wang Nianshuang completed his Chengche University doctoral dissertation—*An Examination of Hong Mai's Life and his* Record of the Listener (*Hong Mai shengping ji qi* Yijian zhi *zhi yanjiu* 洪邁生平及其夷堅志之研究). As the title suggests, a major focus was biographical, yet it contains some extremely valuable research on the *Record* itself. Wang dealt with textual history, content analysis, themes and motifs, authorial intent, and Hong's sources. His chapter on textual history was the first of its kind. Furthermore, his detailed analysis of Hong Pian's topicalized edition is of particular value to students of textual history. The dissertation also includes useful research tools, such as a list of informants—albeit nonexhaustive—for which there was available biographical material at the time of writing.

Katherine Kerr was the first Western scholar to produce a major study on the *Record* with her 1998 doctoral thesis from the University of Sydney entitled *The Yijian zhi: An Alternate Perspective*. This is a four-chapter study which tends to focus on interpretation and thematic analysis. Drawing on postmodern theories, particularly semiotics, Kerr argues that Hong imbued selected accounts with allegorical import. In her 1987 *Papers on Far Eastern History* article entitled "*Yijian zhi*: A Didactic Diversion," Kerr examined the didactic themes discernible throughout the text.[202] She furthermore argued that Hong's spatio-temporal markers were mere literary devices that dressed fictitious tales as fact. Needless to observe, her ideas regarding allegory stand in marked contrast to my own.

The last few years have witnessed a plethora of articles about the *Record* from the People's Republic of China which, unfortunately, tend to be rather descriptive. I will not, therefore, review them all here. There are, however, a few exceptions worth mentioning. The work of Zhang Zhuping 張祝平 is especially noteworthy. Zhang contributed to work on textual history with his 1997 articles entitled "Fenlei *Yijian zhi* yanjiu" "分類夷堅志" 研究 (Examining the *Topically-Arranged Record of the Listener*) and "Wenyan xiaoshuo pingdiande yaoji: timing Zhong Xing ping *Xinding zengbu Yijian zhi* pingyi" 文言小說評點的要籍: 題名鐘惺評 "新訂增補夷堅志" 評議 (A Pivotal Work of Classical Literary Criticism: A Critical Appraisal of Zhong Xing's *Newly Edited and Expanded Record of the Listener*).[203] The former article discusses the compilation and publishing of a topically-arranged edition published in the Ming Dynasty, while the latter reviews a hitherto seldom-cited edition also published during the Ming. Its editor, Zhong Xing 鐘惺 (1574–1624), appended commentaries for many accounts in which he arbitrated on matters such as content and theme. Zhong's commentary embodies perhaps the most lucid appraisal of the *Record*'s literary merit and affords a valuable insight into the reasons for its influence on Ming literature. Zhang's 1999 article, "*Yijian zhi* cailiao laiyuan ji souji fangshi kaoding" 夷堅志材料來源及搜集方式考訂 (A Study of Methods of Collecting Material and Sources of the *Record of the Listener*), discusses possible sources of Hong's accounts and includes a handy list of precursor texts. Zhang's 1997 *Wenxue yichan* article about a hitherto missing version of a *Jia zhi* account has been discussed already in this chapter. His 2003 *Wenxian* article, "Zhu Yunming chaoben *Yijian ding zhi* dui jinben *Yijian yi zhi* de jiaobu" (Supplementing the Current *Yi* Installment of the *Yijian zhi* with Zhu Yunming's Manuscript-copy of the *Yijian zhi*'s *ding* Installment), compares and contrasts Zhu Yunming's manuscript with the recent 1981 edition. Zhang furthermore replicates portions of the text which differ from the 1981 edition.

Japanese scholarship on the *Record*, while mostly not as recent as the above-surveyed mainland Chinese scholarship, has been extremely penetrating. Ōtsuka Hidetaka's 大塚高秀 *Kō Mai to Ikenshi—rekishi to genjitsu no hazama nite* 洪邁と夷堅志—歷史と現實の狹閒にて (Hong Mai and his *Record of the Listener*—between History and Actuality), published in 1980, discusses the *Record* in the context of Hong's career as an official. Ōstuka furthermore addresses issues such as textual history and authorial intent.[204] He carefully examines momentous events in Hong's life, right down to the month and day where possible.

Suzuki Kiyoshi's 領木靖 1990 article, "Kō Kō to Kō Mai" 洪皓と洪邁 (Hong Hao and Hong Mai), explores possible influence received by Hong Mai from his father in regard to the writing of the *Record*.[205] As with Ōsuka's work, much valuable biographical information is made accessible to the Japanese-speaking reader.

Okamoto Fujiaki's 岡本不二明 1989 article "Kuiche zhi yu Yijian Zhi; kexue yu zhiguai zhiyi" 睽車志 與 夷堅志—科学與志怪 之一 (*Cartload Full of Ghosts* and *Record of the Listener*: The Imperial Examination System and *Zhiguai*, translated into Chinese by Wang Zhizhong and Lu Zhonghui), attempts to trace the source of selected *Jia zhi* accounts to a round of prefectural examinations held in the Song capital Lin'an in 1160. As I mentioned in chapter 1, if correct, this provides valuable evidence that Hong was still working on the first installment in 1160. Okamoto also explores thematic issues as well as the relationship between the imperial examinations and *zhiguai* accounts found in these two sources. He furthermore undertakes a close reading of selected accounts. The 1994 article by the same author entitled "*Yikenshi kōshi nijū ken no seiritsu katei ni tsuite*" 夷堅志甲志二十卷の成立課題について (Questions about the Compilation of the First Installment of *Record of the Listener*), provides valuable biographical data on *Jia zhi* informants.[206]

Most recent among Japanese scholarship is Fukuda Chikashi's 福田知可志 2000 article: "*Ikenshi jijo o meguru mondai ten*" 夷堅志自序をめぐる問題点 (Unresolved Questions about the Prefaces of *Record of the Listener*) in *Chūgoku Gakushi*: *Osaka shiritsu daigaku chūbun gakkai* 中國學志 (大阪市立大学中文學会). In this, Fukuda explores what he sees as significant issues surrounding six *Yijian zhi* prefaces which he translated into Japanese.

The *Record*'s detractors, as we have seen, rejected the improbable nature of the work's content. The irony that its unusually large quantity of anomalous events undermined their very strangeness was not lost on some of these critics. Yet the rejection of what they saw as "fictitious" or "unreliable" content implicitly reveals an expectation of historical factuality. This is significant in light of Hong Mai's professed desire to achieve historical factuality, not to mention his frequent references to the *Record* as unofficial history. More, however, will be said about this in chapters 4 and 5. Given, nevertheless, the widespread acceptance of ghostly and *guai* phenomena throughout premodern China, rejection of "fictitious" content suggests that those who articulated such criticism ranked among the skeptics.

Conversely, the *Record*'s positive reception would seem to have been both broad and far-reaching, as can be seen by the imitation works it inspired as well as the influence it exerted over later literature. Ming and Qing editors of the text, all experts on Song literature, appreciated it for thematic profundity and its historical framework, not to mention its edifying moral content. I will return to these critical voices, as well as the author's own, in ensuing chapters.

CHAPTER THREE

Themes

As one opens the cover and commences reading, the very first account one finds in the *Record* narrates the story of a would-be official who meets up with his brother-in-law. Some time elapses, however, before the absent minded protagonist realizes that his brother-in-law has already died. The subsequent plot development reflects contemporary religious ideas about death and how some people were called to serve posthumously as otherworldly officials. Well may the modern reader wonder what this first account heralds in terms of theme and authorial intent. After several chapters, however, recurring ideas manifest themselves. This chapter will explore the major themes that reappear throughout the corpus. I do not, however, pretend that the *Record*'s themes can be restricted to those I explore here. Indeed, a myriad of subtle ideas form a complex matrix throughout the text. Nevertheless, those which I have selected are of particular concern due to their recurring nature.

While exploring themes, we should be mindful of the extent to which the original text has been lost. It is therefore no longer possible to make unqualified pronouncements about what the original in its entirety may have been like. Nevertheless, since the present corpus is a composite of three series written over an extensive period of time, what has survived should provide a reasonably faithful reflection of original themes and motifs. After having read the entire corpus, to my mind the most pervasive themes are: retribution (*bao* 報), destiny, and loyalty to the Song state, that is, anti-Jurchen sentiment. I will therefore focus on these three themes.

RETRIBUTION

Belief in divine retribution for misdemeanors perpetrated in life was widespread during Song times and is particularly well documented by the *Record*. As one sifts through the numerous accounts featuring retribution, it is often difficult—if not impossible—to distinguish between cases of retribution in its Buddhist or Taoists forms and those associated with popular religion. Indeed, retribution as part of a "folk" tradition had been promulgated in China as far back as the Warring States period via philosophical works such as the *Xunzi*. Liu Xiang's *Garden of Stories* (the *Shuoyuan* 說苑) from the Han period also contains numerous narratives about retribution. Yet those accounts from the *Record* which we can clearly associate with Buddhist-influenced ideas about karmic retribution (*yinguo* 因果) indicate that Buddhist influence was much more deep-rooted during Song times than many modern scholars might realize. To be sure, Western-trained scholars have tended to view the Song as a golden age of Taoism given the Song ruling elites' enthusiasm for Taoism during certain periods, particularly the reigns of the Zhenzong and Huizong emperors (r. 997–1022 and 1100–1126 respectively), not to mention the occasional suppression of Buddhism that occurred during Huizong's reign, for example. Nevertheless, whether reflecting Buddhist, Taoist, or popular religious ideas about retribution, the *Record* displays numerous purportedly factual accounts in which a transgressor's preallotted life span is shortened, which are reminiscent of the punishments proscribed in books such as the *Ledgers of Merit and Demerit* (*Gongguo ge*), although Hong Mai never cited any such work directly. I would estimate that accounts featuring various forms of retribution total approximately one-fifth of the extant corpus, and a plethora of motifs act as vehicles for its propagation.

Anecdotes about contact with deceased relatives through dreams, or ghostly apparitions which convey their need of penance-like offerings, were copious. The following account illustrates this well.

The Mountain of Crabs

The mother of Instructor Sha, a physician from Hu Prefecture, loved to eat crabs. Every year when the crabs were abundant, she would buy several dozen a day and place them in a large earthenware vat. Then she would gather around with her son and grandchildren to look at them. If the desire to eat one arose, she would pluck one out and commend it to the cauldron. She died in the seventeenth year of the Period of Continued Ascendancy (1147). Her son organized a Taoist *jiao* ceremony at the Heavenly Felicitation Temple and all the family attended. There was a ten year (*sui*) old grandchild who, alone, saw the old lady standing outside the temple gate. Her entire body was bleeding.

"I have been convicted of eating crabs," the elderly matron explained to her grandchild. "No sooner had I died, I was driven to a mountain of crabs to be punished. The crabs were piled as high as a mountain and the netherworld guards prodded me to stand on top. The multitude of crabs vied to nip me with their pincers, not stopping for an instant. I cannot begin to describe the pain. Just now the officials from the dark regions escorted me here to receive your offerings, but the wall god will not allow me to enter."

The child told its father who, in tears, prayed to the wall god. After a while, the old lady appeared where they had placed her name plaque.

"How can I endure such pain any longer," she cried. "Print a divine memorial of the Nine Heavens in my stead and burn it for the crabs so that they can use it to be reborn. Then I may be spared."

She then disappeared, not to be seen again. Her family had a divine memorial carved [and printed] that very day. They burned a hundred copies every evening and did not stop until the closure of the funeral ceremonies. Xu Fu told this story.[1]

No doubt the *jiao*-holding Taoist priests of the Heavenly Felicitation Temple would have profited enormously from stories such as these. The same may be said for the block carvers and printers of "divine memorials," sutras, and the whole gamut of products that were printed and burned as offerings to the deceased. Hence, accounts such as these both reflected and perpetuated the idea of retribution for killing life.

Other instances of karmic retribution, predicated on the Sino-Buddhist idea of the transmigration of the soul, were played out when both victim and murderer, or murderess, were reborn. In cases when the perpetrator died for his or her wickedness, the reason is often revealed in a dream or through divine intercession. Consider the following short account from the first chapter.

THE MAN FROM THREE RIVERS VILLAGE

Zhang Wei's courtesy name was Zheng Lun and he came from Three Rivers Village in Yanshan (modern Beijing). When my father first went to Taiyuan as an envoy, Wei accompanied him as magistrate of Yangqu. He once said that, in the *yisi* year in the Period of Spreading Harmony (1125), he knew of a villager from his home county who was well read and cultivated mulberry trees for a living. He was over sixty years old.

One night he woke from a nightmare. Shaking uncontrollably, he told his wife, "My life is at an end."

Alarmed, his wife asked the reason.

"Just then I dreamed of walking among the fields," he explained. "I saw seven barbarian horsemen on the road. One of them was dressed in white and was riding a white horse. He addressed me angrily, saying, 'You were once a soldier of Cai Prefecture during the Tang Dynasty in a previous life. I was a loyal citizen when Wu Yuanji rebelled, and I was helping repair the town moat when you murdered me. I have harbored hatred for a long time. Today I have finally ran into you, and although generations have passed, I will kill you in recompense.' He then took a bow and his arrow tore into my heart. I woke as I fell. I certainly shan't avoid it. Tomorrow I will go far away to flee from this disaster."

"A dream in the night isn't worth believing in!" said his wife. "It's been brought about by you unchecked thoughts."

Figure 5.1. Chin Ch'u-shih (1127–79). Hanging Scroll: One of the Kings of Hell. Ink and color on silk. H. 44; W. 18-3/4 in. Inscribed: "Painted by the Household of Chin Chu'u-shih, Carriage Bridge . . . Ming-chou, Great Sung Dynasty."

Figure 5.2. Chin Ch'u-shih (1127–79). Hanging Scroll: One of the Kings of Hell. Ink and color on silk. H. 44; W. 18-3/4 in. Inscribed: "Painted by the Household of Chin Chu'u-shih, Carriage Bridge . . . Ming-chou, Great Sung Dynasty."

Figure 5.3. Chin Ch'u-shih (1127–79). Hanging Scroll: One of the Kings of Hell. Ink and color on silk. H. 44; W. 18-3/4 in. Inscribed: "Painted by the Household of Chin Chu'u-shih, Carriage Bridge . . . Ming-chou, Great Sung Dynasty."

Figure 5.4. Chin Ch'u-shih (1127–79). Hanging Scroll: One of the Kings of Hell. Ink and color on silk. H. 44; W. 18-3/4 in. Inscribed: "Painted by the Household of Chin Chu'u-shih, Carriage Bridge . . . Ming-chou, Great Sung Dynasty."

Yet the old man's fears increased. He rose before dawn. As his family was poverty stricken, he bade only a small grandson carry his quilt, hoping to take refuge at a friend's home some sixty miles away.

The pair went along a grassy pathway for thirty miles or more before coming out onto the high road. After another few miles they came upon several people whom they joined. Suddenly, several riders came galloping up and yelled out repeatedly for the group to stop. They all did. The old man looked back and saw seven horsemen. Among them was one attired all in white, astride a white horse—just like the one in his dream. The old man was, therefore, terrified and he began to walk briskly away from the path. The riders called out menacingly for him to stop, but he did not listen. The white-robed one was livid. "This idiot!" he roared. He whipped his horse and gave chase. Drawing up before him, he lifted his bow and fired. The arrow struck the old man's heart and he died instantly. The seven horsemen were all Jurchen.[2]

While the reasons for the old man's impending death were explicitly outlined toward the beginning of the narrative, he ironically contributed to his own death by running off on his own and ignoring the rider's warnings to stop. In other accounts, ghosts sometimes act as the agent of retribution.[3]

Such stories about karmic retribution were, of course, not new. Yet the agents of retribution in this account, Jurchen horsemen, reflect the Southern Song's distinctive social and political context. This certainly helps claim a unique place in Chinese literary history for the *Record*. I would furthermore argue that the enormous number of accounts in which Jurchen atrocities formed a subtle backdrop to anomalous events and the consequent repetition thereby engendered created a subtle yet powerful anti-Jurchen undercurrent. I will explore this later in this chapter.

Hong was careful to ensure that the "laws" of the religious system were not violated when recording accounts dealing with karmic retribution. Accordingly, if reported events were not in accordance with accepted norms, he would mention this in an end commentary. An account from the twelfth installment, in which the ghost of a mistreated concubine brought about the death of both her master and mistress, illustrates this well. Not only does Hong voice disbelief, he also outlines his reasons.

THE CONCUBINE OF LEGAL OFFICER ZHU

Zhu Zong was a legal officer from Scenic Waters in Chu Prefecture, and he owed his official rank to his grandfather Zhu Daqing's legacy. He was transferred to the post of adjutant in Linjiang in the *wuwu* year in the Period of Continued Ascendancy (1138).

He had a concubine who his wife, Madame Wang, could not tolerate and would cruelly abuse both day and night. The girl eventually cut her own throat. After this not a moment went by when Zhu would not see her ghost, and he grew despondent and fearful.

He called on a Taoist from Mt. Gezao to exorcise her. The Taoist sent a restraining order to the Temple of Walls and Moats, after which he warned Zhu,

"From this day forth, you will be unable to enter the Temple of the Five Peaks, milord."

There were no more sightings of her after this.

Then one day, all the district officials went to say prayers and were caught in a rain storm en-route. They just so happened to be outside the Temple of the Five Peaks, and so the entire entourage went in to seek shelter. Zhu followed too. After a short while the rain abated and they ventured outside. There, suddenly, Zhu ran into his former concubine. Without any formal greeting, she came directly up to him, her face brimming with hatred.

"Since your death," stammered Zhu, "I have been filled with pity. You should know that I had nothing to do with it."

"How could I have come to this had I not been the servant of an official?" answered the concubine.

Zhu went home and told his wife. He fell ill and died soon after. Madame Wang followed him to the grave.

Of their three sons the eldest was but six years and so there was no-one to conduct the funeral. There was a relative, however, who was an official in the neighboring district. When he heard of it, he immediately came to put affairs in order. He also had Taoists and the like come to conduct investigations. They saw Zhu standing there, wearing a robe and holding a bamboo-strip scroll. Two women had their heads in cangues and were being interrogated. When the time came for the cortège to leave the gate, a neighbor's girl saw a woman behind the two coffins—her hair disheveled and her clothing unfastened. Shaking her fist, she laughed heartily then disappeared. The girl was shocked and so told her parents. She became a mute after that and never spoke again.

This story was told by controller-general Huang Xiang who was from Zhu's village.

As for both master and mistress paying with their lives for the death of one concubine, the powerful Temple of the Five Peaks being unable to control a single ghost yet allowing it to come and go at will, and a girl becoming mute after speaking of an apparition—I consider all this to be highly questionable.[4]

Hong, quite rightly, pointed out how ghosts were not supposed to pass door gods. Yet, when they did, as in the incident which occurred within Hong's own family in Xiuzhou, there tended to be a "logical" caveat, such as incompetent deities. Hong Mai's expectation of logic, no doubt shared by his readership, can often be seen in his end comments. And given his aim for "reliability" as expressed throughout his prefaces, such a remark is hardly surprising. Hence, internal logic, at least logic predicated on China's traditional religious system, became a "tool" with which Hong gauged the plausibility of given accounts.

Like the *zhiguai* of the Six Dynasties, the *Record* contains innumerable accounts which saw wrongdoers summoned to the Taoist netherworld or the Buddhist hell—it is invariably impossible to distinguish which. There they were expected to answer for misdemeanors whereby departed souls had lodged writs against them. Elsewhere an innocent person may be called as a witness in these netherworld trials, while their subsequent return to the mortal realm may have coincided with sudden resurrection from the dead. The example below involves a case of mistaken identity in which an innocent soul was returned to the world of the living as soon as the error had been discovered.

THIRD MISTRESS ZHANG

Ye Jifu, a physician from Dexing (Dexing county in Jiangxi), had a wife named Madame Zhang who was ranked number three. She suddenly developed fever and died during the Heavenly Way period (1165–73) yet revived before being placed in her coffin.

"I was accosted by a green-clad official," she explained. "We went into the wilds. It was dim and shadowy, and I didn't know where I was. After a while we came upon a government building and I fell before the audience hall in tears. There was a high-ranking official seated in the center. The green-clad one proffered him a document. The official was struck with rage and ordered that the green-clad one be held to the ground while a jailor beat his feet with a bramble cane. The powerful official berated him.

"I originally ordered you to summon Third Mistress Zhang from the Xu household of Golden Mountain Borough in Leping County, yet you have bungled. Why? This woman has twelve more years yet to live and still has two sons to bear. How could you have brought her?"

"He then had another accompany me back. After that I woke up."

Jifu was pleased that she had revived and had not the time to make inquiries at the Xu household. After this, Zhang indeed bore two sons and passed away precisely twelve years later. Jifu is still alive.[5]

While the miscreants of many *zhiguai* accounts found it difficult to escape divine justice, the otherworldly bureaucracy was not without an occasional error, which is aptly illustrated in this account.

Numerous other accounts record retribution visited on those who might have slain many animals—sometimes in an unnecessarily cruel manner. Not surprisingly, butchers were often the target of such moralizing. Below is the story of a butcher named Dong Bai'e.

DONG BAI'E

Dong Bai'e hailed from White Stone Village in Leping County in Rao Prefecture. Dong earned his living by slaughtering cattle and the number he had killed was innumerable. He contracted a malady in the autumn of the twenty-third year of the period of Continued Ascendancy (1153). Whenever he suffered an outbreak, people would have to fetch rope and tie his head, hands and feet between some posts. They would thoroughly beat him with a cane, and only then would he readily forget his illness. This went on for seven days until he died.

When Dong was alive, he used this very same method to kill the cattle. And the manner of his death was said to be no different from the way the cattle died.[6]

While we might appreciate narratives sufficiently well crafted to have influenced later literature and drama, accounts such as these are reminiscent of what Lu Xun referred to as the roughly-wrought, simplistic narratives displayed by *zhiguai* accounts from the Six Dynasties.[7]

In contrast to killing animals high up on the food chain, such as cattle, other accounts tell of how a person might suffer retribution—often resulting in death—for killing smaller animal life, as shown below.

REVENGE OF THE TURTLES

At the beginning of the Xuande era the Honourable Huai Jingyuan from Qiantang set up an office of supply for Cai You[8] at the Many Treasures Monastery in Xiuzhou. Huai was passionately fond of eating turtle and he had a servant who was an excellent chef. Before cooking a turtle, the man always slashed its throat and let it bleed; he claimed this enhanced the flavor. The man subsequently developed scrofula. His head grew so large that he could not hold it up, and it protruded in front of him as he walked. The condition grew worse with the passage of time. His skin became gangrenous, and eventually his head fell off and he died. It was as if his head had been severed with a knife. Jingyuan did not dare eat turtle again after that.[9]

To twenty-first-century readers, this account seems improbable indeed. Yet, given the widespread belief in retribution for killing animal life, the chef's untimely end is a logical outcome of his actions. Certainly the manner of his wound and Jingyuan's reaction demonstrate the link between killing turtles and the perpetrator's death.

Given that Cai You was the son of the infamous Cai Jing, he counted among the notorious ministers of Huizong's court who were later blamed for the demise of the Northern Song. Furthermore, since the clique headed by Cai Jing implemented the Shenzong emperor's (r. 1067–1085) institutional reforms—albeit in a diluted manner—they were further vilified by officials loyal to the conservative ministers (known in Chinese as the Yuanyou 元祐 faction and later, as I will discuss in the last section of this chapter, the "little Yuanyou faction" 小元祐黨) who opposed the reforms. An account about the demise of someone remotely connected with Cai You may well have piqued the interest of contemporary readers who identified with the conservatives.

Similar accounts purportedly demonstrated retribution for killing even the tiniest animal, as in the case of the artisan who killed spiders so as to use their "blood" (*xue*) for his paintings.[10] Animals ear-marked for slaughter would often plead for their lives in human voices, as in the case of thirteen frogs which were consequently released.[11]

Not unlike many other *zhiguai* texts, the retribution theme in the *Record* was used to propagate Confucian morality. In other words, things which the Master (Confucius) did not speak of were used to reinforce the Master's teaching. Accordingly, numerous accounts documented retribution for unfilial behavior, including unburied fathers, as in the following account.

Luo Gong is Reprimanded by the Netherworld

> Luo Gong was from Southern Sword Sand County and was at the Imperial University during the Great Vision period (1107–1110). There was an extremely efficacious shrine at the University and Luo would pray both morning and evening about his future.
>
> One evening, he dreamed of a god who told him, "You have offended the netherworld and should speedily return to your homeland. You need not inquire about your future."
>
> Luo had always kept himself free of any misdemeanor and wished to be told the reason for his having caused offense.
>
> "You have committed no other misdemeanor. It is only because your parents have gone for a long time without burial," the god explained.
>
> "There are brothers in our family," countered Luo. "Why should I alone shoulder the blame?"
>
> "It is because you practice propriety and righteousness as a Confucian," replied the god. "Therefore, you are the one to suffer the consequences. Your brothers are all weak and not worth admonishing."
>
> When Luo realized what had happened, remorse overcame him and he hurriedly packed his belongings to return home. His compatriot who was in the same study hall asked him, and so Luo told about the dream. He died before reaching home.
>
> Cao (character missing in the original) told this story. Luo was his great-uncle.[12]

The corpses of the scholar's parents here may well have been temporarily lodged at a Buddhist temple, given that temporary storage of the deceased was among the services provided by the Buddhist church to the community during the Song. The scholar's death in this account would almost certainly have acted as a warning to others who may well have been less blameless. The account that follows this also deals with the theme of retribution for an unburied parent;

although, in this case, the protagonist survived to pass the imperial examinations after having attended to the burial. Punishment for unburied fathers is, therefore, perhaps best thought of as an example of *ganying* (stimulus-response 感應) more so than *bao* (retribution for misdemeanors), since human action was thought to affect one's relationship with "spiritual" beings, such as when family fortunes were thought to be affected by the location of a relative's burial site according to *fengshui* 風水 (geomancy).

Accounts featuring retribution for unfilial behavior often employ lightning as a retributive agent. This no doubt reflects the increased popularity enjoyed by lightning cults since the Five Dynasties (907–960), and the high number of such accounts is a distinctive feature of the *Record* when compared to works of a similar genre—particularly pre-Song texts. Certainly there are only a handful of accounts in the lightning section of the *Extensive Records*, only one of which resembles Hong Mai's use of the motif as a retributive agent in instances of unfilial behavior.[13] To be sure, if lightening featured at all in Six Dynasty (420–581) *zhiguai* accounts, it was rarely used to convey moralistic warnings against unfiliality. A typical account in the *Record* might see an unfilial son or daughter-in-law struck dead by lightning soon after an unfilial act.[14] Conversely, predestined death by lightning could be averted due to filial behavior, as in the following example. Hence the didactic message operated both ways: death for the unfilial and reward for the filial, or those who—like Dickens's Scrooge—mended their ways.

> During the sixth month of the twenty-ninth year of the Shaoxing era (1159) there was a thunderstorm in Yanguan *xian*. On the day before the storm, Miss Zhang—who was the wife of Gu Deqian, a saltworker at the Shangguan flats—had a dream in which a spirit admonished her for something she had done in a previous life. He said: "You'll be struck dead by lightning tomorrow." She woke up, terrified and weeping with despair. When her mother-in-law questioned her, she declined to answer. Her mother-in-law became angry and said: "How could it have come to this? Is it because I've borrowed something from you and have failed to return it?" Miss Zhang began to explain, but her mother-in-law would not believe her. The following day, when a fierce wind arose and the sky grew dark, Miss Zhang thought she was about to die. She changed her clothes, then she went outside and stood beneath a mulberry tree. She thought to herself: "I can't avoid being struck by lightning. But mother-in-law is very old, how will she survive the shock?" From amid the thunder and gloom, a voice from the sky called out to Miss Zhang and said: "You were meant to die. But because of your filial thought just now heaven has forgiven you." And then it said: "Go home and continue the good work by telling people about this."[15]

Here is but one example of how an account of a filial daughter-in-law acted as an agent for propagating Confucian morality.[16] It is not difficult to understand how accounts such as this would have encouraged uneducated, and perhaps gullible, women to dutifully care for their mother-in-laws, thus perpetuating the patriarchal system which often reduced wives—particularly those of lower socioeconomic status—to menial positions in their husband's household. And while—to twenty-first-century readers—the reasons for the daughter-in-law's reprieve may seem to undermine the very concept of karmic retribution, the idea that misdemeanors could be mitigated by good deeds was articulated in texts such as the *Ledgers of Merit and Demerit*.[17]

This two-way street of reward and punishment is particularly well illustrated in accounts involving sutras. The Sino-Buddhist idea whereby recitation of sutras and mantras could mitigate misdemeanors was not unlike the concept of doing penance in medieval Europe, and in at least one of Hong's accounts retribution is visited upon those who are insufficiently devout in this regard. The account entitled "Chen Tilian" from the eleventh installment, for example, tells of how a man dies after failing to heed a dream-warning about insufficient recitation of sutras.[18] Other accounts illustrate reward for those who regularly recite sutras, even simple ones.[19] Countless more "document" instances whereby malevolent entities were repelled through the recitation of sutras or mantras. In the following account, a man saves himself from sacrifice to a malevolent snake spirit by reciting the Mantra of Great Compassion and invoking the name of the Guanyin bodhisattva for salvation.

> The son of a Mr. Wang from Qimen (southern Anhui) was traveling from Poyang to Chi Prefecture (southern Anhui), planning to spend the night at Jiande County. Before he had gone thirty or more miles, he passed by a relative's ancestral home and so, sending his baggage on ahead, he stopped by to have a drink. Having finished drinking, alone, he mounted his horse and moved on. Then he lost his way and was unable to rendezvous with his retainers.
>
> He ventured far along a narrow path flanked by dense undergrowth while the sky grew dark. Suddenly, several men rushed out and accosted him. They took him ten miles or so until reaching an old temple deep in the mountains. There they bound him to a pillar. Burning incense and heating wine, the several men prayed before the deity's image, elated.
>
> "Come, take him, Oh Great One," they intoned, after which they closed the temple gate and left.
>
> Wang realized that they were sacrificing him to a demon and sank into uncontrollable despondency and terror. He had been in the habit of reciting the Mantra of Great Compassion. When it came to this, all he could do was chant it silently—pleading for salvation.
>
> In the middle of the night, a great storm arose which shook the trees. With a rumbling akin to thunder, the gate crashed open and a being entered. Its eyes were like torches, illuminating the halls and passageways. Wang took a look at it, and found that it was a giant python. It slithered forward with open jaws, making straight for him. Shaking in fear, he recited the mantra with even greater fervor. When there was about a meter or so between him and the serpent, it was as though there was something blocking the monster's

path. It backed away only to approach again. This happened three times, after which it turned away and went out.

With the approach of dawn, the men came from outside toting drums and flutes. They had come to partake of the sacrificial wine they had offered the deity and were mortified to see Wang still there. They asked him what had happened, and he told them the whole story. They looked at each other and exclaimed,

"This official possesses good fortune. We should not have tried to sacrifice him."

They untied him and apologized, then accompanied him to the high road with admonitions not to tell anyone. After his release, Wang was never able to trace the villains.

Wang Jiasou told this story.[20]

The efficacy of mantras and their power over local cults could not have been lost on contemporary readers. The above account is but one example of human sacrifice to malevolent entities found in the *Record*. Others tend to be somewhat lurid. Nevertheless, the Buddhist church did not posses a monopoly over efficacious sutras and mantras. In other accounts, Taoist incantations (*zhou* 咒) were used with similar results, as in the case of an official who warded off a ghost by reciting the incantation of the stellar deity Tianpeng.[21]

A PARADOX

Not every misdemeanor, however, resulted in the type of sure-fire, often swift-footed retribution displayed in some of the examples above. There are a minority of accounts in which the perpetrator evades retribution after killing animal life or committing murder. This would seem to constitute a hitherto unaddressed paradox meriting further investigation.

Let us first consider the narrative entitled "Chao is Haunted by Toads," in which a scholar residing at a Buddhist temple sees an unusually large frog and kills it. As a result, both the protagonist and his son are haunted by various manifestations yet, inexplicably, escape retribution.

> Master Chao of North Qi (the north of Juye in Shandong) lived in the Five Luck Temple in Fu Prefecture. He was taking a stroll out on the marshland behind the temple when he saw a toad the size of a plate crouching amidst the grass. Thinking it abnormal, he killed it. But no sooner had he returned to his dwelling than he heard magpies calling between the eaves. Then it was as though thunder reverberated throughout the whole sky, without ceasing for what seemed an eternity. Chao went out but saw nothing. Yet the sound which filled his ears continued as before. Chao, however, still didn't think that there was anything untoward afoot.
>
> That night, his son was reading by the window when the lamp suddenly went out. Something was standing next to him. In the darkness, the boy

struck out at it with a ruler, yet it took the ruler from him and went out. Chao then realized that the toad was haunting them. Chao then sent the boy to bed, but before he was fully asleep, he felt his bed shudder. Feeling with his hands, he found that the bed had left the floor by ten meters or more and was almost touching the ceiling. After this, the toad would laugh and cackle among the rafters, sing and dance in the air, and would change into innumerable shapes. Chao called in Taoist priests and shamans to exorcise it, yet not one achieved any success. He then moved to other lodgings, but the haunting continued. Chao, therefore, commissioned a portrait of [the stellar deity] Zhenwu. Both night and day, he would diligently make offerings of candles and incense and, after some months, the haunting ceased.[22]

Given the numerous accounts documenting retribution for killing animal life throughout the *Record*, Chao's escape from retribution here seems remarkable—particularly when contrasted to the fate of Huai Jingyuan's hapless servant featured above whose head fell off as retribution for killing turtles. Cases such as Chao's undoubtedly went far to promote the cult of Zhenwu, of which Hong Mai himself may have been a devotee given, as we saw in chapter 1, that his father worshipped this deity. Recourse to a deity, therefore, held the hope of averting retribution that would have otherwise been meted out. This seems all the more plausible when we consider stories such as the above-mentioned saltworker's wife who escaped karmic retribution through a filial thought. Hence, in harmony with the *Ledgers of Merit and Demerit*, pious deeds sometimes had the power to avert retribution.

What is special about Chao's case is (implied) divine intervention. And, to be sure, his is not the only such example. The Taoist priest, Wang Juchang, for example, was forewarned in a dream of impending death as retribution for having killed someone in a previous existence. He was told to call upon the name of the Great King of Seeking in the Mountains (*soushen dawang* 搜山大王) to attain salvation. Wang did as instructed and was spared.[23] In another account promulgating the power of the Buddha, a Buddhist devotee is similarly forewarned about the impending enactment of karmic retribution and received instructions which he used to save himself (I present a full translation of this account in chapter 5).[24] In the case of Liu Huasheng, the protagonist avoids karmic retribution for having killed two women in a previous life. Through prayer to what seems a popular deity, the Universal Protection King (*Guangyou wang* 廣佑王), Liu's life is extended for twelve years due to his having diligently performed a ten-day Buddhist *zhai* ceremony (during which time only vegetarian food was consumed).[25] In yet another account, a poor man's wife had an affair with a male deity who brought her riches. When the local magistrate discovered this, he arrested both the woman and her husband and put them on trial. They were, however, released after the deity caused various manner of mayhem, including rocks falling like rain on the government offices.[26] In all these accounts, miscreants escape karmic retribution or retribution for immoral behavior through either divine intervention or as a reward for piety.

Nevertheless, the narratives entitled "Yang Zheng's Concubines" and "Han Zhuangmin Eats Donkeys" are somewhat baffling as neither divine intercession nor piety play a pivotal role. The subject of the first account is the Southern Song general, Yang Zheng 楊政 (1098–1157), who fought the Jurchen alongside the famous commander Wu Jie 吳玠 (1093–1139) during the Jianyan period (1127–1130).

> Yang Zheng was a famous general of Qin (central Shanxi) during the period of Continued Ascendancy (1131–1162). His renown was on a par with the two Wu's and he eventually attained the rank of a grand guardian. Yet he was cruel by nature and took pleasure in murder. Having received his command on the Day of Xingyuan, he threw a banquet for his supporters and protégés. One of them, Li Shujia, rose to visit the privy during the festivities while an attendant soldier took a candle and led the way. They took several twists and turns as though proceeding down a narrow alleyway. Li looked at both walls on which appeared the faint outline of human forms. He thought that they had been painted, but when he took a closer look, he could not find the trace of any brush, nor were there any faces or eyes. Altogether there were about twenty or thirty of them. Not knowing what to make of it, he asked the attendant soldier. The soldier looked both in front and behind. Secure in the knowledge that nobody was coming, he said in a hushed voice,
>
> "The master's dozens of concubines are all musically and artistically gifted. But if they incur the slightest displeasure, he's sure to beat them to death. Then, from head to foot, he skins them and nails their skins to these walls. When the skins dry out and harden, they are taken down and thrown into the river. These are the traces they have left." Shuyong left terror-stricken.
>
> Yang had a favorite concubine which he loved as a first wife. He fell ill in his final years and was therefore confined to his bed. He asked nothing about the affairs of the world, but was solely concerned with this concubine and would have her constantly serve by his side. All of a sudden, he said to her,
>
> "My illness has gotten as bad as this and I surely won't recover. I have given you my all. What will you do in the future?"
>
> Yang's breathing was very weak at the time, and much of what he said was unintelligible. Crying, the concubine replied,
>
> "Force yourself to take some more medicine, my lord. Should you not recover, I am willing to follow you to the Yellow Springs."
>
> Yang was elated. He sought wine to give to his concubine and each of them drank a cup. The concubine returned to her room and groaned. Deeply regretting her folly, she planned to go into hiding while Yang, his breath coming in fits and starts, closed his eyes. There was a high-ranking general related to him who taunted him thus:

"In life your lordship slew people as though you were squashing ants and lice. You were truly a great man. Now that your destiny has run its course, you are all sentimental. Where is your resolve now?"

Yang called out his concubine's name. "Just wait for her to die first," he said. "I will follow."

The great general understood his meaning. He had someone say to the concubine, "The master is calling you." He also summoned a burly fellow to bring a noose and hide behind the bed. When the concubine arrived, they swiftly slipped the noose around her neck and in a short while she was dead. Yang died as her corpse hit the ground.[27]

The death scene described here, in which Yang's favorite concubine is strangled so as to follow him into the next world, is reminiscent of pre-Qin times when slaves and servants formed part of the sacrificial inventory sealed inside a ruler's tomb. Given the swift and sure-footed retribution visited upon the subjects of other accounts, the ability of Yang Zheng to escape such reckoning for torture and murder is surely remarkable, unless perhaps his death could be construed as retribution. Yet death in old age can hardly be considered this way, especially when contrasted to the fate of Luo Gong, whose life and career were cut short due to unburied parents.

Similarly, the account about Han Zhuangmin below documents cruelty to animals that—inexplicably—fails to incur retribution. In the narrative entitled "Han Zhuangmin Eats Donkeys," the reader is told of Han's partiality to fresh donkey intestines which necessitated his chef extracting them while the animals were still alive.

Zhuangmin was a posthumous title bestowed on Han Shen 韓慎 (1019–1097), cognomen Yuru 玉 汝, who was an influential minister during the Northern Song. Although Han enjoyed a successful career in the civil service and served in some extremely high-ranking positions, he was well-known for his cruelty and once had a commoner beaten to death.

> Vice Grand Councilor Han Zhuangmin enjoyed eating donkey intestines. In the interests of variety, he would have intestines served in many different ways. When put into the wok, if the intestines were overcooked they would be soft and mushy. And if the timing was not just right, they would come out too hard. The chef was afraid of punishment, so he would tie a live donkey to a pillar and, when wine had been prepared, he would cut open the donkey's stomach, extract the intestines and wash them. He would then cook them in stock for a short time before removing them to be served with five spices. Then, taking some paper money, he would look through the joint between the bi-fold doors, waiting until the Vice Grand Councilor had finished and set to rest his chopsticks without any complaints. Only then would the chef burn the money as an offering to heaven [for the repose of the donkey's soul].
>
> When Han was in Qin Prefecture (Tianshui County in Gansu), there was a guest who left the banquet hall to go to go to the privy. He passed by

the Grand Councilor's kitchen and saw several donkeys prostrate by the pillar. All their stomachs had been cut and their intestines removed, yet they were still alive. The guest had been born in the passes (modern Shanxi) and had often eaten this type of meat. But from then on, he didn't let a morsel pass his lips again. . .[28]

Although the narrative provides a recipe for the perfectly-cooked intestines, it is unclear how extracting them from live donkeys could have helped. Nor is it easy to understand how Han or his chef could have escaped the punishment meted out to, for example, Dong Bai'e the butcher for similar misdemeanors. No doubt the chef's offering paper money could be construed as salvation through a pious act, as in the case of the crab-eating woman. Yet this does not explain how Han himself escaped the same retribution meted out to beef-eaters who indirectly caused animal deaths even though they did not slaughter the beasts themselves,[29] or to Huai Jingyuan, who had his chef kill turtles in a particularly cruel manner. We may remember that, in Huai's case, the chef suffered retribution while Huai, seemingly warned by the chef's untimely demise, exhibited remorse by henceforth abstaining from turtles. In Han's case, however, while his chef escaped retribution—probably due to his burnt offerings, Han displayed no penitent behavior yet astonishingly avoided retribution.

Han's escape appears even more inexplicable when compared to the fate of Wang Tiangong, whose story is documented in the account below.

THE HAUNTED HILL OF EFFICACIOUS SPRINGS

Wang Tiangong was a pacification clerk from Jianyang and was residing at Efficacious Springs Temple on the county border. In front of the temple was a field and in the field was a small knoll. On the knoll grew ten or more enormous trees, all of them several feet in diameter and covered in vines and creepers. The villagers thought them to be animistic spirits. Secluded and dark, they were somehow awe-inspiring. During festivals and on special occasions, there were those who would make offerings to them.

Wang was about to fell them for firewood. He called on field laborers to take to them with their axes, but nobody dared go. Wang grew angry and wanted to beat them, so they had no choice but to comply. However, no sooner had they swung their axes a few times than blood began to flow from the wood. Terrified, they stopped and went back to tell of what had happened.

Wang beat the two ringleaders.

"It's only sap seeping from old bark," he said. "How could it be blood?"

Knowing that they could not avoid it, the laborers bought paper money and burned it. Then they let down their hair and felled the trees. With every fall of the axe they chanted, "Pacification Clerk Wang compels us." When the copse was cleared, the timber retrieved amounted to three thousand bundles.

This occurred during the thirteenth year in the Period of Continued Ascendancy (1143).

After a month, a malignant growth appeared on Wang's back and he himself claimed to have seen an apparition. But the haunting did not go away even after his death. The community attempted pacifying the spirits by replanting the site with other trees. Now it has grown into a thriving forest and the haunting has ceased.[30]

The story of Wang Tiangong's misdemeanor is strikingly similar to that of Han Zhuangmin's; in both cases the underlings who perpetrate the misdemeanors avoid retribution seemingly due to their having been compelled by a higher authority, in addition to their having burned paper money. Yet, in Wang's case, he displays no remorse and so pays with his life. Han, in contrast, somehow avoids retribution. And although the burning of paper money in both these accounts may explain the lack of retribution for those carrying out orders, it is clearly not applicable to Yang Zheng's story.

Perhaps the lack of retribution in these two accounts points to an overriding consideration more important to Hong Mai than the didactic function of literature: that is, historical factuality. Given Hong's professed claim of reliability as articulated in his prefaces, in addition to his scruples as an historian, if the subject of an account was not known to have suffered retribution-like misfortunes, surely Hong would not have invented any. I would argue, therefore, that lack of retribution in the stories of both Han Zhuangmin and Yang Zheng further indicates Hong's desire to achieve an accurate record of what many contemporaries believed to be largely plausible, if not factual, accounts. To be sure, the edited version of "The Female Knight-Errant," which I discussed in chapter 2, demonstrates Hong's willingness to excise didactic content when reported events were (presumably) contradicted by historical fact. Therefore, while didacticism is an extremely important aspect of the *Record*, what was more important to Hong was historical reliability.

As we can see, cases of retribution are particularly prevalent throughout the *Record*. Not only do they reflect Song religious ideas, but they are also inextricably linked to Hong Mai's seeming didactic intent. Yet these didactic accounts, rather than function as fictional, Aesop Fable-type parables, relied on historical factuality for their persuasive punch. In other words, the idea that said accounts supposedly occurred lent weight to their didactic thrust. In this respect, their function may be thought of as similar to "boogieman" stories used to influence children's behavior in the West; the difference being that, in premodern China, almost everyone believed in the boogieman.

DESTINY

The idea that one receives a predetermined allotment of years is a major theme permeating the *Record* and is closely related to omens and prognostication, which assumed political significance due to the mandate of heaven. To be sure, founder of the Song Dynasty, Zhao Kuangyin, summoned all self-professed prognosticians and astronomers to the capital shortly after the establishment of the dynasty. He then conferred state recognition and employment to the worthy while banishing the incompetent. Zhao's act is testament to the continued importance placed on destiny and omens during the early Song and Five Dynasties, not to mention both earlier and later periods. And since this theme was in accordance with orthodox Confucian thinking, accounts of this nature could hardly have been seen by skeptics as quite so improbable as those which dealt with ghosts or other such paranormal activity.

A few accounts dealing with destiny focus specifically on circumstances surrounding a protagonist's birth and subsequent biography, apparently to "prove" the hypothesis that the time and place of one's birth affects one's destiny, as in the following example.

> Hubei's (Jinghu Circuit north) Chief Fiscal Commissioner, Zhou Zi, was from Wuxing (Wuxing in modern Zhejiang). He was the son of Gentleman-in-Waiting Zhou Yan'guang. Born in the *renzi* year of the period of Continued Ascendancy (1132), he passed away in the *guichou* year of the Continued Prosperity Period (1193) at the official rest post in E Prefecture (in modern Hubei). The controller-general of Biling (in modern Jiangsu), Yu Fang, was born in the same year as Zhou and was secretly worried [to hear of Zhou's death]. His friends and relatives all comforted him, saying that destiny according to the five elements is different for people born on different times of the same day of the same month of the same year, not to mention thousands of people of the same age. In the end, Yu was not comforted by any of this.
>
> There was an education officer in Fu Prefecture, Chen Fang, who had been born a year before Yu. Since he had come to take the autumnal (prefectural) exams, Yu went to supervise them. The two were especially close. In the fourth month of that year, Yu went again to E [Prefecture] and Chen invited him to his home. After some convivial conversation, Yu looked at his son.
>
> "I feel that my back is so itchy, I can't bear it," he said. "Can you take a look?"
>
> The son lifted up Yu's garments after which he made an obeisance before Chen and asked him to look together. The middle section revealed a swelling which initially resembled the size of a peach. They hurriedly called a physician adept at ulcers and boils, yet kept on talking as if nothing was wrong. When the physician arrived, the swelling had grown to the size of a fan.
>
> "It has come on at the speed of greased lightening," exclaimed the doctor in alarm. "This is not something that can be cured with acupuncture. Only a mixture of mugwort will do it."
>
> He ordered garlic and mugwort crushed which he applied all over, covering almost the whole of Fang's back. They waited until the inflammation subsided and the swelling went away. The physician, however, was a military one

and his technique was shoddy. The meridian point which he had used during the acupuncture had been opened excessively. The inflamed ulcer flared up again with a vengeance and there was nothing which could be done to save him. Yu died before three days were up.

Yu's clan was wealthy and he had been fond of ingesting golden cinnabar which gave him a ruddy complexion. Therefore, when the ulcer's poison began to spread, it took hold thus rapidly.[31]

The end-commentary of this account gives a physiological reason for Yu's rapid deterioration. Yet his having been born on the same day as another official who died in the introduction links Yu's death to his preallotted lifespan (due to time of birth). The skepticism offered by Yu's family engenders a binary opposition between skepticism and "belief." Perhaps Hong's intention, therefore, was to enhance the doctrine of predestiny's persuasiveness by incorporating and thereby overriding possible counterarguments. The second onset of inflammation after initial success was possibly read by contemporary readers as further evidence for the inescapability of destiny, despite human intervention.

A similar account from the eleventh installment tells of two men from scholar-official families born during the same hour on the same day of the same year. Rather than die at much the same time, as did Yu Fang and Zhou Zi in the above account, they died within three years of each other. This discrepancy was explained due to one of them having taken a later examination and, consequently, having received an official posting slightly later in life.[32]

One account from the first installment is unambiguously entitled "Good and Bad Fortune Cannot be Avoided." In this Hong juxtaposes two reports, apparently to demonstrate fate's inevitability.

Gentleman-in-Waiting Li Sizhi said that, "Since the great catastrophe, a gentleman's good or bad fortune has become predestined."

In the *dingwei* year of the period of Founding Glory (1127), Minister Fu Guohua was magistrate of Shu Prefecture when he heard reports of bandits in Wuchang. Wuchang was only separated from Shu by Qin and Huang Prefectures, and Fu was afraid they would make an incursion into his jurisdiction. He had furthermore acted as an envoy to Korea on several occasions and had many prized possessions in his home. Wishing to preserve them, he bade his younger brother remove his family to Jiangning (modern Nanjing). When they arrived, they moored their boat beside the riverbank.

"There are many local bandits about," warned the boatman. "We had better go inside the water-lock." At the time, Yuwen Zhong was in charge of Jiangning and was on good terms with Lord Fu. Thereupon Fu's family had word sent to Yuwen so as to borrow the key to the lock. The boat thus gained access and they thought themselves free of danger.

That night however, Zhou De—a common soldier—rebelled. The rebels plundered Fu's boat and his whole family was killed; only an elderly maid-servant survived. Shu Prefecture's walled citadel, however, remained unscathed.

Gu Yancheng of Wufang was in charge of transport in Liangzhe when the Hangzhou soldier, Chen Tong, had incurred pent-up anger at the gentlemen of government and was about to rebel. This happened to be the time when Lord Gu had gone on an inspection of Wuxing. Chen, therefore, suppressed his mob and had them wait until he returned. An entire month passed before Gu arrived and the Hangzhou officials and members of the transport authority all came out to greet him. That night the rebels struck and the officials and clerks were slaughtered to a man. Lord Gu and his family, however, had their boat moored outside the city walls at a temple where they were participating in Buddhist ceremonies, and so he had not entered the metropolis. When he heard of the rebellion, he went back to Hu Prefecture (the vicinity of Wuxing in Zhejiang) and escaped.

Lord Fu had it in mind to avoid disaster, yet his whole family could not evade it. The Hangzhou soldiers waited for Lord Gu an entire month, yet he was able to escape. All this is not something that can be controlled by men.[33]

The juxtaposition of these two stories as evidence that good or bad fortune cannot be avoided aptly illustrates the theme underpinning a great many accounts in the *Record*. It also demonstrates how unrelated coincidences were construed by contemporaries, even erudite scholars such as Hong Mai, as evidence of the workings of destiny.

Yet even destiny, it seems, was not so straightforward. Occasionally one's preordained lifespan might be shortened for misdemeanors, as proscribed in the *Ledgers of Merit and Demerit*. Consider the case below of the eldest brother Qian, whose preallotted lifespan was to be cut short because of greed, yet contrition helped him partially redeem himself.

THE THREE TAOISTS OF JADE FORD

It was during the Period of Great Vision (1107–1110) that the brothers Qian, gentlemen from Suzhou, traveled to study at the Imperial Academy. Spring had just blossomed. They had some time to spare while waiting for an exam, and so they went on a jaunt to the Jade Ford Gardens.

There they met three Taoists who greeted them, and they began a conversation. The Taoists had prominent foreheads and long eyebrows. Their words were pure and fresh—pleasing to the ear. After a while they took their leave, saying, "We have a brew of some small reputation which we would like to share with you, but unfortunately the sun is already low. Let us meet here again tomorrow at high noon and we can entertain you then. Don't be late or you may miss us."

The Qians agreed. Then, with a laugh, the smallest Taoist remarked, "Should you miss the appointed time, you can dig up the ground here to find us." Thinking this a joke, the two of them laughed heartily and took their leave.

The following day the Qians were detained on other business, and it was evening by the time they reached the place of rendezvous. There they found the remains of a feast strewn untidily about. The Taoists were nowhere to be seen. Despondently, they remained there for quite some time until the younger of the brothers asked, "Could they have been immortals?"

So saying, he fetched a spade and began to dig away at the ground. He had not gone down more than a foot or so when he came upon a stone casket. Opening it, they found images of three Taoists. Their head-dresses majestic, they looked just like the ones the brothers had met the previous day. Beside the casket was a book of esoterica which contained the formulae for transmuting mercury into silver.

The younger brother suggested, "Brother, you take the book. I would like to have the images. After my return, I will make them offerings of incense." The elder brother eagerly agreed.

When the exam came only the younger brother met with success. The older one returned to Suzhou where he tested out the formulae. There was not one which did not repay his efforts. Within a few years he had bought thousands of acres of land and became a wealthy man.

One day, however, while sitting under the eaves of an outer pavilion, the arrival of three Taoists was announced. No sooner had he received them when one of them rose and addressed him thus, "Do you remember our meeting in the Jade Ford Gardens all those years ago? You took our book of celestial learning, but rather than use it to aid the poor, you exploited it for the sake of your own insatiable greed. Already your wealth has far exceeded its allotment. Heaven, therefore, decrees that you be cut off, and today is the day of your reckoning. If, however, you change your ways this very day, then you may look forward to three more years. If not, you will die in the space of a day. We have been banished to the world of mortals for revealing heaven's secrets, so naturally it falls on us to carry out this sentence."

After they had left, Master Qian was struck by a wave of remorse. He immediately burned the book and smashed his alchemist's stove. He closed the door of his laboratory, never to open it again.

The next day, the smallest Taoist returned. Before Qian could sit down with him, he was told that his concubine had just given birth. Rushing in to see her, he saw that she had produced a boy. Returning to his guest, he found that the Taoist was nowhere to be seen. He questioned his servants, but they knew nothing.

Qian died within three years.[34]

According to the logic on which this narrative is predicated, Qian's preallotted lifespan was to be shortened as retribution for greed. Here, then, is a warning to others. Yet Qian's remorse brought about an extension, albeit by only a few years, which offers hope of reward for "good" deeds. This narrative, like so many others in the *Record*, both admonishes and encourages in the same breath. Nevertheless, the account demonstrates the idea prevalent during Song times that even destiny could be altered by human action in much the same way that a filial thought might avert retribution in the form of lightning.

Physiognomy often acted as a prophetic agent in destiny-related accounts, as in the case of Jiang Zhiping. In this account, the protagonist (Jiang) died within a year of a physiognomist predicting his death due to a minor misdemeanor.[35] Jiang's crime was granting preferential treatment to a relative who undertook an examination which Jiang had supervised the previous year. Hong Mai's tongue-in-cheek end-comment about many similar cases hints at widespread nepotism in the imperial examinations. Hence, even this theme could be harnessed for didactic moralizing.

It should be obvious by now that destiny, throughout the *Record*, was often combined with other themes, particularly karmic retribution. The above-related account in which the old man from Three Rivers Village was forewarned of his impending death by a prophetic dream is as good an example as any. This account also displays the futility of human action to escape one's fate, unless, of course, recourse to deities was made or sufficient contrition was shown by which the doomed protagonist may have attained salvation. And conversely, if one's preallotted years were not up, one might even escape a snake demon, as in the account of Mr. Wang of Qimen's son who was thought to possess good fortune, with, of course, a little help from Buddhist sutras. Or else the case of Zhang Sanniang who was returned from the netherworld since she still had another twelve years to live. Such was the power of a preallotted lifespan.

A great many accounts combining themes of both prophesy and destiny are often related to the imperial examinations. This, no doubt, reflects the literati's concern for the exams, in addition to the growing importance of the examination system as a vehicle of social mobility from Song times onward. A typical account might see the protagonist dream of the circumstances surrounding his future success, which proved correct at the conclusion of the narrative.[36] Sometimes the protagonist felt it necessary to change his name, as this was thought to exert a positive influence on his fortunes: hence the idea of causality between one's name and one's fortune are vividly illustrated in the *Record*. In some of these cases, the dream language conveyed itself in the form of a pun on the dreamer's name, as in the following account.

ZHANG ZHU'S DREAM

> Zhang Zhu was from Shaowu. During the autumn exams in the *dingmao* year of the Period of Continued Ascendancy (1147), he dreamed of one with a chopstick stuck in his hair which had been tied into a high bun. The dream-figure told him,
>
> "Should you wish to receive recommendation for a high level exam, then you must be like this."

He pondered it deeply after waking up. "My given name is Wang. If, however, you place a dot above the character, it becomes 'Zhu' [a synonym of 'chopstick']."

So he changed his name to Zhu. That year he did manage to attain a recommendation to sit for an exam. Then, when he was about to undertake the spring exam, he had another dream. This time it was about a small, green-clad boy who, emerging from a swaddling cloth, pulled at his clothing and exhorted him, "Don't go. Wait for me."

And so it happened that he was unsuccessful. It was not until the *jichou* year of the Heavenly Way Period (1169) that he was able to sit for another exam, this time without recommendation. It just so happened that a fellow countryman, one Ding Chaozuo, went with him and the two of them made the grade. As Chaozuo had been born in the *dingmao* year, he began to realize the meaning of his previous dream. Jokingly, he teased Ding, saying, "You little bugger kept me waiting twenty-one years." The both of them had a good laugh.[37]

In this account, Candidate Wang changed his surname from Wang (汪) to Zhu (注) after dreaming of someone with hair fastened by chopsticks (*zhu* 箸).

To summarize, destiny was a major theme underpinning a great many narratives throughout the *Record*. It was often framed within other themes, notably those of retribution, and encouraged good deeds at the same time that it warned against immorality. And although preallotted lifespan seemed to be an influential idea during the Song, a person's actions in life, whether good or bad, were potentially more important, since misdemeanors were thought to curtail one's predestined good fortune while good deeds could mitigate one's misdemeanors.

LOYALIST VOICES

As I observed previously, the *Record*'s strong anti-Jurchen theme has been all but ignored by most scholars. Yet numerous accounts contain some degree of anti-Jurchen import, even if as subtle as an anomalous event framed within a military atrocity, or else an oblique reference to the "caitiffs" (*lu* 虜), that is, the Jurchen. This important theme is no less pervasive as that of retribution and certainly merits considerable attention. I will, therefore, devote the next section to an analysis of this issue.

The fall of the Northern Song capital, Kaifeng, to the Juchen in 1127 and the consequent loss of territories north of the Huai River certainly exerted a long-lasting effect on subjects of the Song *imperium* for the remainder of the twelfth century (and beyond). After the Jurchen armies were eventually checked and the court of the Gaozong emperor established, Gaozong pursued an appeasement policy toward the Jurchen which saw the rapid rise of Qin Gui as grand councilor. To say that this horribly divided literati opinion, leading to ceaseless acrimony and political witch-hunting, only begins to describe the enormous effect the humiliation had on the Southern Song ruling elite. Many officials were henceforth polarized into two broad "factions," the "war party," which advocated war as a means to recover the lost territories, thereby regaining lost pride, and the "peace party"—which advocated appeasement of the Jurchen in return for peaceful coexistence. As mentioned above, the Gaozong emperor, once having adopted pacifist policies, remained faithful to this resolve for the remainder of his reign. 1162 saw the ascension of the Xiaozong emperor who, perhaps partly motivated by the war which had broken out with the Jurchen the previous year, eagerly adopted an aggressive policy toward them. This led him to welcome war party officials at court. By that time, however, even had the Song possessed armies able to defeat the Jurchen, the lack of capable military leaders eventually led Xiaozong to reinstate the pacifist policies of Gaozong. Certainly the Song's military debacle at Fuli 符離 in 1163 exposed the deficiencies of Song military leadership. Consequently, once pacifism became entrenched at Xiaozong's court, aggressive policies were not pursued again until war faction minister, Han Tuozhou 韓侂冑 (1151–1202), came to exert his influence over the court of Ningzong (r. 1195–1224) in the early thirteenth century. This was, however, after Hong Mai's death and so need not concern us.

Given the widespread hatred toward the Jurchen and the desire to reclaim the northern Song "ancestral" lands (that is, the "central plains" north of the Huai River), loyalist sentiment consequently found a voice in the vast amount of literature that blossomed throughout the first half of the Southern Song period. Many of Lu You's poems, as well as those of Xin Qiji 辛棄疾 (1140–1207), are particularly well known examples.[38] And just as the *Record* faithfully reflects social history during the late Northern/early to mid-Southern Song era, so too does it reflect anti-Jurchen sentiment.

While no conclusive evidence exists, we can be fairly confident that Hong Mai was sympathetic to the war faction, if not a member himself. As I mentioned in chapter 1, his father, Hao, was appointed an emissary to the Jurchen court in 1129 by the chief councilor at the time, Zhang Jun. Zhang led the war faction during this period and openly advocated recovery by force of the lost territories until the Gaozong emperor chose the path of peace. After this, Zhang had little choice but to relinquish his post. Hao's appointment to a mission so vital as peace negotiations by the head of the war faction strongly suggests affiliation with this group. Furthermore, as pointed out in chapter 1, after his return from captivity he soon raised the ire of Qin Gui, which saw him banished to the south where he eventually died in 1155—ironically shortly before Qin's own death. Since Qin's power rested on a policy of peace with—and appeasement of—the Jurchen, he was understandably unwilling to allow Hao too close a relationship with Gaozong, possibly for fear of Hao's precipitating a change of foreign policy, given his intimate knowledge of Jurchen culture and politics. We may also remember that Hong Mai was forced to quit his first official post in 1145 after having been criticized by the censor Wang Bo for giving his father undue support: Qin was well known for using imperial censors to attack and cause the demise of his political enemies. All this strongly suggests that both father and son were sympathetic with, if not members of, the war faction.

Hong was furthermore closely acquainted with both Lu You and Xin Qiji, both of whom were known for their anti-Jurchen poetry.[39] Lu You, in particular, later cultivated a close association with the anti-Jurchen minister, Han Tuozhou. Famous poet and scholar-official, Fan Chengda, had enjoyed a close relationship with the Hong family since his appointment to Huizhou (modern Xin'an, Anhui) as an administrator of revenue. There he earned the patronage of the prefect at the time, none other than Hong Mai's brother Gua. Gua was in a good position to support Fan, given his successful civil service career which later saw him rise to become grand councilor under Xiaozong for a brief period.[40] Fan was known to have sent Hong Gua anti-Jurchen poetry, strongly suggesting that the Hongs were receptive to such sentiments.[41] Furthermore, during Hong Mai's peace mission to the Jurchen in 1162, his insistence that the wording of diplomatic documents reflect the Song court's status as an independent power not subservient to the Jurchen is further evidence of his loyalist sentiments. Hence, we can be fairly confident that Hong's sympathies lay with the war faction.

Significantly, many of Hong's informants were known members of the war faction and/or served as ministers under Zhang Jun after the Xiaozong emperor recalled Zhang to the post of chief councilor in 1162. Some of these informants were very famous, including Han Yanzhi 韓彥直 (dates uncertain), for example, who told Hong several stories and was son of the famous general Han Shizhong 韓世忠 (1089–1151). Han shared a close relationship with Hong from an early period. The above-mentioned war faction minister and loyalist poet, Fan Chengda, gave Hong at least two accounts, which appear in the first and third installments (as noted in chapter 1, the third installment was completed in 1171).[42] Jiang Fu 蔣芾, chief councilor for a time under Xiaozong, told Hong two stories which appear in the second installment (completed in 1166). Although Jiang advocated war early in his career, he advised against it after becoming chief councilor in 1167—by that time the tide was turning against the war party.[43] Yu Yunwen 虞允文 (1110–1174), who became Xiaozong's chief councilor following the death of Zhang Jun, presided over preparations for a second expedition to recapture the lost northern territories in the mid-1160s; he told two stories which appear in the first and second installments.[44] Apart from these few, there were many others whom we know about.[45]

All the above-mentioned were ministers at court early in Xiaozong's reign when the emperor was more amenable to anti-Jurchen, loyalist voices, as compared to later on when he decided to reinitiate the appeasement policies of Gaozong. Significantly, the accounts provided by these officials are recorded mainly in the second and third installments, while a couple of accounts are recorded in the first installment. In other words, they were told between 1160 (probable time of completion for the first installment) and 1171 (known year of completion for the third installment)—some extremely close together, indicating that Hong Mai was in contact with them throughout this period. The appearance of Yu Yunwen's accounts in the first installment is indicative of Hong's long-term acquaintance with Yu, who later rose to become one of the most trusted chief councilors under Xiaozong, while Fan Chengda's account from the very first chapter of the *Record* reflects Hong's friendship with Fan from 1143 or earlier, when he first began work on the *Record*.

This is not to say that *all* of the accounts provided by these war faction members were of anti-Jurchen import, but it does indicate Hong's close association with this faction. Little wonder that the *Record* so strongly manifests loyalist feeling. And these are only the ones we know about; there were almost certainly more, but lost installments make it impossible to say so with certainty. Furthermore, Hong's long-standing association with members of the war party, not to mention his father's political affiliations, certainly suggests that Hong was at least sympathetic to this faction, if not a member himself.

A comparison of Hong's prefaces with the content of his work reveals a discrepancy between his professed intent and that to which he actually attended. Although an overwhelming number of accounts reflect loyalist views, Hong never articulated loyalist sentiment or anti-Jurchen opinions in any of his thirty-one prefaces; at least to our knowledge, based on what has survived. He was, however, certainly vocal regarding his love of the strange, his methodology, and attempts to achieve historical accuracy. This paradox could not have been accidental. The most likely explanation is, of course, the pervasive pacifist sentiment that characterized Southern Song politics. Although Hong's first preface is no longer extant (probably completed in 1160), it would be surprising indeed were it to have contained any loyalist sentiment, given the Gaozong emperor's unswerving adherence to pacifist policies ever since Qin Gui's installation as chief councilor. Hong's prefaces to the second and third installments, completed in 1166 and 1171 respectively, did not discuss the issue either, although at this time Xiaozong was employing war faction officials at court in preparation for a second campaign against the Jurchen. Hence, this was an extraordinarily favorable period for Southern Song loyalists ever since Gaozong's initial employment of Zhang Jun and what became known as the "Little Yuanyou" faction (*xiao Yuanyou dang* 小元佑黨) early in his reign when he fought to reestablish the Dynasty. Following Yu Yunwen's death in 1174, however, Xiaozong decided against aggressive policies. He henceforth readopted pacifist ones, which were to endure until the early-thirteenth century when Han Tuozhou came to power. Under circumstances so favorable to the war faction, the lack of loyalist sentiment in either of these two prefaces is itself a paradox. Nevertheless, given the subsequent pacifist policies that prevailed and the employment of more and more peace faction ministers at court, Hong Mai probably wished to avoid such sensitive political issues, particularly when we consider that the famous scholar-official Chen Liang 陳 亮 (1143–1194) was scoffed at by high-ranking ministers of Xiaozong's court for having submitted a pro-war memorial to the throne after 1174. Nevertheless, powerful loyalist sentiments discernable throughout the text reveal a gap between Hong's professed intention and what he actually recorded.

His love of the strange, or *guai*, was nevertheless undoubtedly genuine. Yet, to a large extent, *zhiguai* elements and motifs camouflage loyalist ones. Whether Hong consciously promoted anti-Jurchen sentiment, or whether such feelings were so pervasive in early Southern Song society that they came to be spontaneously reflected in the *Record*—or both—is impossible to determine. Nevertheless, the echo of loyalist voices is one aspect of how the *Record* faithfully reflects contemporary social issues.

I will now turn to the cultural artifacts themselves. Close readings of selected accounts in the following section will demonstrate how loyalist themes were articulated. Many accounts recorded the virtuous and patriotic deeds of women. Some women, upon capture by Jurchen troops, chose death rather than submit to personal humiliation or recognize Jurchen suzerainty, while others offered successful resistance to advancing Jurchen armies. The following account is an example of the latter.

Villagers Kill Barbarian Horsemen

In the *gengxu* year of the Founding Glory period (1130), barbarian horsemen[46] raided Jiangxi, while people from the villages, counties and prefectures looked on in fear. Many had their hands bound behind them and were executed. Yet there were those among them who fought back without a care for their own safety, often achieving the upper hand. Even women and girls displayed bravery.

A band of resisters went to Sword Lake in Fengcheng where armored horsemen advanced along the high road without cessation for the entire night. This is probably what caused our band to hear them, although they were not certain how many there were. One of the riders had two women between his arms and was coming through a thicket, alone. Another woman pointed at the deserter, yelling, "Attack him." Our band, therefore, raised their staves and beat him from his horse, whereupon they set about pulverizing his brains. His horse was whinnying ceaselessly, as though searching for its owner. The band chased after it and tied it to a well, thus preserving it.

There was another barbarian who kidnapped a woman and forced her to fetch well water, but the woman was from a wealthy family and protested that she couldn't. The barbarian swore savagely at her. Seizing a vessel, he lowered his head and proceeded to draw water. The woman pushed him in the back. He lost his footing and fell down the well.

Master Ai of Yugan's whole family was enslaved. Then two barbarians lit a fire and were about to burn his house down. Ai said to himself, "If they incinerate the house, there'll be nothing to come back to even if we can somehow escape." He then called to his son and, together, they attacked the barbarians with staves. They then tied and suspended them and, taking their barbarian hip knives, decapitated them. The whole family was thus saved.[47]

On a surface level, narratives like these "document" Jurchen atrocities such as pillage, rape, execution of the innocent, enslavement, and wonton destruction. Hence, readers could be outraged by such atrocities that, no doubt, actually occurred; although—in this instance—we cannot be sure about Hong's source and must bear in mind that the said events occurred sixty-six years prior to their having been recorded here. Yet, on a deeper level, they must have almost certainly shamed those officials who endorsed a policy of appeasement. Given that "even women" and common villagers could overcome the odious "barbarians" "without a care for their own safety," how much more could be achieved by influential government ministers?

Furthermore, Hong's use of emotive language, such as "barbarian" (*hu* 胡), embodied the disdain and hatred felt toward the Jurchen by contemporaries. Elsewhere he uses the term *lu* (虜), sometimes translated as "caitiff," which also embodied much interethnic hatred.

Another example which apparently attempts to shame court officials by drawing an implicit contrast between them and those who actively resisted the Jurchen is that entitled "Junior Guardian Wang." In this account, widow of the illustrious general Wang De (1087–1154) goes to make sacrifices at Wang's grave during the Cold Food Festival in 1161 (significantly just prior to the outbreak of renewed hostilities). En route she hears that her husband, accompanied by General Han Shizhong and former chief councilor Zhang Jun, was seen leading a spirit army against "barbarian bandits" (*fanzei* 番 賊), that is, the Jurchen.[48]

Junior Guardian Wang De is buried several dozen miles from Jiankang. In the thirty-first year of the period of Continued Ascendancy (1161), his wife—Lady Li—traveled to his grave for the Cold Food Festival. The evening before the festival saw her staying outside the city walls. At the fifth watch, she went walking and came to the home of a villager where she rested awhile. The dawn had not yet broken. The villager recognized her as a member of the Junior Guardian's clan and addressed her,

"The Junior Guardian only just passed here in the night and has not gone far."

Alarmed, Lady Li asked the reason.

"Several dozen horsemen passed the gate in the middle of the night," he replied. "Three distinguished gentlemen dismounted and knocked on the gate. They bought fodder for the horses to the tune of five thousand in cash and lingered for quite some time before leaving. They didn't appear to be easily trifled with. I discreetly asked one of the troopers, 'Where are these officials from? Where do they wish to go?' The trooper replied, 'They are Dukes Han [Shizong] and Zhang [Jun], and Junior Guardian Wang. As there are barbarian bandits planning to invade, they hasten to lead troops north of the Huai River to resist them.'" Lady Li bade him retrieve the money they left which proved to be the kind of paper notes used in ancestral sacrifice. Heart-broken to the core, when the festival had concluded, she returned home, contracted a malady, and passed away.

I was in Lin'an during the fourth month of that year. I heard the story from a Madame Liu, who was a matchmaker. I dared not speak of it to anyone, but secretly related the story to Han Ziwen. When autumn came, the caitiffs actually did invade.

The underlying message of this type of account appears similar to that of women resisting the Jurchen, that is, deceased loyalists would "turn in their graves" at the policy of appeasement, thereby shaming pacifist ministers by patriotic deeds. Such a critique is made possible through a blending of loyalist themes and *zhiguai* motifs. There is an additional theme of destiny here, given that the Jurchen actually invaded later during the year in question. To be sure, the underlying antipacifist message encoded here hides behind the theme of destiny which is overtly marked by the final line.

Hong's use of the terms "caitiff" and "raid" (or "invade," *rukou* 入 寇) further implies that despicable low-life carried out an immoral assault on the Song Empire. Also significant is the villager's description of the Song generals: their attitude and demeanor "appeared as though they were not to be trifled with" (*yi mao shu bu kuanqu* 意 貌 殊 不 款 曲). Even in modern Chinese, the term *kuanqu* refers to the deference displayed by a host to his/her guest. The implied social relationship—host and guest, I would argue, is analogous to the vassal relationship the Song was forced to endure following the peace of 1141, and the consequent deference the Song emperors were forced to exhibit toward their "overlord." Hong's use of this description, therefore, seems to imply a contrast between Song military leaders and pacifists at court, implying that the former were morally stronger than then latter.

Zhang Jun, however, was still alive at the time—at least according to official history sources, so it would have been impossible for him to have led the spirit armies recorded in the narrative according to contemporary religious ideas. What is curious, however, is how Hong could have been in any doubt about whether Zhang was dead or alive, given the latter's fame. Furthermore, according to *Collection from the Eastern Lattice Window* (*Dong chuang ji* 東 窗 集), Wang De's wife was surnamed Yin rather than Li.[49] Nevertheless, here is one example of Hong's inclusion of the unreliable, not to mention erratic dates, which I will discuss further in chapter 5.

Hong's professed fear of telling this story to anyone but his trusted confidant, Han Shiwen, furthermore points to what must have been the oppressive atmosphere at the pacifist court of Gaozong *vis-à-vis* the Jurchen question. Yet why he waited so long to publish this account—as previously noted, the third (*Bing*) installment was published in 1171—is, however, unclear, given the aggressive policies adopted by the newly-installed Xiaozong emperor following his ascension to the throne in 1162. One cannot help wonder if Hong fabricated this particular account, possibly to drum up support for the loyalist cause at a time when imperial policy was reverting to pacifism. Given that the Xiaozong emperor's resolve to recover the lost territories had already waned by 1171, this account could be read as an attempt to lampoon pacifist officials or engage in an anti-Jurchen discourse as was often pursued in the poetry of Lu You and Xin Qiji.

This account also demonstrates the blending of several motifs and themes into a matrix of frames, in the sense of Goffman's theory of frames.[50] The anti-Jurchen import is framed by the encounter-with-ghosts motif, which also encompasses a theme of destiny. The above account about the old man from Three Rivers Village is also a good example of this, as it frames an anti-Jurchen theme within that of karmic retribution within that of a prophetic dream.

The final example I will examine takes Suzhou's famous *Canglang ting* 蒼浪亭, or Blue Wave Pavilion, as its spatial setting. Significantly enough, the account was told by Hong's close confidant and member of the war party, Han Ziwen. It is, therefore, a fine example of loyalist literature told by a known war party member. Hong glosses the history of the house in the introduction, telling us that it was built during the Five Dynasties period (907–960) and once belonged to the famous scholar-official Su Zimei 蘇子美 (courtesy name Shunqin, 舜欽 1008–1048). By the time events in Hong's account occurred, the property had already passed into the ownership of Han Shizhong. Given that Han Ziwen had presumably lived or was living in the house, he would have been intimately familiar with stories surrounding the property—assuming that he did not fabricate the story as Ye An attempted to do. The temporal setting is, however, somewhat ambiguous: Hong simply states that the house "now belongs to Han Shizhong."

> The Blue Wave Pavilion in Suzhou was originally the residence of Su Zimei and it now belongs to Han Shizhong. When the Jurchen invaded, there were some citizens who tried to escape by taking refuge in the back garden, but they all perished in the pond. Most of the Pavilion's residents have, therefore, encountered disturbances.
>
> Later, when Han himself took up residence, on every moonlit night they would be sure to see hundreds of figures emerge from and disappear into the pond. Some were monks and some were Taoists. There were women as well as merchants. They would all sing and wail in a fearful cacophony, sighing and moaning for what seemed an eternity before ceasing.
>
> The caretaker was an old soldier. He had only just got to sleep when he was borne away by several dozen of them and was about to be thrown into

the pond. The soldier was from Shaanxi and had always been brave. He knew they were ghosts. Yet he had no fear and addressed them solemnly.

"It has been a long time since you all died here. I could speak to the master for you and ask him to collect your bones and re-bury them on high ground. Buddhist ceremonies for your salvation could then be performed, and you would no longer have to haunt this stagnant pit or harm the innocent. What say you to this?"

Ashamed, they all expressed their thanks, "This is indeed our wish."

They left him and withdrew. The following day the soldier went in and told the master who then ordered ten carts to remove the pond water. The putrid mud was dug up and the rotting bones were collected and placed in large, bamboo baskets. Eight were needed in all. The bones were then placed into a large coffin to be buried.

That night there was one remaining male. Leading the old soldier into a bamboo grove, he said, "The others have all gone, yet I have two arms here. Please help me."

These also were recovered according to his directions and buried to the east of the town, while rites of water and earth were performed at the Rock of Souls Temple. The haunting ceased from then on.[51]

If read as "straightforward" unofficial history, the account documents both a war crime committed by the Jurchen during their pillaging of Suzhou as well as the supposed ghost story it gave rise to. The *zhiguai* element evokes the time-worn motif of ghostly haunting due to corpses not having received proper burial. And, as with the other accounts, readers could have felt indignant about the appalling tragedy which befell so many "innocent" noncombatants. Significantly, however, the event occurred on a property which came to be owned by an illustrious Song general who, together with the ill-fated Yue Fei (1103–1141), achieved a high degree of military success against the Jurchen. Furthermore, the agent of the ghost's salvation was a former soldier, albeit anonymous, who may well have fought in Han's army. If accounts about women resisting the Jurchen aimed to shame pacifist officials, then perhaps this account might have conveyed a secondary message: that is, those oppressed by the Jurchen could find salvation through military leaders willing to fight.

The examples I have selected here are but a minute sampling of numerous others found throughout the extant corpus of the text. Certainly anti-Jurchen sentiment had not abated by the closure of the twelfth century judging by the loyalist narratives collected by Hong in his later installments. Hong's accounts not only documented war crimes committed by Jurchen troops, but also acted to shame court officials for their pacifism by comparison to less influential members of society, not to mention the ghosts of deceased Song generals. Yet what cannot be appreciated from the tiny sample presented here is the reoccurring nature of loyalist motifs—resistance by villagers, atrocities, and the like, which often formed an imperceptible backdrop to foregrounded *zhiguai* themes. The repetition of such motifs must surely have exerted a profound effect on contemporary readers, particularly those who suffered personal loss due to the invading "barbarians."

CHAPTER FOUR

Genre

As can be seen from Hong Mai's prefaces and the scant textual reception out-lined in chapter 2, historical factuality seemed an extremely important consid-eration to both author and readership. This aspect is all the more significant considering the recent utilization of the text as a source for secondary studies on Song social history. Before given accounts from the *Record* can be applied appropriately to given theses, a sensitivity to what Paul Katz refers to as a liter-ary work's "textuality" appears essential, that is, the literary aspects and social contexts which inform the way texts were written and interpreted.[1] The exam-ination of truth versus falsity issues which I will undertake in the following chapter is, therefore, crucial to an intimate understanding of the text.

But before this can be adequately addressed, we first need to arrive at a clearer understanding of the text's generic affiliations. Hong furthermore, in his prefaces, implicitly referred to the *Record* as a work of *baiguan xiaoshuo* (unofficial history) which was later echoed by those such as Chen Li and Shen Qizhan. Yet both Zhao Xibian and Wang Jingwen explicitly referred to it as *zhiguai*. And in the twentieth century, Valerie Hansen discussed it in terms of notebook literature (*biji*).[2] Given such divergent opinions, some clarification of the issue would seem appropriate in any case. In this chapter, therefore, I will first examine these and other relevant literary categories and then evaluate their applicability to the *Record*.

Before proceeding further, I would like to acknowledge my debt to Bakhtin-influenced genre theory and its accommodation of open-ended genres. In contrast to Aristotelian theory which defines genres exclusively by form according to a text's stylistic and compositional features, Bakhtin con-ceptualizes speech genres as flexible and open-ended systems which lend themselves to creative manipulation by their performers (authors). Of par-ticular importance is Bakhtin's idea of dialogic genres, whereby given genres may encompass differing voices derived from diverse cultural, historical, and personal perspectives. Conversely, monologic genres contain but one such per-spective. The dialogic nature of many genres gives rise to the concept of what

Briggs and Baumann refer to as "intertextuality," whereby a given genre will share common linguistic features that signal an individual text's association with other texts of the same genre. This in turn opens the possibility of intertextual gaps. Depending on how closely a text (be it verbal or written) conforms to a receiver's expectations in relation to generic affiliation, there might be a large or small intertextual gap. The gap might be large, for example, in cases where a written text has been adapted from an oral performance and vice versa. A performer (or author) might wish to maximize intertextual gaps for various creative purposes. Campany's solar system metaphor is a useful way of conceptualizing the theory. According to this, the distance of planetary bodies from their centre is akin to the degree of affiliation which literary works may display in relation to a *prima facie* example of a recognized genre.[3] Such theory enables texts to be read and written within a specific historical and cultural context, and allows for fluidity in the way recipients relate to texts and the way texts relate to each other. This paradigm is especially useful when dealing with literary works, like the *Record*, that exist on the margins of orthodox classification.

CHINESE TRADITIONAL BIBLIOGRAPHICAL CLASSIFICATION AND THE *RECORD*

As Benjamin Penny has pointed out, even in modern Chinese there is no lexical item which corresponds exactly to the Western concept of "genre." The nearest one, as suggested by Penny, is *wenti* 文體.[4] Yet this also refers to the style or form of literary works. Of far greater importance during the premodern period was the *Sibu (zhulu) zhi fa* 四部著錄之法, or the four-fold classification system under which texts were catalogued as classics (*jing* 經), histories (*shi* 史), philosophical texts (*zi* 子), or belles letters (*ji* 集) respectively in both private and official bibliographical catalogues.

This system, however, was riddled with inconsistency. Ban Gu's failure to include Buddhist texts in the *Bibliographic Treatise of the Han* (*Han yiwen zhi* 漢藝文志) is one example. While this reflected the staunchly anti-Buddhist sentiment of the time, the denial of an entire group of texts is hardly objective. And given the unorthodox nature of *Romance of the Western Chamber* (*Xi xiang ji* 西廂記), in addition to the colloquial language used (considered inappropriate for texts written in literary prose, or *wenyan wen*), this work was omitted from the *Supplementary Bibliographic Treatise of the Liao, Jin and Yuan* (*Bu Liao, Jin Yuan Yiwen zhi* 補遼金元藝文志), the *Supplement to the Three Histories* (*Bu san shi* 補三史), and the *Supplement to the History of the Yuan* (*Bu Yuan shi* 補元史). For similar reasons, the *History of the Ming* (*Ming shi* 明史) did not list the *Water margin* (*Shuihu zhuan* 水滸傳). In the *Bibliographic Treatise of the Song* (*Songzhi* 宋史藝文志), the *Secret Methods of the Five Geomantic Dragons* (*Dili wulong mifa* 地理五龍密法) was classified as geomancy (*dili* 地理) under the broader category of history, despite its clear focus on the five elements; in other words, the five elements subgenre would have been a more appropriate place to categorize it. There are many other examples of erroneous and inconsistent classification too numerous to discuss here.[5] Nevertheless, what should be readily clear are the limitations of a four-fold system and its respective subcategories to classify marginal literary works. On the contrary, the entire system—perhaps not surprisingly—militated against unorthodoxy.

As one can probably guess after having read Hong's prefaces, the *Record* was classified as *xiaoshuo* in the philosophers section of both official and private bibliographical catalogues.[6] This term now refers to modern fiction of the type produced ever since the May Fourth Movement. As I noted in chapter 2, however, it was originally used by Ban Gu in his *Bibliographic Treatise in the History of the Han* to denote works whose sources were the minor talk (*xiaoshuo*) and alley-way gossip (*xiangyu* 巷語) of petty officials (*baiguan*) and had no connotation with "fiction" in the modern sense. It was, rather, associated with unofficial history, that is, works which—while not canonical—were nonetheless valuable in so far as they addressed matters not found in official history.

Hu Yinglin remarked that the earliest work in the *xiaoshuo* subcategory of the philosophers section was the *Yuzi shuo* which, as mentioned in note 111 in chapter 2, was considered a Taoist work in twenty-one chapters.[7] Yet the later literary classification of *xiaoshuo* works became so varied that their classification seems somewhat erratic. For example, works which now tend to be accepted as *zhiguai* (the *Record of the Search for Spirits* [*Soushen ji*], for example); works which are regarded as *chuanqi* (such as the *Golden Oriole* [*Yingying zhuan* 鶯鶯傳]); those which are considered as miscellaneous notes (or *biji*, itself an ambiguous label, such as Fan Zhen's 范鎮 [1007–1087] *Records from the Eastern Studio* [*Dongzhai jishi* 東齋記事], as well as Hong Mai's philological *Rongzhai suibi*); as well as works which could be viewed as unofficial history (such as Zhou Mi's *Miscellanies from Guixin* [*Guixin Zashi*]). Hence, the *xiaoshuo* category encompassed a wide range of similar and dissimilar works. While many of these tended to be narrative in nature, others—such as the *Rongzhai suibi*—were virtually devoid of narrative. Therefore one cannot claim narrative structure as an essential element in these diverse works.

In order to impose a semblance of organization on this nebulous category, Hu Yinglin devised a six-fold subcategorization system in his *Essays*. Hu's first subgroup was "*zhiguai*," of which he cited Gan Bao's *Record of the Search for Spirits* and Duan Chengshi's *Miscellaneous Morsels from Youyang* as examples. "*Chuanqi*" was his second subgroup, among which he cited the *Golden Oriole* as one example. "Miscellaneous (or informal) notes" was his third subgroup, among which he counted Liu Yiqing's 劉義慶 (403–444) *New Accounts from the World* (*Shishuo xinyu* 世說新語, hereafter *New Accounts*) as an example. Among his fourth group, which he termed "collected discussions," was Hong Mai's *Rongzhai suibi*. Hu's fifth group, "textual criticism," included the Song *biji* work entitled *Chicken Ribs* (*Jilei* 雞肋)—originally a seventy-chapter hodge-podge compiled from material secretly circulated before the fall of the Northern Song. Interestingly enough, this work was not without its share of *zhiguai* accounts. Finally, works pertaining to clan rules and coda were cited as belonging to his sixth group, "admonitions and rules." Almost in anticipation of Bahktin, Hu was sensitive to the fluid boundary between categories, particularly those of *chuanqi* and *zhiguai*, in addition to collected discussions and informal notes. In the case of the former, he noted how a given collection might contain both *zhiguai* and *chuanqi* material, while any given story might contain motifs from both; he did not, however, explicate what he conceived of as *zhiguai* or *chuanqi*. Therefore, Hu argued, it is the *focus* of a given work which determines its appropriate categorization.[8] Nevertheless, Hu's refinement did not eradicate the fundamental problem of the amorphous nature of the category as a whole. And even if subgrouping according to *topoi* imposes a degree of organization on an otherwise hodge-podge of disparate works, it still does not enable one to delineate between a genre of *xiaoshuo* and other literary genres, such as *biji* or unofficial history (which I will discuss below). Given this disparity, I would argue that *xiaoshuo* was a residual category. That is, it was broad enough to be a category under which works could be classified when there seemed nowhere else to put them, particularly when the only alternatives offered by the four-fold system were classics, history, other subsections of the philosophers, and belles letters. Perhaps, therefore, it was seen by premodern bibliophiles as the place for many noncanonical texts that were not officially designated as Confucian classics, official history, or belles letters. If this is correct, textual reception became more important than considerations of form—in contrast to Aristotelian theory in the West.

As mentioned above, Valerie Hansen referred to the *Record* as a *biji* text, the writing of which proliferated throughout the Song period.[9] *Biji* was a genre which flowered during the Six Dynasties. To my knowledge, Liu Xie 劉勰 (c. 465–c. 520) was the first to use the term in his *The Literary Mind and the Carving of Dragons* (*Wenxin diaolong* 文心調龍).[10] When discussing *biji* in *Some Aspects of Chinese Private Historiography*, Franke comments that they required no organization of material and observes that some scholars wrote them to supplement official histories. Yet he also tells us that many scholars included both paranormal events and "scholar's gossip." He furthermore discusses authorial intent, citing such things as the desire to entertain and to illustrate traditional ethics by giving examples of behavior both laudable and blamable.[11] All these observations would seem highly relevant to the *Record*. Hong's haphazard arrangement, his professed intention of supplementing local gazetteers, the extremely high instance of paranormal events, as well as his didactic themes, all correlate with Franke's observations.

Y. M. Ma, while recognizing that *biji* texts display both brevity and casualness, further classifies them into three basic groups: fictional, historical, and philological. He gives the *Miscellaneous Morsels from Youyang*, the *Record of the Search for Spirits*, and the *New Accounts* as examples of the fictional group, Wang Shizhen's 王士禎 (1634–1711) *Occasional Talk from North of the Pond* (*Chibei outan* 池北偶談) as an example of the historical group,[12] while I would consider Hong Mai's *Rongzhai suibi* as an example of the philological group according to Ma's classification.

The term *biji* itself suggests that form is more important than *topoi*. Hence, it is broader than Hu Yinglin's subcategories of *xiaoshuo*. And in regard to *zhiguai* or *chuanqi*, the distinctive formal structure of both these genres would seem to preclude their pigeon-holing as *biji*, given that brevity and casualness are supposedly the essential features of the latter. In other words, while some *zhiguai* accounts were extremely brief, their conformity to quasi-historical structural form precluded casualness, even though their arrangement in any given collection may have been haphazard.

Yet, given that brevity and casualness are the essential hallmarks of this genre according to both Franke and Ma, *biji* would seem impossible to define as a genre in its own right; indeed, Ma himself observes that there are no hard and fast rules for defining *biji* literature.[13] And if it is not possible to define clearly what *biji* literature is, neither is it possible to distinguish *biji* from *xiaoshuo*, or from *zhiguai* for that matter. Certainly the gamut of works which we intuitively consider *biji* is classified as *xiaoshuo* in the traditional four-fold system. And while many modern theorists lump both *biji* and *xiaoshuo* together, as in "*biji xiaoshuo*," due to shared narrative form and supposed "fictitious" nature, discursive modes of writing found within *zhiguai* collections (of which the *Classic of Mountains and Seas* contains particularly many)—not to mention the discursive form and philological focus of *xiaoshuo* works such as the *Rongzhai suibi*—belie attempts to impose modern notions of fictionality or narrative form on this diverse group of texts. Furthermore, when the term *xiaoshuo* is linked with *biji* (as in *biji xiaoshuo*) in regard to works which emphasize characterization and narrative, a conflict with the supposed essential characteristics of *biji* as being both brief and casual thereby arises. And, as I have just observed, literature in the narrative mode tended to conform to a quasi-historical form since the earliest extant narratives found in works such as the *Commentary of Gongyang* (the *Gongyang zhuan*). And if *biji* confirmed to an expected form, then it could not at the same time be casual.

Given, therefore, the wide variety of texts which have been regarded as *biji*, I would argue that it, like *xiaoshuo*, is a residual category, a label attached to works not because of what they were, but because of what they were not. Therefore, while the *Record* would seem to share the above-mentioned generic traits with the *biji*, characterizing it in this way no more illuminates its precise nature than does the term *xiaoshuo*.

Although Hu Yinglin was formerly regarded by Western scholars as the first to use the term *zhiguai* as a formal classification for literature,[14] he does not directly use it in reference to the *Record*. In his *Essays*, he labels the *Record* as a work of *xiaoshuo* and discusses it alongside Zhang Hua's (232–300) *Treatise on*

Curiosities (*Bowu zhi*) and Liu Yiqing's *New Accounts*. The *Treatise on Curiosities* was classified by the editors of the *Four Libraries* as miscellaneous sayings (*suoyu* 瑣語) and the *New Accounts* as miscellaneous stories (*zashi* 雜事), both subgenres of *xiaoshuo*. The *New Accounts*, as noted above, was regarded as an example of fictional *biji* by Ma. Nevertheless, the bulk of Hu's critique of the *Record* in his *Collected Essays* focuses on Wang Jingwen's preface to the *Other Record of the Listener* because, he argues, the preface affords a broad insight into the *Record*'s compilation. As discussed in chapter 2, Wang Jingwen not only labeled the *Record* as *zhiguai*, he also considered it the paragon of all such works. He then gave his own reasons for writing *zhiguai*. As I noted in chapter 2, Wang's reference to the *Record* as *zhiguai* is the earliest such reference. Wang's reference also displays greater precision in terms of classification than the amorphous *xiaoshuo* of traditional bibliographical classification. His use of the term was echoed by Zhao Xibian and, in more recent times, by Lu Xun. Hu Yinglin's quoting of Wang's preface indirectly endorses Wang's use of the term.

Furthermore, Chen Zhensun intimated that the *Record* belongs to the *zhiguai*. Although he avoided direct labels, his use of the term *guai* when he observed that the degree of abnormality (*guai*) displayed by the *Record*'s accounts was undermined by their high frequency, implied that he too saw the *Record* in the *zhiguai* tradition.[15]

Hong Mai also seems to have regarded the *Record* in this light, although he too avoided direct labels. We saw in chapter 2 how, in various prefaces, Hong used the terms *guai* 怪, *yi* 異, and *qi* 奇 when referring to either the work itself or to accounts contained therein.[16] *Yi* is closely related to *guai* since scholars throughout the imperial period considered the two synonymous, while *qi* is obviously semantically connected. Hong's comments suggest that he considered the terms *guai*, *yi*, and *qi* to be appropriate labels in terms of content, although he clearly did not refer to genre.

THE NATURE OF *ZHIGUAI*

We can see, therefore, that several influential premodern scholars saw the *Record* in terms of *zhiguai*. And, to be sure, Confucius's disdain for discussing spirits ensured a contradictory reception for *zhiguai* texts: Confucian-trained scholars felt obliged to outwardly follow Confucius's example and to not take such texts seriously; yet the sustained writing and reading of the texts is indicative of the fascination they engendered in the minds of the literati. While the *zhiguai* grew from official historiography and were originally classified as a subbranch of history in the *Bibliographic Treatise of the Sui Dynasty* (*Sui yiwen zhi*), their status was later down-graded ever since Ouyang Xiu expunged them from this category in his *New History of the Tang* (*Xin Tang shu*). Yet, as Hong Mai so eruditely observed in his prefaces, orthodox texts considered as classics and official histories, such as the *Commentary of Zuo* (*Zuo zhuan*) and the *Records of the Grand Historian* (*Shi ji*), abound with *zhiguai* material. Perhaps it was easy for traditional literary theorists to absolve the presence of anomalous material in works regarded as "classics" or "official histories" that were canonical. Certainly such texts did not focus on *zhiguai* material for its own sake, as did many works which contemporary scholars consider *zhiguai*. In other words, a relatively minor amount of *zhiguai* material was acceptable in its proper place, that is, in a recognized, orthodox text, particularly when used in a phenomenological manner that reported rather than endorsed the *zhiguai* content. On the contrary, once authors began to focus on the *zhiguai*, their undertaking was no longer acceptable according to Confucian sensibility—as may be seen from the apologetic tone of so many *zhiguai* prefaces from Gan Bao's *Record of the Search for Spirits* to Ji Yun's *Close Scrutiny*.

Nevertheless, the question still needs to be addressed: what did premodern scholars mean when they spoke of *zhiguai*? Although luminaries such as Hu Yinglin were wont to use the phrase, none deigned to define it. And as DeWoskin has pointed out, it is an extremely difficult genre to delineate.[17] The term comprises two components, the characters *zhi* 志 and *guai* 怪 respectively. The former can be translated as either a verb meaning "to record" or a noun meaning "record." It has been used in generic titles for orthodox literary genres—particularly historical works such as local gazetteers and the bibliographic treatises of dynastic histories. Campany has argued convincingly that the term acted as an intertextual device which signaled the presence of *zhiguai* material to the prospective readership of Six Dynasties *zhiguai* accounts.[18] Then there is the *guai* component, generally translated as "anomaly" or "strange." As a compound, the term has been translated as "recording anomalies."[19]

The prefix *zhi* indicates conformity to established form as an essential criterion to membership of this genre, reflecting its early affiliation with history writing. Indeed, Campany incorporated form as one of his criteria for membership in the *zhiguai* genre.[20] Nevertheless, since *zhiguai* texts were distinguished from other literary genres primarily due to their focus on motifs containing or embodying *guai* elements, an examination of the precise meaning of this term is crucial to the task at hand. Given the disdain held toward *zhiguai* works throughout the imperial period under the guise of Confucian morality, it would seem appropriate for us to commence with Confucius's remarks on the subject. Below is his famous quote from D. C. Lau's translation of the *Analects*.

> The topics the Master did not speak of were prodigies, force, disorder and gods.[21]

子不語怪力亂神

The English translation of the terms prodigies, force, and disorder is ambiguous and requires further explanation. Waley translated the same line thus:

> The Master never talked of prodigies, feats of strength, disorders or spirits.[22]

Although he used the same term "disorder," he clarified it in a footnote: "disorders of nature; such as snow in summer, owls hooting by day, or the like."[23] Below is Legge's translation:

> The subjects on which the Master did not talk were extraordinary things, feats of strength, disorder and spiritual beings.[24]

Legge then attempts to clarify the terminology thus:

> *luan* "confusion," meaning rebellious disorder, parricide, regicide and such crimes. Chu Hsi makes *shen* here *guishen zaohua zhi ji* 鬼神造化之跡, the mysterious, or the spiritual operations apparent in the course of nature. Wang Hsiao 王蕭 (died c.e. 266), as given by Ho Yen (He Yan), simply says *guishen zhi shi* 鬼神之事; the affairs of spiritual beings. For an instance of Confucius avoiding such a subject, see XI. xi.[25]

Legge's definition of *luan* corresponds with the *shu* 疏 commentary to the *Analects*, which explains it as regicide and patricide.[26]

The term *shen* has been frequently translated into English as "gods" or anthropomorphic "spirits." In other parts of the *Analects*, it has been used in connection with *gui*—a term frequently translated as "ghost" (i.e., an anthropomorphic spirit) or "demon" (as in pestilence demons and the like).[27] The concurrent usage of both *gui* and *shen*, or gods and ghosts, reflects the idea that humans have the potential to be posthumously elevated to either the status of a deity or to be denigrated to that of a ghost. Hence, *shen* may be used in matters relating to gods as well as ghosts and demons. According to the *Record of Rites*, *shen* also referred to animistic spirits.

> Mountains, forests, rivers, valleys and hills may produce clouds which bring rain and wind. The anomalous things 怪物 [therein] are called spirits 神.[28]

The He Yan commentary tells us how such spirits received offering due to the benefit they were thought to bring mankind. Hence, both Waley and Legge translate *shen* as "spirits."[29]

Arriving at a definition of the term *guai*, however, presents greater difficulties and the above two translations are not particularly helpful. Legge's translation of "extraordinary things" unfortunately reflects the ambiguity of the original Chinese term. Both Waley and Lau's rendering as "prodigies" is unsatisfactory for our purposes since its semantic field is too constrictive; in modern English "prodigies" often carries connotations of birth abnormalities or child prodigies. And while there are reports of abnormal births and anomalies of size throughout the corpus of *zhiguai* literature—the *Record* included—the term *guai* clearly has broader connotations. And when we consider another nuance of the word prodigy—that is, marvelous—we return to the problem of ambiguity.

Recourse to Chinese dictionaries, glosses, and commentaries on the *Analects* is initially unhelpful. The *shu* commentary to the *Analects* defines *guai* as *guaiyi* 怪異, another ambiguous term. The *Great Chinese Dictionary* (*Hanyu da cidian*) defines this compound as: 1) *qite* 奇特 (peculiar) or *qiyi* 奇異 (extraordinary), and 2) *qiyi fanchangde xianxiang* 奇異反常的現像 (strange and extraordinary phenomena; *fanchang* literally means "counter to the norm" which is significant in relation to the opinions I will discuss below). Yet another definition offered is: 3) *yaoguai guishen* 妖怪鬼神; roughly translatable as "monsters, prodigies, ghosts and gods."[30] In regard to the third definition, leaving aside the term *guai* itself, monsters, gods, and ghosts would clearly form part of most social groups' concept of *guai*, be they contemporary Western scholars or Song Dynasty literati. And, in respect to *guai*, there were a number of classical texts which offered similar examples of *guai* phenomena.[31]

According to the etymological *Shuowen jiezi* 說文解字 (*Explaining Written Language and Analyzing Characters*, hereafter the *Shuowen*), *guai* corresponds to *yi* 異 whose meaning approximates "difference."[32] This is reminiscent of the second definition above. Yet it leads to a problem of reference—how is "difference" to be defined and to what is it different? Nonetheless, this idea concurs with one of Chen Zhensun's criticisms of the *Record*, which I discussed in chapter 2; that is, what was considered strange (*guai*) was the rarity (*han* 罕) of given phenomena which ran counter to what was considered normal (*fanchang fanwu* 反常反物) throughout heaven and earth.[33] In other words, *guai* should be defined by contrast to what was considered normal—that is, normality defined by high frequency of occurrence. Here Chen gave us an insight into what at least he himself considered as *guai*. Interestingly enough, this corresponds with the usage found in Han Dynasty Confucian philosopher Dong Zhongshu's 董仲舒 (c. 179–c. 104 B.C.E.) biography according to the *History of the Han* (*Han shu* 漢書). According to this, *guaiyi* phenomena are said to warn of dynastic collapse, which is in harmony with Confucian ideas about heavenly mandates.[34] Paradoxically, *guai*, conceived in this manner, would take the "genre" outside the boundary of what one might intuitively think of as *zhiguai*, that is, literary motifs pertaining to "paranormal" phenomena. According to Chen, therefore, *guai* need not necessarily equate with what post-Enlightenment scholars might consider as paranormal.

The reason for this, I believe, is traceable to early usage of the character *guai* when used to describe tributary objects collected from the periphery of the "civilized" pre-Han world. Campany argues that the rise of *zhiguai* writing in the Six Dynasties was linked to tours of inspection made by the ruler of the political centre to its periphery, in addition to the tribute system as discussed in such works as *Yu's Tribute* (*Yugong* 禹貢). According to this, governance of the civilized centre in ancient China depended on collecting "the periphery": that is, its anomalous and exotic objects, customs, creatures, songs, events, and the like. And, once having collected them, the recording of these little-known items thus civilized the periphery not only through heightened awareness, but also through quantification and standardization, in short, by objectifying the periphery. Early works such as the *Canon of Shun* (*Shundian* 舜典) tell us how the ruler would make religious sacrifices during such tours of inspection, thereby spreading orthodox religious beliefs while paying respect to local deities and spirits. To be sure, the early tribute system could be seen as a potlatch-type arrangement, which resulted in reciprocity between the central ruler and his subjects throughout the far-flung corners of the known world. Reports of portents were also collected which, due to ideas about the mandate of heaven, were crucial for the maintenance of central authority. Those reporting auspicious portents from the periphery were rewarded, while the reporting of adverse phenomena could be controlled. Thus, the tribute system, along with the tours of inspection, the collection of portents, and collection of popular songs under the auspices of such administrative organs as the Music Bureau (*Yuefu* 樂府) served as a vehicle whereby the central ruler could proliferate central culture, religion, and—ultimately—control over these distant regions.[35]

I mentioned above *Yu's Tribute*, which described tribute-paying lands as well as the goods collected therein. It also constructed a topographical schema whereby the world was hierarchically graded in concentric zones surrounding the centre. Significantly, when discussing unusual tributary objects, the character "strange" (*guai*) was used to describe certain goods, such as strange stones from Qingzhou.[36] Unusual local customs were also mentioned. The nature of these "strange" items would not, however, seem to equate *guai* with "paranormal" events, but is rather closer to Chen Zhensun's conception of something anomalous due to rarity.

Herein, I would argue, lies the confusion about the precise nature of *guai*. On the one hand *guai* referred to phenomena of a cosmological nature and included ghosts, deities, animistic spirits, legendary creatures, and "supernatural" entities in general—in short, matters about which the Master did not speak and which post-Enlightenment, Western-trained scholars would understand as paranormal. Yet, on the other hand, *guai* also referred to rare objects and customs, particularly at a time when the tradition of what we now recognize as *zhiguai* literature was coming into being.

Even if phenomena constituting *guai* could be unambiguously delineated, the following point is, I believe, crucial to our understanding of the term in relation to literary texts: what *zhiguai* authors did not write about was equally significant as what they did. To be sure, traditional religious practices of performing offerings to ancestral spirits—particularly during the Ghost Festival, offerings to household deities during New Year celebrations, offerings to animistic spirits as well as local earth gods, supplications made by the emperor on Mt. Tai, and the like—demonstrate a widespread belief in ghosts, deities, and ancestral spirits since early times. Yet none of these observances are the subject of *zhiguai* accounts unless, of course, they form the setting or backdrop to a main narrative.[37] Furthermore, *zhiguai* authors tended not to regale their readership with narratives focusing on the making of such offerings or prayers as motifs in their own right. This strongly suggests that it is not merely the presence of a ghost or spirit (or any of the *guai* phenomena discussed above or in the notes) in a given account which imbues it with the "property" of "*guai*." Rather, it is the intrusion of such beings into the mortal realm and vice versa that constitutes *guai*. In other words, it is not the phenomenon itself that is *guai*—since their existence was seen to have been part of the natural world as conceived by the Chinese since antiquity. But when such phenomena transcend the limen separating the mundane realm from that of the spirit world and interacted with the living, then this encounter can be labeled *guai*.

If one uses the above concept of *guai* as contrary to that which is normal, routine offerings to ghosts and spirits would not merit the label "anomaly." Furthermore, idioms such as "the living and the dead are of different substance" (*youming li shu* 幽明理殊), or "people and ghosts follow different paths" (*regui dao shu* 人鬼道殊), often cited in relation to *zhiguai* works, would seem to support the idea that the *guai* element lies in the disorderly or unpredictable traffic between these two realms rather than the mere presence of the "paranormal."

In his commentary to one of the earliest *zhiguai* works, the *Classic of Mountains and Seas*, Guo Pu 郭璞 (276–322) offered a comparatively detailed discussion of what is meant by *yi* which supports this idea. Although Guo discusses the term *yi* rather than *guai*, the two were more or less interchangeable according to the *Shuowen*'s definition. His discussion is framed in an apology for the apparent suspicion with which the *Classic*'s seemingly fantastic content was held. He then cited the *Mutianzi zhuan* as a precedent for works focusing on such motifs, after which he referred to the preservation of historical material as a justification for their writing.

> What the world refers to as strange (異) is itself unaware of what it is which renders it strange. And what the world calls not strange (不異) is itself unaware of what it is which renders it not strange. Why is this so? Things are not inherently strange; they are strange by virtue of one's perception of them. The property of strangeness is, therefore, with me and not with the thing itself. It is for this reason that barbarians accept cloth but are suspicious of hemp, and the people of Annam accept flannel but are fearful of thread. They believe in what they are familiar with but marvel at what is rare. This is a common fault of human nature.[38]

While Guo's contention shares common ground with Chen Zhensun insofar as he attempts to define *guai* against a yardstick of what was perceived as commonplace, his argument differs somewhat, given his emphasis on the percipient's role. To Guo, things (物)—that is, inanimate objects and animals—are not inherently strange or anomalous; on the contrary, labels of anomaly depend upon the observer. Guo's dialectic between "strange" and "not strange" supports my observation above that *guai* relies on traffic between an observer and an object.[39]

Such a conception of *guai* is reminiscent of Jauss's concept of "aesthetic experience" in relation to reader-response literary theory. Unlike a philosophical concept, an aesthetic experience occurs when textual meaning is recreated in the mind of the receiver and cannot necessarily be linguistically defined.[40] I would, therefore, argue that *guai* is an "aesthetic experience": something one perceives but cannot articulate. On the one hand, the intrusion of paranormal phenomena into the mundane world—such as ghostly apparitions and the like—obviously merited the label. But on the other hand, nonparanormal phenomena such as unusual rocks or little-known objects from the periphery could also be considered *guai*, depending on prevailing social constructs. I would therefore argue that this dualistic nature of what could be intuitively considered *guai* is the reason why writers and theorists have found it so difficult to define a genre of *zhiguai* literature.

One final point which should be made before moving on, and one which seemingly escapes detection, is the pejorative nature of the term *guai*. As stated by the Ming writer of vernacular short stories, Feng Menglong, "[a]ll in all, *guai* is not a pretty thing."[41] Therefore, rather than translating *guai* as "anomaly" as English-speaking scholars have tended to do, perhaps "abnormality" would serve better since it fully renders the derogatory nuance of the term.

THE CONCEPT OF *GUAI* IN RELATION TO THE *ZHIGUAI* OF CHINESE LITERATURE

According to the above discussion, integral to the formulation of *guai* phenomena is the presence of humans, for—as succinctly articulated by Guo Pu—*guai* are themselves unaware that they are *guai*. It is rather the human agent who perceives and confers the *guai* element to a given object or phenomenon. It is little wonder, then, that *zhiguai* texts embrace many thematic elements related to human behavior and the human condition.[42] Furthermore, in terms of *topoi*, texts generally considered *zhiguai* are a blend of what is "normal" and what is not. As Campany pointed out, many Six Dynasty *zhiguai* narratives were set in a framework of normality which served to heighten the effect of *guai* phenomena.[43]

The practical and instructional applications of *zhiguai* texts did not escape the attention of Guo Xian 郭憲 (an early Han *fangshi* 方士), thought to be author of the *Record of the Han Emperor Wu's Penetration into the Mysteries of Outlying Realms* (*Dongming ji* 洞冥記). In the preface to this work, Guo states:

> I maintain that remnant data from ancient times should not be thrown away when obtained. This is even more the case [when one recalls the example of] Han Emperor Wu, a brilliant and singular ruler; for [his advisor] Dongfang Shuo[44] relied on humor and the "insubstantial and absurd" (因滑稽浮誕) to correct and admonish him.[45]

In other words, the moralizing didacticism of many such works was not without a contribution to Confucian morality. And, as we saw in chapter 2, Guo's words find an echo in the critique offered by the authors of the *Four Libraries* that the *Record*'s didactic aspect was not without merit.[46]

Apart from moralistic intent, the writing of *zhiguai* texts was also a control mechanism whereby unusual or abnormal entities which were little understood, and therefore beyond the control of officialdom, could be contained. As Attali has observed, "Recording is a means of social control, a stake in politics, regardless of the available technologies."[47] Accordingly, Guo Pu observed that the people of Annam were suspicious of—and therefore possibly frightened by—those qualities of cloth which they did not understand. Similarly, the Han Chinese inhabitants of "civilized" (Sino-centric) far antiquity held apprehension toward, what to them, were unusual and/or abnormal objects in much the same way they viewed the intrusion of ghosts into their everyday world. Furthermore, such activities as the collecting of the songs by the Music Bureau during the Han Dynasty, along with the collecting of little-known objects from China's periphery, was arguably no different from the awarding of titles to local deities by the emperor (especially prevalent throughout the Song period), or the performing of ancestral sacrifices. These were all arguably smaller parts of a larger system of control meant to categorize, understand, pacify, and thereby encompass the *guai* (unusual, abnormal, and perhaps spooky) phenomena. To be sure, one major purpose of offerings to ancestral spirits was, surely, to pacify and prevent them from becoming "hungry ghosts" which may have wrought harm on the living. And while active human participation was an integral part of such rituals, action or manifestation on the part of the spirits was neither expected nor desired. Hence, such rituals can be seen as a control mechanism.[48]

The same can be said about offerings made to animistic and anthropomorphic spirits. The state canonization of deities was clearly another method by which such spirits could be encompassed, and therefore controlled, by the state, while those cults and deities not officially sanctioned were liable to be persecuted.[49] Yet, when the "proper" demarcated boundary between the living and the spiritual was crossed, professional religious practitioners were often called upon to exorcise the afflicted in what Dutch anthropologist de Groot termed the "war against the specters."[50] Such stories became the stock-and-trade of *zhiguai* accounts. Therefore, stories about demonic and spiritual possession—often leading to sickness and/or death—no doubt bolstered the standing of Taoist priests and lay exorcists in their communities. Indeed, their livelihoods would have depended on the perpetuated belief in spirit possession and the efficacy of the Taoist clergy to relieve such conditions.

THE *RECORD* AS A WORK OF *ZHIGUAI*

Accordingly, if *guai* may be understood as the disorderly intrusion of little-known, unpredictable, and potentially dangerous entities which incorporate both objects as well as spirits (both animistic and anthropomorphic) into the everyday world of the living, it would follow that literary texts often exhibiting such motifs could be seen as *zhiguai* texts. Attempts, however, to classify texts as *zhiguai* based purely on motif would seem unsatisfactory since the distinction between them and other genres would be too blurry. In other words, the resulting intertextual gaps would be so small as to render it impossible for readers to delineate the two. To be sure, Hong Mai played upon the fluid boundary between the *Record* and official (canonical) historiography in his prefaces. I would, therefore, argue that additional criteria be considered.

The work Campany has done on the *zhiguai* genre is of particular importance in this regard. In his monograph, *Strange Writing*, he developed a generic formula for *zhiguai* literature based not only on motif, or what he refers to as content, but also on what he calls form, style, status, and the presence (or absence) of intertextual markers. I will summarize his schema below and then discuss it in relation to the *Record*. To be sure, Campany's schema was formulated specifically for Six Dynasty texts, yet it would appear perfectly applicable to those from later periods. Each criterion is sufficiently broad as to accommodate period variation, such as the inclusion of poetry within a narrative that tended to occur from the Tang onward. In devising his formula, Campany has applied what he calls a blend of Aristotelian and Bakhtin-influenced genre theories. As he points out, the former approach lacks the tools to contextualize the works, while the latter places insufficient importance on the texts themselves.[51]

According to his first characteristic, form, *zhiguai* texts comprise short narratives and/or descriptions, as opposed to continuous narratives such as are found in treatises and essays. His second characteristic is style. To belong to the genre, texts should be written in "mostly non-metrical or loosely metrical but non-parallel, non-rhyming, classical prose." His third characteristic, content, requires texts to display a primary focus on "phenomena that are in some sense anomalous." His fourth characteristic, status, requires that *zhiguai* texts are not considered canonical. Hence, the perception of contemporary scholars as to the nature of the text in question was an important consideration and one which reflects Bakhtin's theories as well as those of reader-response literary critics.[52] The fifth characteristic, the presence of intertextual markers, refers to such things as generic features present in the titles which would indicate the inclusion of *zhiguai* motifs to an intended readership. Therefore, there might be explicit references in titles to a "continuation" of a previous work; explicit references in metatexts or in the body of texts to other *zhiguai* works; quotations or paraphrases from, or allusions to, other *zhiguai* accounts.[53]

To belong to what Campany calls a "core" of (Six Dynasty) *zhiguai* texts, a given work could be expected to exhibit all of the above five characteristics. Yet, conceding to an open-ended conception of genre, Campany gives examples of works which he considers marginal to the genre since they displayed some but not all of the five characteristics.[54]

According to Campany's schema, the *Record* would seem to belong to the *zhiguai* genre. Its form comprises short narratives and descriptions. Its style displays mostly nonmetrical, nonrhyming, classical prose. Its content focuses primarily—but not exclusively—on "phenomena that are in some sense anomalous." Nor was it considered a canonical text. Finally, its title bears the intertextual marker *zhi*, also present in numerous other works which could be considered *zhiguai*.

Nevertheless, as I have previously argued, neatly pigeonholing the work in this way tends to obscure other possible affiliations. Furthermore, as should be obvious from my above discussion of the nature of *guai*, since the construction of *guai* was so broad (encompassing both the paranormal as well as simply the unusual), it is difficult to determine the boundary between what might have been considered *guai* and something which was simply newsworthy or worthy of preservation. And while Hong Mai often professed interest in what he called "the strange" throughout the *Record*'s prefaces, he never—as far as we know— labeled the *Record* as "*zhiguai*." Rather than neatly pigeonhole the *Record* thus, I propose to adopt an open-ended approach to its generic formulation and examine its affiliations with other literary genres—particularly history.

ALTERNATE PERSPECTIVES

We saw from the *Record*'s prefaces how Hong Mai implicitly referred to his work as *baiguan*, or unofficial history. In the preface to the twenty-first installment (the *Sanzhi jia*), he provided a list of what he referred to as unofficial histories and compared the speed of their compilation with that of the *Record*. By doing so he implied that the *Record* could also be considered a work of unofficial history. Furthermore, in the preface to the thirteenth installment (the *Zhijing zhi*), through a supposed dialogue between himself and one of his sons, Hong referred to himself as a writer of unofficial history. And as I have already pointed out, the Qing scholar Shen Qizhan, in his preface to the Zhou edition, informed us that contemporary "scholars and men of letters who search for forgotten records would speak of it [the *Record*] in the same vein as unofficial history."[55] While Shen intimated that the work transcends the category of unofficial history and is, in some way, superior to other such works, he implied that there were other Qing scholars who saw the work as part of this tradition. The scholarly literature on the *Record*, which I outlined in chapter 2, certainly demonstrated the expectation of historical factuality on the part of several influential men of letters. Why would scholars such as Zhou Mi and Chen Zhensun expect a high degree of historical factuality to be displayed by a work of *zhiguai* anyway, particularly if one were to equate *zhiguai* with "fiction"?

In chapter 2 I discussed Gardner's views on what constituted unofficial history. I will not, therefore, delineate the concept further here. Suffice it to say that while unofficial histories may have included *zhiguai* material, since allowances were made for the inclusion of what Gardner refers to as "spurious material," the examples he gives—secret matters and personalia of all kinds which might be classified as dubious—show that the range of their subject matter was broader than that of the *zhiguai*. Furthermore, the subject of an unofficial historian's brush, while being unusual enough to attract and hold the attention of both author and reader, may not have necessarily described unusual events and phenomena which ran contrary to what was considered normal. As noted in chapter 2, Gardner's characterization of unofficial history aptly encapsulates several aspects of Hong's methodology, that is, venturing beyond his documents and observations, the inclusion of spurious material, examination of secret matters and personalia, and comparative freedom from the restraints of orthodox historians. Furthermore, Hong's self-professed motives for collecting and recording oral material, also discussed in chapter 2, correlate with what Vansina has identified as the motives of oral historians: "The goal is to save sources from oblivion."[56] The same can be said of Hong's professed desire to preserve written material.

Furthermore, a significant number of accounts found throughout the *Record* do not necessarily equate with *guai* according to the above discussion. The inclusion of this material appears to be due to its newsworthiness, or possibly because of Hong's self-professed desire to preserve stories which were in danger of being lost. Such accounts tend to focus on banditry, local folklore, the wars between the Song and the Jurchen, sea-faring, and various miscellaneous anecdotes.[57] And while the themes displayed therein may be linked—albeit tenuously—with the encompassment of disorder by order, they are certainly devoid of any cosmological element. Apart from these, there are numerous accounts detailing medical cures, which seem to have been included so as to preserve and popularize their usage: not because they seem to have been considered *guai*.

There was, furthermore, much biographical material which could broadly be divided into two categories: biographies and hagiographies of Taoist transcendents/recluses (not unlike those found in the *Lives of Divine Transcendents* [*Shenxian zhuan* 神仙傳] or the early Song *Record of Remarkable Personae of the Jianghuai Region* [*Jianghuai yiren lu* 江淮異人錄], for example) and those pertaining to virtuous women (similar to those found in the *Classic of Female Martyrs* [*Lienü zhuan* 烈女傳]). Narratives belonging to the former category were once classified as unofficial biographies (*zazhuan* 雜傳) according to the traditional four-fold classification system before their relegation to that of *xiaoshuo* after the compilation of the *New Bibliographic Treatise of the Tang*. This was presumably due to their containing *zhiguai* motifs. Yet the narrative structure of these hagiographies, due to their biographical nature, is demonstrably different from that of typical *zhiguai* accounts. Accounts about virtuous women furthermore seem closely affiliated with the biographies in the *Classic of Female Martyrs*, which was classified as "biography" (*zhuanji* 傳記) under the traditional classification system. Indeed, the *Record of Remarkable Personae of the Jianghuai Region* was still classified as an historical work under this system. Hence, even according to the traditional classification system, the *Record* contains material of disparate categories. All this strongly suggests that the *Record* is not purely and exclusively focused on *zhiguai* phenomena.

The strong loyalist, anti-Jurchen sentiment discernable throughout the corpus, which I discussed in chapter 3, is also a relevant consideration. On the one hand, these anti-Jurchen motifs reflect then-contemporary public feeling and help mark the *Record*'s unique contribution to Chinese literature. Yet, on the other hand, these patriotic themes are so overwhelmingly strong in the *Record* that they suggest an alternate ontological purpose: that is, the *Record* as a work of anti-Jurchen, patriotic literature which may well have influenced the hearts and minds of its readership against the pacifist policies of the Southern Song court. Although Hong never discusses this theme in any of his prefaces—understandably so, the anti-Jurchen sentiment was so powerful as to almost eclipse his "love of the strange." Hence, labeling the *Record* as a work of *zhiguai* would possibly blind us to alternate perspectives such as these.

As I indicated at the beginning of this chapter, the marginal nature of the *Record*'s classification (i.e., *xiaoshuo*) excluded the possibility of clear-cut classification, as was the case with orthodox genres. The residual nature of the category, the unorthodox nature of Hong's subject matter, his method of collecting and presenting material, as well as the variety of subjects displayed throughout the text—*zhiguai* among them—ensured the marginalization of his work. The intertextual gaps were large enough to create associations with several genres, particularly with unofficial history. Hong, furthermore, made several metatextual references to unofficial history throughout his prefaces. And the close affiliation the *Record* exhibited to works of unofficial history, in regard to content as well as authorial approach, should be clear by now—that is, Hong's penchant for verifying information, his attempts to achieve what he referred to as historical reliability, and the like. Given all this, we should not be surprised that he made a claim of historical reliability for his accounts in the preface to the second installment; what else would a scholar writing unofficial history hope for, if not a record which had a "factual" basis? Therefore, while I do not wish to deny the *Record*'s obvious links to what modern scholars intuitively understand as *zhiguai*, taking Hong Mai's lead, I would hesitate to label the work as exclusively *zhiguai* since this closes other possible generic affiliations—particularly that of unofficial history—and would perhaps lead readers to overlook the work's subtlety.

CHAPTER FIVE

Questions of "Reliability" and Transmission

Now that we have arrived at a clearer understanding of the *Record's* generic affiliations, we may proceed to examine that which seemed extremely dear to Hong Mai's heart: the factuality of his accounts. As can be seen from his prefaces, this is something which Hong pondered deeply. And, given the *Record's* close connection with unofficial history, historical factuality is a particularly pertinent question meriting detailed scrutiny. An exploration of the temporal and spatial settings, along with featured personae, will furthermore shed light on the circumstances surrounding the telling and circulation of selected accounts, be they based on oral or written transmission. In this way, circumstances discussed by Hong in his prefaces may be aptly illustrated.

Judging by the prefaces which I reviewed in chapter 2, Hong made several references to what may be understood as "reliability," a summary of which would be useful before proceeding further. We may remember that from the preface to the second installment, after reference to other works displaying *zhiguai* motifs, which he asserted were illusive/insubstantial and allegorical (寓言), he boldly claimed that his stories were all based on factual sources (*jie biaobiao you juyi zhe* 皆表表有據依者). And while the phrase "*jie biaobiao you juyi zhe*" is sufficiently ambiguous as to open Hong's words to various interpretations, I have chosen to read this phrase as "reliability," given his frequent reference to what is obviously historical factuality—something hardly surprising in view of Hong's background as an historian and his approach to the *Record* as a work of unofficial history. He returned to the same question in the preface to the third installment when he apologized for the inclusion of material which he told us was not according to what was said. While this points to the inclusion of unreliable material, it nevertheless implicitly reveals Hong's sincere intent to achieve reliability. We should also remember that he henceforth began questioning spurious material or citing known precursor texts; hence, his professed intentions are supported with action. In the preface to the fourth installment, he implicitly disclosed his search for evidence through the words of an interlocutor who accused him of seeking proof for the spurious. In the preface to the fifth installment, he gave an example whereby an associate, Ye An, attempted to dupe him with a tall tale. Hong's lamentation that such was inevitable is a further admission of the probable inclusion of the unreliable, yet it again reveals his desire to avoid the spurious. In the preface to the eleventh installment, he refuted anonymous or fictitious allegations that he borrowed extensively from previous works, and then looked to the *Zhuangzi* for defense. In the preface to the fourteenth installment, he wrote of having unsuccessfully attempted to verify selected accounts and his footnoting of such attempts. Again, had Hong not sincerely wished to achieve historical factuality, neither would he have gone so far as to verify information passed on to him, nor would he have footnoted doubtful material. In the preface to the fifteenth installment, he discussed fictionality in an account from the *Annals of Lü Buwei* (*Lüshi chunqiu* 呂氏春秋). In the preface of the twenty-third installment, he talked about the possibility of *Record* accounts being included in gazetteers, hence implicitly affirming his faithfulness in their veracity. In the preface to the twenty-sixth installment, he again discussed his attempts to verify information given him. In the preface to the twenty-eighth installment, he replicated an account from the *Imperial Digest from the Era of Great Peace*—which in turn replicated one from the Six Dynasty *Records of the Living and the Dead*—and compared it to one in the *Bing* installment with the admission that they were alike. This was a major apology for his previous claims, from the preface to the eleventh installment, that no two accounts were alike, again raising questions of original versions as is the case with text-based transmission of stories as opposed to oral traditions. And finally, in the preface to the thirtieth installment, Zhao Yushi summarized Hong's discussion of "mistakes" found in the *Extensive Records* and the *Encyclopedia of Art and Literature* (*Yiwen zhi leiju* 藝文志類聚); once more Hong's penchant for philology and textual criticism—so noticeable in his *Rongzhai suibi*—comes to the fore.

Reliability, of course, has several connotations. The surface meaning of the phrase "*jie biaobiao you juyi zhe*" would seem to simply refer to Hong's accounts having been based on contemporary events rather than having been fabricated from the author's mind. Nevertheless, given Hong's attempts to verify information as summarized above and his excising of accounts which he later found "untrue," he clearly seemed concerned about whether the events actually occurred. Therefore, I use the term "reliability" in the sense that his accounts were understood as true to historical events (historically reliable), that is, the expectation of both author and his actual readership—skeptics aside—that reported events either actually took place or were likely to have taken place according to the Chinese religious system.

As can be seen from the above summary, Hong clearly valued reliability and factuality. We may furthermore remember that in his *Rongzhai suibi*, he raised doubts about the truthfulness of one of the *Record*'s accounts and expressed regret at having included it.[1] Another important aspect of Hong's treatment of his material—and one which would seem to reflect his adherence to historiographical principles—is his inclusion of not only the name of the protagonist and other parties involved, but also of the event's temporal setting and the name of the informant or source. The presence of at least one of these three features as criteria for inclusion is discussed in the preface to Wang Jingwen's aforementioned *Other Record of the Listener*, which is quoted by Hong Mai in the preface of the *Ren zhi*.[2] In this, Wang informed us that Hong was sure to include at least one or two such criterion—which would place the story within the boundaries of historical writing. Conversely, Hong would not record an account if all three were unverifiable.[3] This feature, however, was nothing new and can also be seen in numerous texts throughout the corpus of *zhiguai* literature, in addition to the *chuanqi* texts of the Tang. In other words, it is an intertextual marker shared by many texts intuitively considered as *zhiguai*.

Even Hong's detractors, such as Zhou Mi and Chen Zhensun, expected historical reliability from the *Record* and were disappointed not to find a sufficiently satisfying degree of it. Zhou, we will remember, accused Hong of including "unreliable" material, while Chen likened him to Xu Xuan, who was said to have been tricked into including fictitious accounts in his *Examining Spirits (Jishen lu)*. Chen also accused Hong of "borrowing" extensively from previous works—the *Extensive Records* in particular. Such criticism seems unusual considering that the corpus of Song *biji* literature abounds with accounts which can also be found in other literary works, not to mention the cut-and-paste methods of traditional Chinese historians. Yet, considering that Hong claimed a factual basis—one presumably grounded in an authentic Song Dynasty context—for his accounts, the existence of precursor texts sharing the same plot would understandably undermine his claim of authenticity. It is likely that both Chen and Zhou had this in mind. Given that Hong relied heavily on collecting oral material focusing on social history, in contrast to official history writing which may have featured many cut-and-pasted tracts pertaining to political and biographical *topoi*, it is hardly surprising that questionable material found its way into the *Record*. And, as can be seen from his prefaces, Hong was not unaware of this. Below I will therefore first examine the spatio-temporal settings as well as personae mentioned in the accounts, after which I will discuss selected precursor texts.

PERSONAE AND SPATIO-TEMPORAL SETTING

As can be seen from previous chapters, a significant number of Hong's informants were known historical figures. The same is true for protagonists and "characters." And there is no reason to suspect that those for whom there is no available biographical data were not. To be sure, a Song historian has but to flip through the extant corpus and a plethora of well-known figures will be readily apparent. Some are as famous as emperor Gaozong's long-time grand councilor Qin Gui and the "loyal" general Yue Fei, while others are comparatively lesser known scholar-officials whose names, nevertheless, may still be found in extant official history sources such as the *History of the Song* and the *Important Collected Documents of the Song* (*Song hui yao jigao* 宋會要輯稿, hereafter *Important Collected Documents*).[4] Occasionally one finds a seemingly incorrect name, as in the case of Wang De's wife, whom I discussed in chapter 3; while the account gives her family name as Li, official historical records give it as Yin. While Madame Li may have been a second or third wife, the discrepancy throws doubt on either the official record or Hong's *Record*.

Not surprisingly, the prefectures, counties, and other major landmarks mentioned in the text are all historical. Yet what is perhaps of greater interest is the number of buildings, bridges, gardens, lakes, and the like which prove to have been historical places. To be sure, historians may get a sense of what these places may have been like during the Song from Hong's accounts. We saw in chapter 3 how Suzhou's Blue Wave Pavilion (*Canglang ting*) provided the backdrop for an account from the second installment. According to Hong Mai, the property's ownership had passed from its original owner, Su Shunqin, into the hands of the famous general, Han Shizhong, who was awarded the posthumous title of Han Xian'an 韓咸安. The Blue Wave Pavilion was, and is, an actual place and details regarding its ownership as given by Hong Mai were corroborated by Su Shunqin's *Canglang ting ji* 蒼浪亭記.[5]

Another interesting example is the old Palace of Spreading Beneficence (*Xuanhua lou* 宣華樓) built by Wang Yan 王衍 (901–926) at Chengdu during the Five Dynasties. This acts as the backdrop to an account from the first installment. Wang Yan ruled the area before being overthrown by the Tang general Meng Zixiang 孟子祥 (874–934). Meng lived for only two years after taking control of Sichuan and was succeeded by his third son, Meng Chang 孟昶 (919–965). Meng Chang was still a juvenile when he ascended the throne and governed through officials loyal to his father. After he came to rule in his own right, he conducted a purge of several former ministers, arresting them and their families as well as confiscating their property. In Hong's account, ghosts of murdered palace attendants were said to have been sighted during the twenty-first year of the Shaoxing period (1157) by Chen Jia 陳甲 (dates uncertain), who was a guest of the then-prefect Li Ximei 李西美 (dates uncertain).[6] The palace attendants were said to have served in the Palace of Spreading Beneficence, even though it was no longer in existence at the time of the alleged occurrence. The ghosts furthermore composed poetry which alluded to the palace and one of its pavilions—Welcoming the Immortals Pavilion (*Yingxian* 迎仙)—the name of which can also be found in the *New History of the Five Dynasties* (*Xin Wudai shi* 新五代史).[7] The *Record* story also gives information about the palace's ownership, albeit sketchy, in addition to details about Meng's rule in Sichuan. Although the *New History of the Five Dynasties* does not corroborate the ghost story, it does confirm the existence of the historical setting.

Apart from these examples, one has but to scan through the pages of the *Record* to find numerous others. The Golden Brightness Pond (Jinming Chi 金明池), for example, one of Kaifeng's famous scenic sites;[8] Huizong's Northeastern Marchmount (Genyue 艮岳), a sumptuous imperial garden in which Huizong housed rare animals, not to mention exotic rocks and flowers;[9] or the Jade Ford Gardens (Yujin Yuan 玉津園) in Lin'an where war party leader and influential minister Han Tuozhou was assassinated[10]—all these places were factual and are well known to Song historians.[11]

Hong's dates, however, occasionally betray minor inaccuracies. The same may be said for biographical information. We saw in the account of Wang De (discussed in chapter 3) how Wang was still alive when an account from the third installment presumed that he was already dead. An example of inaccurate dates can be found in a story about the famous general Han Shizhong involving medical treatment he was said to have received in the twenty-fifth year of the Shaoxing period (1155). Han, however, died in 1151.[12] Interestingly enough, 1155 as the year of Han's death is not restricted to this account. Another, now found in the second supplementary chapter, also gives his year of death as 1155.[13] Does this, therefore, suggest an alternate year generally accepted at the time of writing, albeit different from the one given in the *History of the Song*? If so, it would not be the only incorrect date given in the official dynastic history, as was the case with Hong Mai's own biography.

In another account, one of its main figures, Li Hui 李回 (?–1133), had actually died before the story supposedly took place. This account centers around a general, Yang Weizhong 楊惟忠 (1067–1132), who was sent to fight bandits by his commanding officer, Li Hui. Yang fell ill the day following the bandit's surrender and died soon after being taken home. This event was supposed to have taken place in the fourth year of the Shaoxing period (1134) in the vicinity of Poyang (modern Jiangxi). According to official records, Li Hui's last post was in Hongzhou 洪州 (Jiangxi). The spatial setting, therefore, would seem accurate. The dates, however, are not. According to the *Record*, Yang Weizhong died in 1134, yet official records give 1132 as the year of death:[14] a discrepancy of approximately two years. According to official historiography, Li Hui died in the third year of the Shaoxing period (1133),[15] indicating a discrepancy of no greater than one year compared to the *Record* account.[16]

Inaccurate dates, however, do not necessarily discredit a work *in toto* or indicate fictitious content. As Glen Dudbridge has pointed out in regard to the *Record of Extensive Marvels* (*Guangyi ji* 廣異記), such discrepancies reflect the imperfect memory of informants. They furthermore indicate that the recorder of an oral story has been faithful to his source.[17]

PARALLEL AND PRECURSOR TEXTS

We have seen how Chen Zhensun accused Hong Mai of including numerous texts from the *Extensive Records* without significant amendment. Nevertheless, as I have already noted, since Chen did not give any examples—not to mention the loss of almost half the original text—it would seem impossible to fully assess the validity of his claims. Nevertheless, in his preface to the thirty-eighth installment, Hong Mai himself demonstrated that at least one account from the *Extensive Records* shared a common plot with one in the *Record*, hinting that there may have been others like it. And, as I argued in chapter 2, the anonymous criticism outlined in the preface to the eleventh installment—that Hong borrowed from previous accounts—may well be factual, given that it corresponds to Chen Zhensun's comments.

No doubt the existence of such parallel texts would have undermined the *Record*'s supposed reliability; that is, had an account which supposedly occurred in the Song Dynasty shared a plot and narrative syntagms with, say, one from the Six Dynasties, then the account's authentic Song Dynasty context would become problematic. Yet stories in oral traditions tended to claim a life of their own, displaying numerous variations with each retelling, while the oral nature of their transmission ensured the absence of an "original" version. Nevertheless, Chen Zhensun's criticism suggests that, by the Southern Song, when a thriving print culture was undergoing unprecedented development, the recycling of old stories as new was no longer completely acceptable in relation to the writing of unofficial history. Hong's own increasingly apologetic tone when discussing precursor texts and his footnoting of parallel texts supports this view. Hong's professed originality and reliability, not to mention his claim of unofficial history, must have surely fuelled such criticism. Hong was certainly scrupulous when it came to citing known parallel texts. Yet, as I observed in chapter 2, he tended not to do this before the third installment.

Parallel texts can—for convenience—be grouped under five broad categories in regard to historical accuracy (or lack of it): 1) those based on "evidence" (as stated in the preface of the *Yi zhi*) which are corroborated by official histories and other literary sources; 2) those for which Hong cited a precursor text; 3) those whose spatio-temporal markers and personal names were later proven incorrect (such as those he referred to in the preface of the *Zhiding zhi*); 4) those which he considered questionable but still included, appending his suspicions with an end commentary; 5) those whereby informants deliberately attempted to dupe him with overtly fabricated accounts (such as the example he gave in the preface of the *Wu zhi*). Below I will discuss examples from the first three groups. Examples from the fifth group, apart from the one in the preface to the *Wu zhi* and the ones Hong spoke of excising, would not seem possible to conclusively identify. And, as examples from the fourth group have already been dealt with in the prefaces outlined in chapter 2, I will not discuss them further here. Since the *Record* accounts which I discuss below not only share plots, names, and temporal settings, but also correspond partly in verbatim with their parallel texts, I shall provide a full or partial translation of the relevant portions where appropriate.

ACCOUNTS SUPPORTED BY OTHER SONG SOURCES

The case of Huang Gongdu 黃公度 (1109–1156)[18] from the fourth chapter of the fourteenth installment is an instance whereby official history sources corroborate a *Record* account.[19] According to this, a scholar preparing for the imperial examinations named Huang Ying 黃瀛 (dates unknown) dreamed on several occasions of meeting someone named "Number One Scholar Huang" (Huang *zhuangyuan* 黃狀元). Not surprisingly, this caused him great joy since he interpreted it as an omen of his own future success. In the eighth year of the Shaoxing period (1138), however, the number one scholar proved to be Huang Gongdu, after which Huang Ying realized his error. When consulting the relevant entries of the *Important Collected Documents*, while no record of Huang Ying's dream can be found, we can find Huang Gongdu's success recorded there, and the dates correspond exactly to those given in the *Record*.[20]

Valerie Hansen discovered two additional accounts from the first installment which are also corroborated by the *Important Collected Documents* as well as other sources. The account from the former recording the martyrdom of a Song loyalist, Commander Fan Wang, verifies the *Record*'s parallel text not only in narrative detail but also in regard to places and dates.[21]

> At Fort Xunjian in Shunchang County (now Nanbei county, Fujian), [under the jurisdiction of] Yanping, in the sixth year of the period of Continued Ascendancy (1136) of the Gaozong Emperor, a temple was erected. In the eighth [lunar] month of the 28th year (1158), the plaque [inscribed with the words] "Far-Reaching Virtue" was granted. The mad bandit, Fan Ru, rebelled early in the period of Continued Ascendancy and the bowmen of the county were plotting to join the bandits. Wang did not accede and, in a scathing tone, told them,
>
> "Our wives and children are kept warm and well-fed from the bounty of the empire. Unable to kill the rebels for the state, today you wish to become one. Will you not be ashamed to face heaven and earth?"
>
> The recalcitrants were angered by his words, after which they killed him in the market square. His son [also] did not follow them, and so they killed him too. They kidnapped his wife, Madame Ma, who also did not submit to the bandits. They removed her vital organs and dismembered her. After the bandits had been quashed, the outline of Wang's corpse could be seen faintly on the ground and would not disappear. The people of the district were astounded, and they placed his effigy in the Temple of Walls and Moats. The prefecture brought forward a petition, and so they have been given permission to erect a state-sanctioned shrine which may be used for prayer. The temple plaque [inscribed with the words] "Far-Reaching Virtue" has also been granted.[22]

When we compare this to the *Record* version, although the two do not correspond completely, many specific details coincide, including Commander Fan's dialogue.

There was also Commander Fan Wang of Shunchang county (now Nanbei county, Fujian). At the time of Fan Ru's uprising, Yu Sheng and other bandits in the district rebelled. Chen Wangsu of the local militia was a trouble maker, and he wanted to take the bandit's lair to retaliate. Fan Wang scolded the crowd, saying, "Our parents, wives and children obtain their livelihood from the country. Today we're not strong enough to attack the bandits. If we do so, it will help them to be even more terrible. How can you not be ashamed to view heaven and earth?" Angered by his cutting words, the leader of the bullies [Chen Wangsu] killed him.

One son, called Fosheng, was twenty and famed for his courage. The bandits falsely used his father's name to summon him and killed him when he arrived. When Fan's wife, née Ma, heard that her husband and son were both dead, she sobbed in the road. The bandits wanted to rape her, but she resisted. They dismembered her with a piece of wood and divided her into sections. After several months, the bandits were subdued.

The bricks where Commander Fan had been killed retained obscure outlines of his corpse, which were very faint. The people of the district gathered the bricks and joined together to build a shrine to him. They also painted his likeness on the wall of the temple to the god of walls and moats. In 1136 the vice-prefect, Wu Kui from Jian'an [now Jian'ou county, Fujian], petitioned the court about the deity. An edict awarded him the posthumous title of chengxin gentleman and granted permission to build a temple to him.

Then Su Hao, the Shunchang sheriff directing the corvee laborers [building the temple], dreamt that Commander Fan, clothed in the garb of a high official, came to visit him and thanked him for overseeing the work. He said, "At the time I was hurt, my left eye was gouged out by the bandits." He led Su to the place to see it; there was his corpse, clothed in a short white shirt, as well. Commander Fan pointed again to the southeast corner of the temple and said, "The leftover traces are still here. I already have sent a message to the magistrate and hope you will remind him."

The next day Su entered the temple and asked how Wang had died. Everyone said Wang's story was true, but no one had been aware that his eye had been gouged out. The southeast corner was the original site of the shrine. Accordingly he asked and received five bricks, which he brought to the temple.

The district magistrate Huang Liang heard about this and asked his wife, née Cai. She answered, very surprised, "Last night I also dreamt that a purple-clad person visited you in your chambers. You bowed to him to enter the room, and climbed the steps. He then refused and left. His name was Fan Wang. Could that be what the sheriff refers to as leaving a message?"

Commander Fan died as a loyal martyr, and his wife died unmolested. They died but are not forgotten. How can one not believe this?[23]

This story was preserved in the *Important Collected Documents* when the local magistrate petitioned the court to recognize the cult of Commander Fan, as was the custom in regard to popular deities. This particular one happened to be recorded by Hong Mai. Unfortunately I have no information about how Hong collected the story, nor does he disclose his informant. He may have based his account partly on the *Important Collected Documents*, although an additional source is likely considering the greater detail he provides. Hansen considers that the *Important Collected Documents*, although never published in their entirety, were partially available to Song government offices.[24] It is, therefore, possible that Hong had access to them during his first term as an official in the capital when, apart from his office of junior compiler in the National Historiography Institute, he held the concurrent office of an examination consultant in the Recruitment Section of the Board of rites. Since the section containing the story of Commander Fan is preserved in the Rites section (*Li bu* 禮部) of the *Important Collected Documents*, it is possible that a copy of this section was kept there and was available to him.

Another of Hong's accounts tells of an older woman who suffered from an arm complaint. As it corresponds partly in verbatim with a version in the *Tiaoxi ji* 苕溪集 and the *Wuxing jinshi*,[25] it is worthwhile comparing the relevant sections. First is Hong's version.

> An old village woman of Huzhou suffered an aching arm for a long time with no respite. During the night she dreamt that a white-clothed woman came and said: "I am also like this. If you can cure my arm, I can cure yours."
>
> The old woman said: "Where do you live?"
>
> She replied: "I stay in the west corridor of Revering Peace Monastery."
>
> The woman then awoke. She went into town, to Revering Peace Monastery, and told what she had dreamt to the monk Zhongdao of the Western Hall. He pondered and then said, "It must have been Guanyin [the Buddhist goddess of mercy]. Our hall has a white-robed image. Because of a gap in the thatch, her shoulder is hurt."
>
> He led her to the room to perform her obeisance, and indeed one arm was missing. The elderly woman then ordered workmen to repair it.
>
> When the image was complete, the woman's disease was cured.[26]

The *Tiaoxi ji* and the *Wuxing jinshi* record the text of a stele dated 1157 for a Guanyin hall attached to the monastery in question, which corroborates the *Record* account. The name, however, differs slightly—perhaps reflecting an imperfect memory on the part of Hong's informant.

> For a long time there was a statue of the bodhisattva Guanyin in between two pillars on the Western [sic] side of the monastery. Zhang of the prefecture had been sick for three years. One night Zhang dreamt of a white-robed woman who said: "You cannot lift your arm. I also suffer from this. If you can heal my arm, I will also cure your shoulder and give you long life."
>
> Zhang asked her where she lived, and she said: "I live in the west corridor of Heavenly Peace Monastery."
>
> The next day Zhang was carried to the monastery to the statue of the bodhisattva, and it was just as Zhang had dreamt. Zhang looked at the statue

with reverence and was moved to tears. Zhang examined the right arm of the bodhisattva and noticed it had been damaged by a piece of falling wood. Zhang ordered it repaired, and Zhang's illness was subsequently cured.[27]

I find it amusing that the terracotta bodhisattva in this story is able to heal someone else while being unable to heal herself, reminiscent of the popular Chinese idiom that a terracotta bodhisattva finds it difficult to preserve itself [let alone others] when crossing a river (*ni pusa guojiang, zishen nan bao* 泥 菩 薩 過 江 ，自 身 難 保).

Nevertheless, the two versions clearly refer to the same event. The slight discrepancy regarding the cause of Guanyin's damaged arm, as well as the name of the monastery, is of interest. Both these details strongly suggest oral transmission—supporting Hong's end-note that the account was *told* (*shuo* 說) to him by his informant. The stele's inscription was written by Liu Yizhi 劉 一 止 (1078–1160), cognomen Xingjian 行 簡, who was a native of Gui'an County (Jiangxi) and became an official in the capital. Interestingly enough, he appears in a *Record* account from a later installment.[28] Hong names Wu Jie吳价 (dates uncertain) from Huzhou 湖州 as his storyteller. While little is known about him, the *Index to Bibliographical Materials of Song Figures* informs us that someone called Wu Jie held the posts of a fiscal commissioner-in-chief of the Hebei Circuit and an edict attendant (*daizhi Hebeilu duyun shi zhi* 大製 河北路都運使製). It also cites an edict which transferred him to the post of (presumably concurrent) grand master and commissioner of waterways in the palace (*dazhong dafu dushui shizhe* 大中大夫都水使者). No dates, however, are traceable in the originals and whether it was the same person referred to in the *Record* is unclear.[29]

An account entitled *Lin Lingsu* 林 靈 素 (dates uncertain) from the third installment tells of how this famous Taoist successfully prayed for rain at the request of the Huizong emperor (r. 1101–1126) during a hot, dry day in the Northern Song capital.

> Lin Lingsu was adept at the Rites of the Five Thunder Gods. It was once oppressively hot in the capital (Kaifeng) and it had not rained for an entire month. [The Huizong emperor] called upon [Lin] to use his [Taoist] methods.
>
> "Heaven still does not wish it to rain," he replied. "The water sources of the Four Seas and Hundred Rivers have all been locked. I would not dare to attain any were it not for your majesty's command. Only [water from] the Yellow River is not forbidden, but it cannot be used."
>
> "The commoners are in the grip of scorching heat," observed the emperor. "If all you could do was obtain sweet swamp-water to give them just one bath, then what harm would it be if it were muddy?"
>
> Lin received the command, then proceeded to the Supreme Pure Temple. [The emperor] ordered the Hanlin academician, Yuwen Cuizhong, to assist. Lin took one bowl of water. Waving a sword, he performed the Steps of [King] Yu chanting incantations repeatedly.

"You may leave, your Excellency" he said to Yuwen. "If you are slow, you will be caught in a downpour." Yuwen came out the door and mounted his horse. There was a cloud the size of a fan which materialized in the air. After a short while it was the size of a parasol. With a clap of thunder, it rose from the ground. The horse galloped off in fear and had only just reached his home when it began to pour with rain followed by thunder claps in rapid succession. This went on for four hours before ceasing. People's tiles and gutters were all filled with mud and the water had accumulated for about an inch or so on the ground. It was yellow and muddy and could not be drunk, and it certainly did not do the crops a scrap of good.[30]

Hong's storyteller was one Hong Xingzu 洪興祖 (courtesy name Qingshan 慶善, active during the Shaoxing period).

An alternate version can be found in Zhou Hui's 周煇 (1127-after 1198) *Miscellaneous Record from Qingbo Gate* (*Qingbo zazhi* 清波雜志, hereafter *Miscellaneous Record*).

During the Hsüan-ho period (1119–1126), Taoists had access to the palace. The so-called "Golden door immortal guests 金 門 羽 客" were even more powerful than officials. Lin Lingsu was their leader. Taoists held office titles that exceeded those held by the ordinary officialdom.

One day, during the height of summer, the noon sun made it unbearably hot even in the water pavilion. The emperor ordered Lin to make rain by his magic powers. After a while, Lin reported: "Although the Lord on High has sealed off temporarily the four Great Rivers on earth, I may still be able to borrow some water from the Yellow River. But I'm afraid the rain cannot reach beyond the palace." He was urged to do all he could.

Soon came thunder and lightening; rain was pouring down like torrents. But the rain stopped after a little while. Workers who came from outside reported that beyond the inner walls of the palace the sun was beating down hard as usual [sic]. The emperor was amazed as ever.[31]

Zhou was a writer and collector who once acted as an emissary to the Jurchen. In his later years, he lived in the Qingbo Gate precinct of Lin'an, hence the work's title. His *Miscellaneous Record* is a twelve-chapter piece of *biji* literature first published in 1192, approximately twenty-one years after the *Bing zhi* (first published in 1171). This opens the possibility that Zhou Hui's story was based on Hong's account. Yet an examination of literary style reveals differences so great in terms of expression and syntax that the two stories would appear to be different versions of the same "event." Moreover, the conclusion differs: both versions emphasize the event's strangeness, yet Hong focuses on the poor quality of the rainwater—suggesting that its origin was, as Lin Lingsu had stated, the Yellow River. Lin's prediction toward the beginning of the account is "verified" by the result, thus unifying the narrative's beginning and conclusion. In Zhou's account, although Lin stated that only water from the Yellow River was available, he added that the rain would not extend beyond the palace grounds. The conclusion of the narrative vindicates Lin's foretelling and provides the element of the strange. Yet no mention was made—as in Hong's version—of dirty, yellow water unfit for drinking. We can be fairly confident, therefore, that this was, as Hong noted, told (orally) by Hong Xingzu and that the discrepancies in regard to wording, syntax, and narrative syntagms reflect oral transmission and imperfect memory. In other words, this account—and others like it—seemed to have assumed a life of its own, changing over time with each retelling. We do not, however, know the source of Zhou Hui's version.

While the above account was likely to have been in oral circulation during the late-twelfth century, the account I will analyze below is an example of Hong having received written material according to his claim from the prefaces of the fifth and fifteenth installments. A version of this account also appears in Wu Zeng's 吳曾 (?–after 1170) *Casual Notes from the Nenggai Studio* (*Nenggai zhai manlu* 能改齋漫錄). This was a work of *biji* literature initially published four years or so prior to the first publishing of Hong's inaugural installment. The account was, according to Hong, given to him by its author.[32] It records another anecdote about Lin Lingsu.

> Toward the end of the Zhenghe period (1111–1118), Lin Lingsu was lecturing at the Baolu Hall. There were several thousands of Taoists and lay Taoists kowtowing and paying homage before him. Yet there was one Taoist [who] stood there staring at him angrily. Lin was perturbed that he was not kowtowing. "What abilities do you have that you dare act like this?" berated Lin.
>
> "I can do nothing," the Taoist announced.
>
> "Why do you come here?" Lin asked him.
>
> "If you can do everything, why do *you* come here?" the Taoist retorted.
>
> Huizong was listening behind a curtain at the time and his curiosity was aroused. He asked the Taoist what he could do.
>
> The Taoist made his obeisance and answered, "I can grow anything."
>
> An attendant was ordered to find something plantable in the Taoist temple, and a bunch of star-anise was obtained which was given to the Taoist. Two guards were assigned to supervise him. The Taoist planted it in the imperial garden and only then was he allowed to sleep in the Temple. At the third watch, the Taoist disappeared. The following day they went to see the star-anise and it had sprouted into a thicket.[33]

Below is Wu Zeng's version.

> When Lin Lingsu was lecturing at the Pao-lu (Baolu) Hall, a Taoist stood there staring at him angrily. Lin asked him what he could do.
>
> "I can do nothing," the Taoist announced.
>
> "If you can do nothing, why do you come here?" Lin asked him.
>
> "If you can do everything, why do *you* come here?" the Taoist retorted.

This repartee aroused the curiosity of the emperor Hui-tsung. He asked the Taoist what he could do.

"I can grow everything," the Taoist answered.

An attendant was ordered to find something plantable in the Taoist temple, and a bunch of star-anise was obtained. The Taoist was ordered to plant it in the imperial garden[34] and then was escorted back to the Taoist dwelling. At the third watch that night, the Taoist disappeared. The next day, the star-anise was found to have grown into a forest in the imperial garden.[35]

The plot of the *Record* version is the same, as are the characters and setting. In the absence of any specific temporal setting in Wu Zeng's version, Hong provided the approximate time of the event at the beginning of his narrative: "toward the end of the Zhenghe period" (1111–1117). As mentioned above, although both accounts share a common plot, the syntactic order and choice of lexicon occasionally differ—although parts of the text correspond verbatim. Nevertheless, it is clear that one account was based on the other, supporting Hong's claim to have based his account on that of Wu.

This is a rare insight into the way Hong embellished and edited information given him. By comparing the two original texts, we can almost feel his creative hand at work. Given Lin Lingsu's infamy during the reign of the Huizong emperor, stories about him abound—Guo Tuan's *Cartload of Ghosts* contains especially many. Hong Mai was, therefore, understandably willing to include this one in his collection. Thus, in the cut-and-paste manner of the traditional Chinese historian, he recorded it in his third installment. The similarities between the two accounts demonstrate Hong's faithfulness to purported events and source.

He Wei's 何薳 (1077–1145) *Record of Hearsay from a Spring Waterside* (*Chunzhu jiwen* 春渚紀聞, hereafter *Record of Hearsay*) reveals a parallel text which corroborates a *Record* account, although—unlike the above examples— Hong Mai gives no reference to it. He Wei was born in Fujian. His father gained office under the patronage of Su Shi, hence the number of anecdotes about Su in the *Record of Hearsay* are probably not simply due to a general admiration of a literary genius. The work itself could not have been published any later than 1145 when the author died, and it was not widely circulated. It was reprinted in the Ming by Chen Jiru 陳繼儒 (1558–1639). Nevertheless, we know that Hong Mai was aware of at least part of the *Record of Hearsay*'s contents since he cited another of its stories as being a precursor text to one in his third installment.[36] The story in question concerns a National University student named Xu Guohua 徐國華 (dates uncertain) and was set in 1126 during the Jurchen attack on the Northern Song capital, Kaifeng.

Xu Guohua of Jian'an entered the National Academy in the Period of Spreading Harmony (1119–1125). During this time he dreamed of ascending a tall tower. In the tower was suspended a great, golden bell. Standing next to the bell was an enormous armored figure who, upon seeing Xu, struck the bell and cried, "Twenty-seven armored soldiers." Again he struck the bell, "Your official rank will not surpass that of a supernumerary." On the third stroke, he said, "The seventh subject."

Xu awoke. "If I go I will surely attain first division in the exam," he reasoned. "An official rank of a supernumerary would be enough." He therefore recorded it on a bamboo strip scroll, but could not fathom the words "seventh subject" or "twenty-seven armored soldiers."

In the *bingwu* year of the Jingkang period (1126), the barbarian horsemen attacked. The National Academy students contracted beriberi and many of them died. Xu also died of this disease. His compatriot, Dong Zongju, wished to bury him in the Eastern City Cemetery, but there was no spare land for new graves inside the cemetery wall. So he buried him with the other later burials, outside the wall. Dong marked the site of his grave, and it just happened to occupy the seventh plot in the twenty-seventh row.

Dong returned and told Xu's father. He therefore took out Xu's notebook and found that the divine message of the dream was without the slightest inaccuracy.[37]

Below is the *Record of Hearsay* version.

Xu Guohua of Jian'an was about to enter the National Academy in the Period of Spreading Harmony (1119–1125). He dreamed of a tall tower in which was suspended a great golden bell. Standing next to the bell was an armored figure who, upon seeing Guohua, struck the bell and cried, "Twenty-seven armored soldiers." He struck the bell again, announcing, "Subject number seven." Guohua awoke and, in his heart, he was secretly pleased.

"Surely I'll take out the number one place in the exams this time," he said [to himself]. "[Even if] my rank will not surpass that of a gentleman, it doesn't matter." He therefore recorded it at the bottom of a book-box. The only thing he could not fathom was the phrases "twenty-seven armored soldiers" and "seventh subject."

When the *bingwu* year came, the Jurchen pirates plundered [the capital]. Over half the Imperial University students died after contracting beriberi. Xu became ill and died. His compatriot, Dong Zongju, encoffined him and was going to bury him in the Eastern City Cemetery. But when he got there, there were no more plots available; later arrivals were all buried outside the wall. Dong, therefore, recorded the place of his burial.

After his examinations were over and he returned to his village, Dong counted the row [of Xu's grave], and it happened to be the seventh plot in the 27th row. He went back to tell Xu's father and, when he took out Xu's handwritten record, what the god [of the dream] had announced and the burial site showed not the slightest discrepancy.[38]

The plot and narrative syntagms in the *Record of Hearsay* story correspond with Hong Mai's almost exactly and sections of dialogue correspond verbatim. The protagonist's name is the same, as is that of Xu's friend—Dong

Zongju—although the last character is written differently: in the *Record* version it is 董縱舉, while in the *Record of Hearsay* it is 董縱矩. The year of occurrence—1126—corresponds, as does the time of the dream, albeit imprecisely.

While no record can be found of the protagonist or his dream, the death of many National University students following the Jurchen capture of Kaifeng is, however, an historical fact noted by Fang Hao in his *Song History (Song shi)*. The capital fell in the eleventh intercalary (lunar) month of the first year of the Jingkang period (early 1127 according to the Gregorian calendar) amidst winter snow. The consequent grain shortage caused an outbreak of beriberi and Zhang Bangchang 張邦昌 (1081–1127), soon to become a puppet of the Jurchen, sent medical officials to treat the students. Yet from spring to summer, their dead were said to have numbered some two hundred.[39]

The above *Record* account is, therefore, set in an historically authentic background. Yet, unlike many other occasions in which Hong cited a known precursor text, he fails to do so here, although he clearly knew about the content of the *Record of Hearsay*. Why, then, did he not refer to it? Hong gives Shao Desheng (dates uncertain) as his informant, so presumably it was told to him as an oral account. The different characters (homophones) in the protagonist's friend's name also suggest that oral transmission played a part. Yet the extent to which the two versions correspond verbatim alternatively suggests written transmission; that is, the later version was copied from the former. And since He Wei died in 1145, it should follow that Hong's recording was the latter.

Yet we cannot be sure if He Wei's version was added to his text at a later date. Certainly the detail about the dream message betrays signs of textual corruption: Hong's version mentions the twenty-seventh subject, the seventh subject, and also the prediction that the dreamer's rank would not surpass that of a supernumerary (*yuanwai* [*lang*] 員外郎). This last detail is missing from He Wei's version; yet after the dreamer woke up, He Wei mentions his dismissal of the possibility that his rank would not surpass that of "gentleman" (*lang* 郎). A portion of the text is clearly missing here.

Yet the wording and narrative detail differ sufficiently to not rule out the possibility of oral telling by Shao Desheng. I suspect that this was the case. If so, Hong's lack of reference to He Wei's version may well point to the possibility of his having accessed a somewhat different edition (or manuscript) than the modern one—an edition which originally did not contain this account; we will probably never know for sure. If the story was indeed circulated orally, the extent to which Shao was able to memorize several lines verbatim is astonishing. Nevertheless, the precursor text supports Hong's version and is further evidence of his accuracy as a recorder of near-contemporary stories.

PRECURSOR TEXTS CITED BY HONG

Perhaps the most intriguing example of a precursor text is the one Hong quoted in the preface to the thirty-eighth installment. This, we will remember, dealt with Jia Bi who agreed to swap heads with an ugly paranormal being. As Hong noted, this Six Dynasties account shared similar narrative syntagms with the story of Sun Siwen, whom Hong professed to have seen in 1158.[40] Although Hong did not clearly state his informant, it seems to have been Yang Pu 楊朴 (courtesy name Gongquan 公全), as Yang is mentioned toward the conclusion as having known Sun and had commented on his changed appearance. Yang furthermore told two other accounts which both appear in the first installment (*Jia*: 15: 128 and 18: 159).

Given, however, the existence of what Hong himself considered a precursor text from the Six Dynasties period, it is tempting to argue that the *Record* version is somehow derived from the former. If so, it would clearly undermine Hong's purported spatio-temporal setting, as well as the name of his protagonist. Sun Siwen was therefore possibly fictitious, in which case the entire account and its Song Dynasty context may also be fictitious—possibly a retelling of the Six Dynasty account, refreshed with a Song spatio-temporal setting. Alternatively, Sun Siwen was indeed a Song figure and the Six Dynasty story—or a version of it which may have been in circulation at the time—was modified to ridicule his hideous features in a manner akin to malicious gossip.

Significantly, an abbreviated version of this account found on page four in chapter 5 of Guo Tuan's *Kuiche zhi* suggests that—at least this account—was in general circulation during the 1160s and 1170s and was, therefore, an "authentic" Southern Song story. Guo's stated informant was Wei Liangyou 魏良佑 (dates uncertain). While different from Hong's, someone surnamed Wei is mentioned by Hong as an informant for the final account from the same chapter in which the Sun Siwen story appears; unfortunately, Wei's given name has been lost due to poor preservation of the surviving imprint. Since the *Bing* installment (in which the Sun Siwen account is located) was completed in 1171, while the *Kuiche zhi* was completed somewhere in the late 1170s given dates mentioned throughout the text, Guo Tuan's version may have been based on Hong's. Yet the two versions are sufficiently different as to strongly suggest oral or partial-oral transmission. That is, apart from a couple of phrases, the wording is quite different. Furthermore, in Guo's version, Sun's misdemeanor is to ask his wife if he was better looking than the deity, whereas in Hong's version he directs licentious thoughts toward the deity's wife. In addition, rather than having his head replaced, it is Sun's face (*mian* 面) that is replaced by guards and not by the deity himself, as in Hong's account. This disparity points to a different version of the same story.

Nevertheless, the existence of further such antecedents may well call into question the Song Dynasty context of Hong's accounts. Certainly this is Chen Zhensun's contention—that Hong included several chapters of old tales from the *Extensive Records*. Hong evidently came to endorse this view, otherwise he would not have footnoted similar precursor texts or indulged in the type of apologetics seen in this preface.

Below I will examine another antecedent cited by Hong. First is my translation of the *Record* version.

THE VILLAGER FROM JIANGYIN

Lin Mingfu said that in the sixth year of the Period of Continued Ascendancy (1136), when he was residing in Jiangyin, the price of mulberry leaves in the vicinity of the Huai River surged.

There was a villager who lived on a small island in the middle of the river, extremely close to Xixian County in Taizhou. The villager kept several dozen containers of silkworms.

He said to his wife and sons, "Every year I tend the silkworms. The expense is great, yet the return does not cover our costs. It is also very time consuming. It would be better to get rid of the lot. We could transport the leaves to Xixian. It would take no more than three days and the profits would be generous. There would also be no harm done."

His wife and sons were compliant, so he scalded the silkworms in hot water and they all died. He then buried them beneath the mulberry trees. Picking all the leaves, he took a boat and headed North. He was halfway when a carp jumped into the boat. The villager seized it, cut open its belly and rubbed it with salt.

In a short while he reached the bank where officials boarded the boat to search for dutiable goods. They opened the leaves and found a corpse. The villager went over to see and found that it was his own son. Shocked, he began to weep.

The officials thought that he had murdered someone and so arrested him. They interrogated the others who were on the boat, but none of them knew a thing. When they questioned Xu about where he had come from, the villager told them everything from beginning to end.

The county dispatched officials to Jiangyin to investigate. The door was closed when they reached his house. They entered by knocking a hole in the wall, yet all was still and no-one was inside. They dug up the silkworm's burial place and there was his wife, her body already in a state of decomposition. This made it easier to prove that he had murdered his wife and son before absconding. He had no means with which to defend himself, nor did the officials dare dismiss the case. In the end he died in prison.

This story is similar to that of "Wang Gongzhi's Story" in the *Sanshui Xiaodu*.[41]

Below is my translation of Huangfu Mei's 黃甫枚 (magistrate of Ruzhou 汝州 during the Xiantong 咸通 period [860–873] of the Tang Dynasty)[42] account from the *Little Tablet from Three Rivers* (*Sanshui xiaodu*, hereafter *Little Tablet*), which is set in the Tang Dynasty. Hou Zhongyi considers the *Little Tablet* the most significant collection of *chuanqi* from the Five Dynasty period.

It also contains numerous *zhiguai* accounts. According to the *Four Libraries* editors, it was completed in 907.[43]

DISASTER FROM BURYING SILKWORMS

It was the *gengyin* year of the Xiantong period during the Tang dynasty (870). There was a great famine in the capital and the price of grain was exorbitant. People were starving in the ditches and on the pathways. The month of the silkworms came and many of the mulberry leaves were being devoured by pests. One *jin* weight of the leaves was worth one *huan*.[44] There was one Wang Gongzhi from a village to the north of Zirun Dian in Xin'an County. He had several dozen mulberry trees which were profuse and leafy.

Gongzhi said to his wife, "We have become so impoverished that our family is without grain. We labor ceaselessly over these silkworms, yet we do not know whether we will lose or gain by them. According to my calculations, it would be better to rid ourselves of them and sell the mulberry leaves while the price is high. We would be able to get a million in cash, have grain for a month and go into wheat production. Wouldn't this be better than starving?"

His wife agreed. So he took a spade, dug a hole in the ground and buried the several containers of the silkworms which he had raised. The following morning, he took the mulberry leaves to the citadel and sold them, receiving three thousand *wen*. He then bought shoulders of pork and an assortment of loaves with which to return.

Reaching Hui'an Gate, the gate keepers saw that there was a trail of blood dripping from his sack, forming a trail on the ground. They then stopped and questioned him. Gongzhi said, "I've just sold mulberry leaves and got money. I bought some shoulders of pork and some assorted loaves which are in the sack. There's nothing else. You're welcome to search."

So saying, he opened the sack. There was a human's left arm, as though it had been freshly severed. The gate keepers then escorted Gongzhi to the magistrate. The magistrate ordered him be taken before the prefectural authorities of Henan. There the administrator ordered him to be interrogated. Gongzhi spoke freely, "Burying my silkworms, I sold the mulberry leaves and bought some meat to take back. I truly haven't killed anyone. Please verify what I say."

The administrator dispatched his director to go to the village and verify the silkworm's burial site. The director then escorted Gongzhi to his village. He first gathered Gongzhi's neighbors, who all said that they knew of how Gongzhi had buried his silkworms and that there was no foul play. The director and the villagers, together with Gongzhi, opened the burial pit. There, in a corner of one of the boxes, was a corpse. It was missing its left arm. When the severed arm was fetched and compared with the corpse, it fitted perfectly. Following this, the director again escorted Gongzhi to the prefectural office and reported to the administrator.

The administrator said, "Wang Gongzhi, although you are not guilty of murder, you have committed the misdemeanor of burying silkworms. The law permits me to condone this, but my conscience makes it difficult to tolerate. Silkworms are a sacred insect. They are the givers of thread. Exterminating them is no different to killing humans. I will punish you with the full weight of the law so as to expunge your wickedness."

Following this, the administrator ordered him beaten to death in the marketplace. When the officials checked the corpse, they found that it had returned to decomposing silkworms.[45]

Although archetypal motifs were often recycled in *zhiguai* literature over the centuries, the common narrative syntagms displayed by these two accounts, as well as the common dialogues and shared plot, all point to a common source. The most likely form of transmission is oral storytelling—possibly mixed with written transmission over several centuries, which would account for the minor differences in detail. If what we know about Hong Mai and his methods of collecting is anything to go by, it would not be surprising if many other similar texts were also largely based on oral sources; hence, they defy the modern notion of one integral original which renders other version "imitations." Yet, were we to accept that the latter is derived from the former, the *Record* version's Song Dynasty context (i.e., names and dates) then becomes questionable. Hong's names and dates may have acted as a later embellishment to an old tale which was in oral and/or written circulation. Surely Hong Mai recognized this possibility when he decided to footnote the precursor text. Yet he still included it, presumably since it was told to him ostensibly in good faith and was neither illogical in itself (at least according to the Chinese religious system) nor contradicted by other sources. And, as Gardner observed about Chinese unofficial historiography, what was not contradicted was included.[46]

Of course, the *Record* account still displays much verisimilitude, and it reflects contemporary attitudes and conditions. Nevertheless, unlike the Commander Fan or the Huang Guangdu accounts discussed above, the purported events and Song Dynasty context for such accounts were likely to have been historically unreliable. And, as can be seen from Appendix 1, there are many other examples of such parallel texts found throughout the *Record*.

UNCITED PRECURSOR TEXTS

I will now turn to examples which display conflicting spatio-temporal and personal names when compared to antecedents not noted by Hong Mai. The first is again derived from He Wei's *Record of Hearsay*.

THE GOLDEN SUTRA TWICE TESTED

There was one Shen Ergong from Anji County in Huzhou. Before the Jurchen pirates arrived, he dreamed of a monk who told him:

"Retribution for having committed murder in your previous incarnation has arrived. Your family may all escape to far away, [but] you alone must remain to guard the house. When you see a large person, breaking down the door with a sword and entering, have no fear. Address him with the words, 'are you Li Li from Yanshan?' Just stretch out your neck so as to receive the blade and wait for him to spare you. Then you will be released from the previous retribution."

The Jurchen arrived not several days later. His family had already fled with neighbors into the distant mountains to hide. Although Shen wished to go, he could not. He therefore sat at home watching for the bandits' coming.

On the following day there actually was a youth who broke down the door and came in. Seeing Shen, he regarded him with enraged eyes. Shen, unmoving, sat peaceably. Looking up at him, Shen said, "Could you be Li Li of Yanshan?"

The person put away his sword. Looking at him, Li inquired, "I have not yet killed you. How is it that you know my name and where I come from in such detail?"

Shen told him of his dream. Li was astonished when he saw that there was a Buddhist sutra on the table. He asked Shen, "What sutra is this?"

Shen replied, "It is the Golden Sutra which I recite everyday."

Li said, "For how long have you recited this sutra?"

To this he replied, "Twenty years."

Then, from his clothing, Li took out a small bamboo box from which he produced a scroll of the Golden Sutra which had been written in a delicate script.

Pointing at it, he said, "I, too, have been reciting this sutra—for five years. If I kill you because of retribution incurred previously, you will kill me again and the vendetta will run deep: when will it be released? I will not kill you now, but I will become your brother. So long as you remain here peaceably without fear, I will stay and protect you for three days."

When the bandits had all gone, he took supplies, grain, money and cloth and gave it [to Shen] before leaving.[47]

The above story, as suggested by the title, gives details of two such incidents whereby the "Golden Sutra" proved efficacious. I have omitted the latter incident here. Below is the same story as it appears in the *Record*.

SAVED BY THE BUDDHA FROM PAST ENMITY

Master Zhang, who came from Lin'an, once went to a temple. Inside a dilapidated building, he saw an old statue of the Buddha that was without hands or feet. He took it back home where he reverently venerated it and made offerings before it. After about a year or more the statue began to speak[48] and would always foretell of auspicious or calamitous events affecting Zhang's family. This went on for twenty or thirty years.

During the Jianyan period (1127–1130), the Jurchen soldiers sacked Lin'an and Zhang hid in an empty well. There he saw, as if in a dream, the Buddha that he venerated had come to bid him farewell, saying, "Disaster has befallen you and you will die, yet I have no means of saving you. Destiny decreed that in a previous life, during the Revolt of Huang Chao, you killed a man. Now he is known as Ding Xiaoda. He will come here tomorrow and kill you in recompense. You will be unable to avoid it."

Zhang was terrified. On the following day someone did come to the well. Brandishing a spear, he shouted for Zhang to come out. When Zhang did emerge the fellow immediately wished to smite him.

Zhang cried out, "Would you, sir, by chance be Master Ding Xiaoda?"

The fellow was astounded and asked, "How did you know my name?"

Zhang told him everything the Buddha had said. The fellow then cast his sword on the ground, as if in a daze, and said, "Enmity can be unraveled; it can not be tied and knotted. You killed me once before, if I kill you today, in the next life you will kill me again: when can it end? Today I will release you so as to break the chain. If, however, you stay here, you will surely be dispatched by the cavalry following. Come with me and we'll go together."

After which he let Zhang follow him for several days and only when the danger had past did he send him on his way. Master Ding came from north of the Yellow River and was a conscript in the Jurchen army.

These three stories were all told by Chen Jiruo.[49]

The above two narratives not only share the same plot, even sections of dialogue correspond verbatim: they are clearly different versions of the same story. Yet the spatial setting and personal names differ. One is set in Lin'an (Hangzhou at the time of the supposed event), while the other is set in Huzhou. While the *Record* story is set in the Jianyan period 建炎 (1127–1130), which saw the extinction of the Northern Song, the date of the *Record of Hearsay* story is unclear; although it certainly relates to events surrounding a Jurchen invasion—probably the Jianyan period, given that the author, He Wei, died in 1145. Hence, at least in regard to the temporal setting, there would seem to be no overt discrepancy.

Given the *Record of Hearsay*'s publishing year, while Hong Mai probably began work on the *Jia zhi* in 1143, it is highly likely that this story was in oral circulation around the time of writing. I have not, however, been able to locate any biographical information regarding Hong's said informant, Chen Jiruo 陳季若. As with the stories about the silkworms, although these two are clearly derived from the same source, there are enough minor discrepancies to strongly suggest oral storytelling. Yet it seems strange that Hong did not cite this parallel text when we know that he was familiar with the contents of the *Record of Hearsay*, given that he cited several parallel texts from it (see Appendix 1). Perhaps this is because, as I suggested in chapter 2, Hong did not begin to pay careful attention to parallel texts until after he received the actual criticism alluded to in the preface to the third installment. Or, alternatively, the text of the *Record of Hearsay* as Hong knew it was different from our present edition.

There is, of course, the possibility that Hong deliberately adapted it without due citation. Given that he spent eighteen years on the writing of the first installment where the account is found, he would have had ample time in which to adapt old accounts had he wished to do so—as opposed to later on when he began producing them by the month.

I would, however, be inclined to argue that Hong's account was derived from oral sources, given the degree to which the two accounts vary. Perhaps the discrepancy in regard to spatial setting and personal names is due to the imperfect memory of the storyteller, Chen Jiruo. Yet, as with the account about Xu Guohua, the partly verbatim-corresponding dialogues are intriguing. Perhaps Chen Jiruo was able to easily memorize parts of the dialogues since he heard them recited by professional storytellers. Regardless of how Hong came to have heard it and its mode of transmission, the disparity between the spatial setting and the personal names demonstrates that the *Record*—contrary to Hong's professed aspiration—was not always "reliable."

There is another precursor text which shares so many narrative syntagms and micromotifs with a text from the *Record* that the former would seem to be the source of the latter regardless of mode of transmission. In this case, as with the sutra story discussed above, it is uncertain whether Hong was aware of the existence of the precursor text in question. I will present translations of the two accounts below, starting with the *Record* account.

THIRD DAUGHTER XIE

Zhao Feng was commander of the rear in the army at Xingzhou. It was in the spring of the twenty-seventh year in the Period of Continued Ascendancy (1157) when, under orders from the commander-in-chief, he embarked upon an inspection tour of the prefecture's troops. Upon reaching Guozhou, he took up residence at the official's rest house in Nanchong. There he ordered his attendants to set up a camp bed for him in the hall.

The rest house keeper came forward. "The hall is haunted," he warned. "People always hear the sound of crying in the night. Guests usually avoid the hall. Most dare not go anywhere near it. Instead they stay in the west pavilion."

Feng laughed, "I am afraid of ghosts?"

Defiantly, he insisted on sleeping in the hall. When night descended, he heard the sound of sobbing drifting in from outside, as if something was coming right up to the place where he slept.

Feng rebuked it, saying, "Do you have an injustice to report? Speak, and I will put it right for you. Otherwise, make haste and leave!"

It went away. After a while, however, it came again. His attendants all heard footsteps—a hesitant tip-toeing. The following day Feng told the prefect, Wang Zhongfu. But Wang thought that he was jesting.

That evening, Feng attended a prefectural banquet and night had fallen by the time he returned. He was still experiencing the warmth of intoxication. Unable to sleep, he rested on a folding chair. Thereupon the image of a girl, hair disheveled, materialized before him. "I am the third daughter of Controller-general Xie," she said. "My name is Lotus Slave. I am originally from the central provinces, but I came to Sichuan during the time of trouble.[50] I lost my life in the household of Li Zhai who was with the Horse Trading Bureau, and I lived within these very walls."

"Li had a daughter who married Prefect Ma's son, Shaojing, and she took me along as her hand-maiden. Unfortunately, on account of my beauty, I was secretly favored by Master Ma. Madam Li informed her father who had me beaten to death. While there was still life left in me, he ordered a large pit dug. He had me thrown in and buried. Thirty years have since elapsed. I hope that your Excellency will take pity on me and help me to attain reincarnation."

"You have been dead for a long time now," Feng said. "Officials of high rank pass through here everyday. Why did you not bring forward your case earlier?"

To this she replied, "Never for a moment did I forget that my forlorn bones were in need of proper burial. But there are deities on guard in this world who do not allow us to venture out too often. Ten years ago I shed tears in the night in the hope of coming out to make my plaint. The earth god said to me, 'One day a General Zhao will come here. That will be your time to attain justice.' Both day and night have I stood sentinel, waiting for you to arrive. This is why I now make so bold a request of you."

To this Feng replied, "Since this is the case, I will look into the matter for you."

The girl thanked him and took her leave. Feng dispatched people in her wake to see where she went. But, having reached the wall outside the hall, she disappeared without trace.

On the following day, Feng called upon monks to chant Buddhist sutras and perform rites for her, after which he went on his way. By nightfall he had arrived at Dongguan County in Tongchuan, where he broke his journey at the county rest house. The girl came to him again, only this time her hair was arranged into a high bun.

Feng said to her, "I have already performed a Buddhist ritual for you. Why do you pursue me?"

"Your excellency's gift is great indeed," replied the girl. "But my pallid bones still lie beneath the wall outside the hall. Who will be able to recover them, if your excellency does not?"

Feng demurred, saying, "I was but a mere guest there, and I have already taken my leave. How can I possibly make an effort on your behalf now? Why don't you take the matter up with the Prefect, Director Wang?"

To this she said, "It is not that I am unaware of this. There are, however, gods who dwell beside the official gateway and refuse entry for common-place matters. Yes, Director Wang is the only one able to deal with my injustice. But should your excellency refuse to act as my champion in this matter, then how can I possibly reach him?"

"If my bones are not recovered, I cannot be re-born. The recovery of my bones and my rebirth depend on a mere hint dropped in your excellency's conversation with the prefect."

Once again, Feng assented and sent a footman to relate the matter to Prefect Wang. Wang, for his part, sought out those attendant soldiers employed by Li during his time in office. The only one was Tan Yong. Wang therefore delegated to him the task of recovering the bones.

Yong led a dozen or more soldiers to the wall who set about digging for the remains. Nevertheless, after two days of toil they had not discovered their whereabouts. Thus Yong called upon a sorceress. This sorceress called herself the "Sacred Woman" and could act as a medium for spirits.

In a screeching voice, she rebuked Yong, saying, "You buried me with your own hands at the time. Can you truly have forgotten my resting place? It is right here, where you have been digging. I lie not far beneath the surface. When you threw me in, you covered my body with a wooden bed. The wood is still there. Recover the wood, and the bones will follow. Be sure to recover the skull for me, which is furthermost down. If I can not get the skull, I cannot be reborn."

Terrified, Yong confessed his guilt. And sure enough the following day he succeeded in finding the remains. The prefect had these reburied on high ground.

At that time, Shaojing was the deputy prefect of Linshui in Quzhou and was transferred to the post of administrative assistant in Puzhou not long after. There he saw Miss Xie materialize and speak with him of what had transpired that day. Not long after this, Shaojing also followed her to the grave.

Guan Shouqing took up residence in the rest house when he first came as an education officer and it was he who recorded these events. He also said that Shaojing was deputy at the time that Yu Bingfu was prefect of Quzhou.[51]

Here Hong Mai relates an intriguing ghost story and embellishes it with evocative descriptions. The date of alleged events places the story within a few years of the first installment's completion, in which it is located. The place names are all actual ones; Guozhou 果州 is located in present-day Nanchong 南充 (itself mentioned in the account), Sichuan. Hence, in accordance with Hong's stated aim of presenting "factual" stories, this would appear to have been a contemporary account of actual events.

Let us now turn to the piece from the *High-Minded Conversations beneath the Green Lattice Window* (*Qingsuo gaoyi* 青瑣高議, hereafter *High-Minded Conversations*).[52] The *High-Minded Conversations* comprises twenty-seven chapters (including ten chapters of a *houji* 後集 and seven of a *bieji* 別集) and was completed no later than 1077, judging by the latest date mentioned in the text. Publishing details are, however, uncertain. It is a collection of stories and anecdotes on a diverse range of subjects, including many narratives displaying *zhiguai* motifs. Contemporary figures mentioned throughout the text suggest that at least some accounts were written for the benefit of the author's potential patrons and their mentors. The opening account, for example, is a laudatory appraisal of Northern Song official Li Fang 李昉 (925–996). Not all accounts, however, display *zhiguai* motifs and some are extremely short. Others, particularly those located in the *bieji*, could be described as *chuanqi*. Not all the accounts come from the author's hand, in which case authorship is generally acknowledged. Unfortunately, no biographical data about the author, Liu Fu 劉斧, is available.

Master Wei Reburies Forlorn Bones

In the fourth year of the Xining Period (1071), Attendant Gentleman Pi went to take up a posting. The road brought him to the Northern Capital and he took up lodgings in the Military Personnel Bureau for high ranking officers. It was then that he became bed-ridden due to illness. The servants had just brought in medicinal preparations. Then, suddenly, the flames from the fire shot up and the medicine tripod fell to the ground. His lordship was lying down when he saw this, and was rather shaken by it. Soon after a maid, moaning and wailing, fell onto the corridor pavement.

"I am a member of your wife's family," she told him.

At once his lordship brandished a sword and rebuked her. "What demon are you, who dares possess the living?"

The girl replied herself, "I am not a member of your wife's family, I only used this as a means of being received. I am really Xie Honglian.[53] I used to be a second wife. Unfortunately the first wife murdered me as soon as she saw me. She buried my bones here, and I have been unable to be re-born. Since your lordship has come here, I would ask that you devise a plan to remove these forlorn bones."

She spoke no more after this, and the female maid recovered and proved to be alright.

The following day he saw Master Wei and told him everything. "Unburied corpses often have the ability to cause disturbances," pronounced Wei. He then bade officials go in search of the bones. After several days, however, there was not a trace of them.

One night, one of the corvée laborers dreamed of a woman. "My bones are between the kitchen troughs," she said. The laborer told his supervisor, after which they indeed recovered the bones. Yet there was no skull. His lordship thought that she must have met with an unnatural death and so was buried hurriedly. He therefore wrapped them in soft, shiny silk and covered them with colored clothing. He was, nevertheless, mindful that the remains were incomplete since there was no skull.

When a military official came touring from Enzhou, he arrived at the Bureau to see his lordship. His lordship bade him lodge there, and waited for an apparition. It was after midnight, and the moonlight was brilliantly bright. The official saw a woman, without a head, dancing in the garden. The official made enquiries the following day. His lordship gave orders for another search, resulting in the recovery of the skull. He then had a day chosen on which to re-bury the remains on high ground according to protocol.

One night, one of his lordship's retainers, a Mr. Li, dreamed of a woman. Bearing pretty features and clad in splendid apparel, she made obeisance to Mr. Li. "Mine were the forlorn bones from long ago," she told him. "Thanks to Master Wei, my remains have attained repose in dryness and elevation, and the day of my rebirth will come. How can I repay his Lordship's grace by which he had me reburied? Convey my thanks to Master Wei."

"Why go through a third person when you do not thank him yourself?" replied Master Li. "Is it not a trifle disrespectful?"

"I dare not show disrespect," replied the woman. "It is because Master Wei is a public figure, and he is also of elevated position. His residence is protected by guards, and it is due to this that I dare not see him. I therefore sincerely and wholeheartedly implore you."

The following day, Mr. Li conveyed this to Master Wei.[54]

As I noted above, *zhiguai* accounts tended to recycle archetypal macro-motifs even though the plots may have differed somewhat. A shared archetype, however, would not explain the similarities between the above two accounts. The common narrative syntagms strongly suggest that the *Record* account is derived from the *High-Minded Conversations* version, given that the latter was written in the eleventh century. Furthermore, the micromotif of door gods barring a ghost's entry to a building is relatively rare in *zhiguai* literature, as is concern for the recovery of a skull after an unsuccessful initial search. Nor is the shared syntagm about the ghost's appearance—reflecting her changed spiritual state—all that widespread. The combination of all three in the same account makes them all the more rare. Apart from these common features, there are others:

1) The appearance of the ghost of a murdered girl which seeks proper burial.

2) The socioeconomic position of both victim and her mistress.

3) The motive for the murder.

4) Similar sounding names for the ghost.[55]

5) The venue where events unfold, that is, a government residence.

6) The reappearance of the ghost.

The *Record* account therefore, far from being an original narration of near-contemporary events as Hong Mai outwardly intended his audience to have believed (or which he himself believed), was somehow derived from the earlier version.[56]

Oral transmission seems to have played a significant part in this account's telling and retelling, particularly when we consider the similar-sounding name of the ghost. In the *Record* version she is known as Xie Liannu 解蓮奴 (literally "lotus slave"), while in the *Remarkable Opinions* version she is Xie Honglian 謝紅蓮 (literally "red lotus"). The semantic commonality displayed by the given name speaks for itself, although the character meaning "slave" was not an uncommon component of a concubine's name.[57] Perhaps more significant is the homophonic surname, Xie, strongly suggesting oral or part-oral transmission. As I observed in regard the above sutra account, interplay between oral and written sources would certainly not have been improbable, as I will discuss below.

The primary informant for this story was one Guan Qisun 關耆孫 (1148 *jinshi*), courtesy name Shouqing 壽卿, who came from Sichuan and once served as an education official in Guozhou 果州 (modern Nanchong 南充 in Sichuan).[58] He attained a posting as an office manager in the Directorate of Education (*guozi lu* 國子錄) and, in 1166, attained a position as an editorial director (*zhuzuo zuolang* 著作佐郎). He occupied a position as an editor (*jiaoshu lang* 校書郎) in 1167, after which he took up a position as prefect in Jianzhou 簡州 (modern Jianyang 簡陽 in Sichuan).[59] Guan also provided information for other accounts which appear elsewhere in the *Record*.[60]

The other person whom Hong mentions as having known Ma Shaojing 馬紹京 was Yu Yunwen, courtesy name Bingfu 併甫. As I mentioned in chapter 3, he once served as grand councilor under the Xiaozong emperor. Having passed the examinations of 1154, he was called to take up a foreign affairs posting in Lin'an from Quzhou 渠州 in 1158 where he was then acting as a magistrate (at the time, Hong Mai was an official in Lin'an). He served for several terms as vice minister of the Ministry of Rites (*libu langguan* 禮部郎官) as well as a secretariat drafter (*zhongshu sheren* 中書舍人) in the Institute of Academicians (*xueshi yuan* 學士院). He was appointed a councilor to the military (*canmou junshi* 參謀軍事) when the Jurchen invaded in 1161 (Hong Mai was a consultant to the military [*canyi junshi* 參議軍事] at this time) and made a name for himself in the Battle of Caishi (*Caishi zhi jie* 採石之捷) on the eighth day of the eleventh [lunar] month, 1161. After this he served in both military and civil postings.[61] Yu also provided another *Record* account.[62] His father, Yu Qi 虞祺 (cognomen Qinian 齊年, 1115 *jinshi*), was also an official in Sichuan and is featured in another *Record* account.[63]

It is possible to trace this account's transmission immediately prior to its having come to Hong Mai's attention. Toward the conclusion of the account, Hong tells us that it was recorded (i.e., in written form) by Guan Shouqing (most likely during his incumbency in Guozhou). Whether he heard of it from yet another source is, however, unclear. It then seems to have been passed on to Yu Yunwen for, at the conclusion of the eighth account of the chapter in which this account is located, Hong tells us that all eight accounts were told by Yu Yunwen (including this one). This account was possibly widely-circulated and "evolved" with each retelling before having been recorded by Guan Shouqing; both he and Yu Yunwen may have been unaware of the *High-Minded Conversations* version. *High-Minded Conversations* expert Tsiperovitch argues, however, that this work was widely known, although it does not appear in private bibliographical catalogues such as the *Zhizhai shulu jieti* or the *Junzhai dushu zhi*.[64] Nevertheless, it would seem difficult to ascertain its precise circulation at the time of this account's telling. The possibility exists, therefore, that Guan Shouqing heard the story somewhere—most likely in Guozhou during his incumbency—and, unaware of its existence in the *Remarkable Opinions*, passed it on to Hong Mai. The two different homonyms in regard to the concubine's surname certainly support this.

Conversely, the informants for this particular account may have deliberately attempted to deceive Hong. A shred of evidence for this can be found in Hong's metatextual comment—namely Guan Shouqing's assertion that Ma Shaojing was deputy prefect under Yu Yunwen. If the *Record* account was derived from the *Remarkable Opinions*, Ma Shaojing was possibly not an historical figure.[65] Hence, any alleged connection to Ma would seem a fabrication, most likely on the part of Guan Shouqing. Conversely, it is not altogether clear whether this is indicative of isolated embellishment in a tale which Guan had genuinely heard of, or fabrication *in toto*. Alternatively, if Ma did exist, his name may have been appended to the account in a manner akin to malicious gossip, or else to lend the story an air of factuality by connecting it to a (presumably) known figure. This may well be the type of "slander" Hong referred to in the preface of the third installment. If so, it would not be unlike the manner in which the anonymous author of *Tale of the White Ape* (*Baiyuan zhuan*) appropriated the *zhiguai* motif of apes abducting women in order to slander Ouyang Xun's (557–641) parentage.

While it is improbable that Hong Mai consciously adapted the *Remarkable Opinions* account, given his scruples as an historian and the strong possibility that oral telling played a role in the account's transmission, it is unclear whether his informants knowingly deceived him or whether they themselves were unaware of the story's existence in the *High-Minded Conversations* and were simply passing on a story which contemporary Western scholars might understand as something akin to a folktale. Nevertheless, assuming that the latter account was somehow derived from the former, the disparity displayed by the spatio-temporal setting and the personal names undermines the Southern Song context of Hong Mai's account. Hence, here is another example of what Hong Mai himself alerted us to in his prefaces.

As we can see, many accounts that came to be recorded in the *Record* were circulated orally. And, according to the *Record of a Drunken Man's Talk*, which I cited in chapter 1, there would seem to have been a complex interplay between the written and the oral in regard to both professional and amateur storytelling. Given that so many accounts were in oral circulation before being transformed into written form by Hong, one cannot expect an inviolable original akin to modern constructs of intellectual property. Nevertheless, Hong strived for what he claimed was a "reliable" record that was based on "something." He also painstakingly footnoted precursor texts and questionable material. Even so, Chen Zhensun charged Hong with replicating *in toto* numerous accounts from the *Extensive Records*. All this suggests that—by the Song—expectations generated by an oral storytelling culture had begun to change to those of a text-based one. The heightened development of print culture brought about by cheaper book imprints and technological innovation (such as the unprecedentedly widespread use of bamboo paper) may well have contributed to this changing attitude.

For the most part, Hong was a reasonably reliable recorder of events, and his attempts to verify what he intimated to be the factuality of his accounts certainly went beyond previous authors of *zhiguai* or unofficial history who were content to merely footnote their informant or attend to spatio-temporal settings. To be sure, the assertions found in his prefaces are supported by internal textual evidence. Hong, therefore, was not a *fictor* in the modern Western sense or otherwise. Nevertheless, given that he was compiling a large compendium on social history and collected material from a variety of disparate sources, the inclusion of the unreliable was, by his own admission, inevitable. Modern scholars who utilize the text for secondary studies would do well to bear this in mind, although the *Record* undoubtedly displays much verisimilitude in regard to then-contemporary life and religious ideas. Yet the spatio-temporal settings, as well as personal names, cannot in all cases be relied upon. It would, therefore, seem fitting to close this chapter with the words of Zhou Mi:

> . . . When Hong Jinglu wrote the book of *Yijian*, he could not avoid including unreliable stories given his desire for quantity. This was [all] due to an over-zealous curiosity toward the paranormal.[66]

Postscript

As stated at the beginning of this volume, the *Record* is not a text—or series of texts—about which one can easily formulate generalizations. The vastness of the corpus, the variety of accounts in terms of quality and form, in addition to the catholic nature of its motifs, all work against comprehensive hypotheses. Its very genre, compounded by its marginal status in traditional bibliographic catalogues of the imperial period, defies unambiguous categorization. And while Hong's methods seemed not unlike those of unofficial historians, his exuberance toward the strange—and the consequent stigma attached to such pursuits—further ensured the work's marginality.

Hong's professed claim of historical reliability and his ever-increasing efforts to verify information told him no doubt created controversy during his lifetime. And anonymous criticism addressed in certain prefaces seems to have been genuine. We have seen how Hong's collecting of accounts from both oral and written sources displayed a remarkable degree of accuracy when compared to parallel texts and official documents. Yet—by Hong's own admission—the *Record* was not immune to the unreliable. This came in many forms, from outright fictitious tales whereby informants attempted to dupe him for a joke, to others whose spatio-temporal frames proved untrue—perhaps partly due to the imperfect memories of his informants. In other cases, accounts containing unreliable details amounted to slander (libel)—whether deliberately intended by the informant or not. And no doubt the many accounts akin to Buddhist and Taoist miracle tales were so integrally linked to the economic survival of both the Buddhist and Taoist churches that their telling was likely to have provided compelling motivation for fabrication. This was not something which Hong was unaware of, and perhaps is not surprising. Yet, rather than make assumptions about textual historicity—or lack of it—I have explored these issues carefully so as to more fully understand this crucial aspect of the text and its making, given its importance as a source for Song social history.

No doubt Hong's renown as a scholar, author, historian, and high-ranking official from an eminent lineage enhanced the *Record*'s reputation. The vast size of the collection would also certainly have reflected and contributed to its widespread popularity, especially in the 1160s when several editions of the inaugural installment were published. Its form inherited the aesthetic tradition of the Tang *chuanqi* and *zhiguai*, yet Hong did not develop his craft further by introducing stylistic innovation. Perhaps the genre had already reached its zenith by Hong's lifetime, in which case Pu Songling's achievement with his innovative *Liaozhai zhiyi* is all the more remarkable.

If we were to consider the *Record*'s unique place among works of a similar genre, perhaps more than anything else, this lies in its reflection of Song society. Specifically, the strong nationalistic sentiment woven into the very fabric of the text marks the *Record* apart from works of earlier or later periods. The surprisingly high number of accounts featuring lightning as a retributive agent, and the way in which Hong often linked this to filial piety, was also not often seen in similar works which—again—reflected the growing importance of lightning cults since the Five Dynasties. Accounts about Taoists echo the importance placed on Taoism by several of the Song emperors, yet the strong Buddhist element discernable in numerous others suggests that Buddhism was still greatly influential during this period. It is little wonder, therefore, that the literati of the Yuan and Ming turned to the *Record* in their attempts to resurrect a Song culture, adapting so many of Hong's accounts for pieces of drama or vernacular short stories, an influence which can be traced right up to the writing of the *Liaozhai*.

Notes

PREFACE

1. Perhaps influenced by Lu Xun, Guo Zhenyi and Liu Yeqiu also argue for this hypothesis. See Guo Zhenyi, *Zhongguo xiaoshuo shi* (Hong Kong: Taixing shuju, 1961), and Liu Yeqiu, *Gudian xiaoshuo luncong* (Beijing: Zhonghua shuju, 1959). Also, see Shimura Ryoji, "shōsetsu no hatsusei," in *Chūgoku bunka sōsho* 5: *Bungakushi*, ed. Suzuki Shōji et. al (Tokyo: Taishūkan shoten, 1967), 97–107; Takeda Akira, "shikai, denki," in *Chūgoku bunka sōsho* 4: *Bungaku gairon*, ed. Suzuki Shōji et. al (Tokyo: Taishūkan shoten, 1967), 215–28; and *Chūgoku setsuwa to kōshōsetsu* (Tokyo: Daizō shōin, 1992).

2. See Carl Gustav Jung, "The Psychological Foundations of Belief in Spirits," in *Collected Works* (New York: Pantheon, 1960), 8: 301–18. Translated from "Die psychologischen Grundlagen des Geisterglaubens," in *Über psychische Energetik und das Wesender der Trüeme* (Zurich: Rascher, 1948).

3. Mark Elvin, "The Man Who Saw Dragons: Science and Styles of Thinking in Xie Zhaozhe's Fivefold Miscellany," *Journal of the Oriental Society of Australia* (Sydney) 25–26 (1993–1994): 1–41.

4. See Robert Hymes, *Way and Byway: Taoism, Local Religion, and Models of Diversity in Sung and Modern China* (Berkeley and Los Angeles: University of California Press, 2002), 12–13.

5. See Wang, Teh-yi's "Hung Jung-chai hsien-sheng nien-p'u," in *Songshi yanjiu ji* 宋史研究集 (Taipei: Zhonghua congshu weiyuanhui, 1964), 2: 405–74 (originally published in *Yu-shih hsüeh-pao* 3.2 [April 1961]: 1–63). This was based on eminent Qing Dynasty historian Qian Daxin's 錢大昕 (1728–1804) biography, "Hung Wen-min kung nien p'u," in *Ssu Hung Nien P'u*. Hung Ju-k'uei (1909); Wang Nianshuang 王年雙, *Hong Mai shengping ji qi Yijian zhi zhi yanjiu* 洪邁生平及其夷堅志之研究 (unpublished Ph.D. diss., Taipei: Chengche University, 1988); Ch'ang Fu-jui, *La vie et L'oeuvre de Hung Mai (1123–1202)* (unpublished Ph.D. diss., University of Paris V11, 1971)—the location of this dissertation is presently unknown; Ch'ang Fu-jui's chapter on Hong Mai in *Sung Biographies*, ed. Herbert Franke (Wiesbaden: Steiner, 1976), 469–78.

CHAPTER ONE

1. *Liezi*: 5: 6a. The translation is A. C. Graham's. See *The Book of Lieh-tzu* (London: J. Murray, 1960), 68.

2. Hong Mai, *Yijian zhi* (Taipei: Wenming shuju, 1994), 2: 537. The page numbers in this edition all correspond to those of the Beijing Zhonghua shuju edition of 1981.

3. *Wuyou xiansheng* 烏有先生. Literally "this person does not exist." The term was first used in Sima Xianru's 司馬相如 rhapsody "Zixu fu" 子虛賦 ("Sir Fantasy").

4. Hong Mai (1994), preface to the *Yi zhi*, 186.

5. For a survey of Hong's known informants, see Wang Nianshuang, 231–340. For an alphabetical index, see Alister David Inglis, "Informants of the *Yijian zhi*," *Journal of Sung-Yuan Studies* 32 (2002): 83–125.

6. While mindful not to speak for the Song literati, I am grateful to Wilt Idema for this perceptive remark.

7. For an in-depth discussion of oral history and storytelling, see Jan Vansina, *Oral Tradition as History* (Madison, WI: University of Wisconsin Press, 1985). Also, see Jack Goody, *The Interface between the Written and the Oral* (Cambridge: Cambridge University Press, 1987), especially 170.

8. There are different versions of the same account in Guo Tuan's 郭彖 (fl. ca. 1165) *Kuiche zhi* 睽車志 (*A Cartload of Ghosts*), for example. This is a collection of short classical stories, many of which display paranormal motifs. The surviving corpus comprises six chapters and it was initially published at approximately the same time as the first installment of the *Record*. For the reference to parallel texts it shares with the *Record*, in addition to other examples, see Appendix 1.

9. Dangtu 當塗 was an alternative name for Taiping zhou 太平州 (modern Dangtu in Jiangsu) where Hong served as a provincial official from 1189–1190. See Wang Teh-yi (1964), 2: 464–65.

10. Modern Jinan 濟南 in Shandong Province.

11. Modern Luoyang in Henan Province.

12. Hong Mai (1994), 1818.

13. The character "liao" 潦 in this name—as it appears in the 1981 edition of the text—is incorrect and should be "zhen" 溱. Wu Zhen 吳溱, courtesy name Boqin 伯秦 (dates uncertain), was from Poyang 鄱陽. His father's name was Wu Liangshi 吳良史 (dates uncertain). For a brief biographical account, see Wang Nianshuang, 258–59. Lü Deqing 呂德卿, courtesy name Lü Danian 呂大年, was the grandson of the early Shaoxing period grand councilor, Lü Yihao 呂頤浩 (1071–1139) and was himself an active official during this period. For a brief biographical account, see Wang Nianshuang, 261.

14. Wu Zhen provided the material for chapters 7, 8, and 9 of the *Zhigeng zhi* (see Hong Mai [1994], 1211), in addition to a story in chapter 6 of the same installment (see Hong Mai [1994], 1180). Lü Deqing provided the initial ten accounts of chapter 5 of the *Zhigeng zhi* (Hong Mai [1994], 1173), as well as the material for the whole of chapter 3 of the same installment (Hong Mai [1994], 1161). In addition to this, he provided numerous accounts for other installments.

15. Hong Mai (1994), 1135.

16. Luo Ye, *Xinbian zuiweng tanlu* 新編醉翁談錄 (Shanghai: Gudian wenxue, 1957), 1: 3 (*xiaoshuo kai pi* 小說開闢). Cited in Jaroslav Prusek, "Urban Centers: Cradle of Popular Fiction," in *Studies in Chinese Literary Genres*, ed. Cyril Birch (Berkeley: University of California Press, 1974), 283–84.

17. Chen Rihua was also a known contributor to the *Yijian zhi*, having contributed the account that is now found in the *Sanji zhi* 7: 1352

18. See Barend ter Haar, "Newly Recovered Anecdotes from Hong Mai's (1123–1202) *Yijian zhi*," *Journal of Sung-Yuan Studies* 23 (1993): 21.

19. Kang Baocheng 康保成, "*Yijian zhi* jiyi jiuze," 夷堅志輯佚九則 *Wenxian* 29 (1986): 21–24; Cheng Hong 程弘, "Guanyu *Yijian zhi* yiwen ji 'Dongchuan shifan,'" 關於夷堅志佚聞及東窗事犯 *Wenxian* 文獻 32 (1987): 285–86; Li Yumin 李裕民, "*Yijian zhi* buyi sanshi ze," 夷堅志補佚三十則 *Wenxian* 文獻 46 (1990): 172–84; Wang Hsiu-huei 王秀惠, "Guji yu dian'nao fenxi yunyong—yi *Yijian Zhi* wei li," 古籍與電腦分析運用—以夷堅志爲例 *Hanxue yanjiu tongxun* 漢學研究通訊 14, no. 2 (June 1989b): 163–83, and "Vingt-sept Recits Retrouves du *Yijian Zhi*," *T'oung Pao* 75 (1989a): 191–202; Li Jianguo 李建國, *Songdai zhiguai chuanqi xulu* 宋代志怪傳奇敘錄 (Tianjin: Nankai daxue chubanshe, 1997) and *Tianjin jiaoyu xueyuan xuebao* 天津教育學院學報 2 (1992); Zhao Zhangchao 趙章超, "*Yijian zhi* yiwen xiaoji," 夷堅志佚文小輯 *Wenxian* 4 (2004): 134–38.

20. Yuan Haowen was something of an unofficial historian. According to the *Yiwen zhuan* 藝文傳 (*xia* 下) of the *History of the Jin* (*Jinshi* 金史), he built a pavilion and named it the *Yeshi ting* 野史亭, meaning the *Unofficial History Pavilion*, in which he worked (ironically) on the official *Jinshi*. The *Yijian zhi*'s connection with unofficial history will be discussed in this and later chapters, hence my interest in Yuan Haowen.

21. The story about how a boatman foiled an attempt by pestilence demons to infect a rural community in Pu Songling's 蒲松齡 *Liaozhai zhi yi* shares an identical plot with one in the *Record*. See the *Liaozhai zhiyi huijiao, huizhu, huiping ben*, ed. Zhang Youhe, rev. ed. (rpt. Shanghai: 1986), 8: 1139–40. For the parallel text in the *Record*, see Hong Mai, *Jia*: 5: 226–27. For a detailed study of the *Yijian zhi*'s influence on later literature, see Chang Fu-jui's "L'Influence du *Yi-kien Tche* sur les Oeuvres Litteraires," in *Etudes d'histoire et de littérature offertes au Professeur Jaroslav Prusek*, ed. Yves Hervouet (Paris: 1976), 51–61.

22. Hong Mai (1994), *Yi*: 8: 250. The translation is Hansen's. See Valerie Hansen, *Changing Gods in Medieval China, 1127–1276* (Princeton, NJ: Princeton University Press, 1990), 171–72.

23. Ibid.

24. See, for example, Judith Magee Boltz, "Not by the Seal of Office Alone: New Weapons in Battle with the Supernatural," in *Religion and Society in T'ang and Sung China*, ed. Patricia Buckley Ebrey and Peter N. Gregory (Honolulu: University of Hawaii Press, 1993), 241–305.

25. Hong Mai's mother's maiden name.

26. *Yi*: 10: 270

27. See Appendix 1.

28. For a study on Hong Hao's influence over Hong Mai, see Suzuki Kiyoshi 鈴木靖, "Kō Kō to Kō Mai," 洪皓と洪邁 *Hosei daiguku Kyoyōbu kiyō jimbun kagakuhen* 74 (1990), 1–17. Suzuki contends that Hao did act as the inspiration for the *Record*. Barend ter Haar has also raised this possibility. See Barend ter Haar, 21.

29. Tuo Tuo et al., *Song shi* (Beijing: Zhonghua shuju, 1977), 33: 11560–61.

30. *Zhijing*: 8: 944.

31. The formation of "snuff-flowers" referred to an unusual twisting of the wick and was thought to be an auspicious omen. In an occasional poem written for New Year's Eve, 1084, eminent Song poet Su Shi wrote: "Lone lamp—I wonder why—forms a flower. In the middle of the night you send us cakes and wine." *Su Shi shiji* 24: 1303. See Burton Watson, *Su Tung-p'o: Selections from a Sung Dynasty Poet* (New York: Columbia University Press, 1965), 103. Cited in Katherine Kerr, *The Yijian zhi: An Alternate Perspective* (unpublished Ph.D. diss., University of Sydney, 1998), 57.

32. Heng'e was a mythical figure who stole an elixir of immortality and fled to the moon. The name is usually rendered as Chang'e, but in this poem it is written as Heng'e so as to observe the taboo associated with the name of Han Dynasty emperor Wudi (r. 140 B.C.E.–85 B.C.E.).

33. Hong Mai (1994), 944.

34. See Appendix 2.

35. *Yi*: 8: 253.

36. See Appendix 2.

37. See Hong Mai's preface to the *Zhigeng zhi* (the seventeenth installment), 1135. In this, Hong writes that the *Zhigeng* installment was completed in forty-four days from the *gengwu* day of the tenth month to the *guichou* day of the twelfth month. The *gengwu* day refers to the seventh day in the traditional sixty-day cycle, while *guichou* refers to the fiftieth. Hong's method of counting in this case clearly includes the *gengwu* day.

38. Ibid., 185.

39. I am grateful to Anne McLaren for suggesting this possibility.

40. Based on records from the *Songhuiyao jigao* 宋會要集稿, Okamoto Fujiaki identifies a round of prefectural examinations in 1160 as one whose board of examiners was headed by Zhu Zhuo 朱倬. Apart from Hong Mai himself, eleven (twelve actual) out of thirty examiners who were known *Yijian zhi* informants were isolated for approximately forty days due to the supervision of the examination. Supposing that 1160 was the year of completion for the *Jia zhi*, stories provided by the majority of these informants are, as one would expect, found in later chapters of the *Jia zhi*. Because of this, as well as thematic (imperial exams and the *zhiguai*) and spatial (venue) considerations, Okamoto surmises that at least two of the stories in chapter 18 of the *Jia zhi* were told to Hong Mai during this time. See Okamoto Fujiaki 岡本不二明, "Kuiche zhi yu Yijian Zhi; kexue yu zhiguai zhiyi," 睽車志" 與 "夷堅志—"科學與志怪" 之一, trans. Wang Zhizhong and Lu Zhonghui, *Gansu shehui kexue* 甘肅省社會科學 6 (1995): 88–90. This article first appeared in Kagoshima Kenritsu Tanki Daigaku jinbun gakkai ronshu *Jinbun* 鹿兒島縣立短期大学人文学会論集 "人文" 13 (June 1989).

41. See Luo Dajing's 羅大經 *Conversations Carried on at He Lin* (*Helin yulu* 鶴林玉露), quoted from Ding Chuanjing 丁傳靖, *Songren Yishi Huibian* 宋人軼事彙編 (*A Compilation of Anecdotes of Sung Personalities*), trans. Djang Chu and Jane Djang (Jamaica, NY: St. John's University Press, 1989), 650–51.

42. See the *biji*, or miscellaneous notebook work, the *Sichao wenjian lu* 四朝聞見錄. The relevant section has been preserved in Ding Chuanjing. A translation appears in Djang Chu and Jane Djang, 653–54.

43. Chen Junqing provided Hong with an account which appeared in the first installment of the *Record*. See Hong Mai (1994), *Jia*: 15: 135.

44. See Ch'ien Ta-hsin's "Hung wen-min kung nien-p'u," ch. 1. Cited and translated in Djang Chu and Jane Djang, 652–53. Reproduced with permission from Djang Chu.

45. Lu Xun, *Zhongguo xiaoshuo shilüe* (Beijing: 1973), 242.

46. *Zhiwu zhi*: 8: 1114. For a discussion on the Masha printing village during the Song, see Lucille Chia, *Printing for Profit: The Commercial Publishers of Jianyang, Fujian (11th–17th Centuries)* (Cambridge, MA and London: Harvard-Yenching, 2002), particularly 6, 8, 17, and 116–26.

47. This refers to the traditional method of counting days according to the system of earthly branches and heavenly stems. The *gengwu* day refers to the seventh day in the (sixty-day) cycle, while *guichou* refers to the fiftieth.

48. Documented in chapter 20 of the *Qidong yeyu*. Cited and translated in Djang Chu and Jane Djang, 651–52.

49. Hong Mai (1994), 1819–20.

50. The Chinese phrase is *sansheng jieyuan* 三生結願. This is a Buddhist term, linked to reincarnation, which expresses a wish to be married to one's spouse for three incarnations.

51. This is known in Chinese as the *xiongjing chigu* method 熊經鴟顧 in which one was supposed to meditate in a position resembling a bear climbing a tree combined with the look of an owl that glances around without moving the rest of its body. It was thought to be beneficial for attaining long life and good health.

52. Hong Mai (1994), 1820–21.

CHAPTER TWO

1. See Liu Langming, "Hong Mai dui zhiguai xiaoshuo lilun pipingde lishixing gongxian," 洪邁對志怪小說理論的歷史性貢獻 *Wuhan daxue xuebao* 武漢大學學報 (*zhexue shehui kexue ban* 哲學社會科學版) 6 (1996): 93–98.

2. It is unclear whether Hong is referring to the metropolis of Fujian or the province here, although it is most likely the latter.

3. 婺州 (modern Zhejiang).

4. The Southern Song capital (Hangzhou), which literally means "temporary peace," reflecting a hopeful facade on the part of the Southern Song court that the Northern territories lost to the Jurchen would be regained. This was, of course, never realized.

5. Qi Xie 齊諧 is spoken of in the *Xiaoyao you* 逍遙游 section of the *Zhuangzi*, where he/it is linked with the term *zhiguai*. Its significance lies in its being the earliest

recorded instance of the term *zhiguai*. There is no agreement among ancient commentators as to whether the name Qi Xie refers to a literary work of what might now be understood as akin to the *zhiguai* genre or to an author of such a work. For a discussion of the evidence, see Chen Guying , *Zhuangzi jinzhu jinyi* 莊子今註今譯 (Beijing: Zhonghua Shuju, 1983), 3. Chen contends that Qi Xie is the name of a literary work, meaning "The Riddles of Qi" 齊諧.

6. The Taoist philosophical classic.

7. Gan Bao 干寶 (fl. ca. 317) was known to have been appointed as an official historian by Emperor Yuan 元 of the Jin Dynasty (317–322). His *Soushen ji* 搜神記 is generally considered the archetypal *zhiguai* work. In the preface, Gan calls attention to the existence of spirits after alleged personal experiences with the paranormal. See Kenneth DeWoskin, "The Six Dynasties *Zhiguai* and the Birth of Fiction," in *Chinese Narrative: Critical and Theoretical Essays*, ed. Andrew Plaks (Princeton: Princeton University Press, 1977), 22. See also Campany, 55.

8. Niu Sengru 牛僧儒 (779–848) was a political figure and attained the office of prime minister in 823. His *Xuanguai lu* 宣怪錄 contains many *zhiguai* motifs and subsequent writers of *zhiguai* have acknowledged their debt to him. See Karl S. Y. Kao, *Classical Chinese Tales of the Supernatural and the Fantastic* (Bloomington, IN: Indiana University Press, 1985), 387–88.

9. The *Boyi zhi* 博異志. Gu Shenzi 谷神子 literally means "master of the spirit of the valley" and is a pen name. In its preface, the author states his desire to remain anonymous due to the veiled political and social comment which underpinned the work's *zhiguai* content. The author's true identity has not been generally agreed on. Hu Yinglin thought him to be Zheng Huangu 鄭還古 (doctoral degree holder during the Yuanhe period 元和 [806–820] of the Xianzong 憲宗 emperor during the Tang Dynasty [618–906]). For further discussion, see Hou Zhongyi, 侯忠義, *Sui, Tang, Wudai xiaoshuo shi* 隨唐五代小說史 (Zhejiang: Zhejiang guji chubanshe, 1997), 119.

10. The *Hedong ji* 河東記, 3 chapters, by Xue Yusi 薛漁思. The *Junzhai dushu zhi* 郡齋讀書志 catalogue states that the *Hedong ji* records *zhiguai* tales and that it was modeled on Niu Sengru's work, i.e., the *Xuanguai lu*. Although the work had been lost by Hong's time, it was partly preserved in the *Extensive Records*. Due to the number of stories set during the Dahe 大和 period (827–835) of the Tang, it can be inferred that the work was written after this period, possibly in the middle of the ninth century.

11. Zhang Du's 張讀 (834–886?) *Xuanshi zhi* 宣室志. Written between 851 and 874, the content is concerned with gods, ghosts, and retribution. Ten chapters are extant with an additional supplementary one. It takes its title from the venue of the conversation reported to have taken place between Emperor Wu of the former Han Dynasty (206 B.C.E.–8 C.E.) and the *fangshi* (exorcist, or master of esoterica), Jia Yi 賈誼, about gods and ghosts.

12. Xu Xuan's 徐鉉 (915–991) *Jishen lu* 稽神錄 (*Examining Spirits*).

13. The original term is *yuyan* 寓言, literarlly "lodged words," which I have translated as "allegory." For further discussion of this concept as it is applied to premodern Chinese literature, see Charles Hartman's discussion in William Nienhauser Jr., *The Indiana Companion to Chinese Literature* (Bloomington, IN: Indiana University Press, 1986), 946–49. Also see Andrew Plaks, *Archetype and Allegory in the Dream*

of the Red Chamber (Princeton, NJ: Princeton University Press, 1976), particularly chapters 5 and 6.

14. *Wuyou xiansheng* 烏有先生. Literally "this person does not exist." The term was used in Sima Xianru's 司馬相如 rhapsody "Zixu fu" 子虛賦 ("Sir Fantasy").

15. 建安 Modern Jian'ou 建甌 in Fujian Province.

16. See Hartman in William Nienhauser Jr., 946–47.

17. Cited in Pauline Yu, *The Reading of Imagery in the Chinese Poetic Tradition* (Princeton, NJ: Princeton University Press, 1987), 21.

18. See Angus Fletcher, *Allegory, the Theory of a Symbolic Mode* (Ithaca, NY: Cornell University Press, 1964).

19. Andrew Plaks, 1976, 146.

20. Handscroll, ink and color on silk, 11 5/8 x 32 5/8 in. (29.5 x 827 cm), collection of the Metropolitan Museum of Art, New York.

21. Handscroll mounted as an album leaf, ink and color on silk, 9 7/8 x 22 in. (25 x 55.8 cm). Denman Waldo Ross Collection, Museum of Fine Arts, Boston.

22. For a discussion of both these paintings, see Wen C. Fong, *Beyond Representation: Chinese Painting and Calligraphy 8th–14th Century* (New York: Metropolitan Museum of Art; New Haven & London: Yale University Press, 1992), 195–214.

23. Erich Auerbach, "Figura," rpt. in *Scenes from the Drama of European Literature* (Gloucester, MA: Peter Smith, 1973), 29. Quoted from Pauline Yu, 23. For a more detailed discussion of this, see Pauline Yu, 22–24.

24. Ibid., 23.

25. Leo Tak-hung Chan, *The Discourse on Foxes and Ghosts: Ji Yun and Eighteenth-Century Literati Storytelling* (Honolulu: University of Hawaii Press, 1998), 192.

26. This phrase is derived from the *Analects* (the *Yanghuo* 陽貨 chapter [17], 9a). D. C. Lau translates it as: (Confucius responds to a question from Zigong as to whether or not the gentleman harbors dislikes) "He (the gentleman) dislikes those who proclaim the evil in others." Confucius, *The Analects*, trans. D. C. Lau (Harmondsworth, United Kingdom: Penguin, 1979), 148.

27. This refers to narratives which are possibly no longer extant. The only story about a were-bird in the *Jia Zhi* is entitled "Jin Si Catches a Ghost." According to this, a park keeper catches a were-vulture that has been guilty of poaching. See *Jia*: 8: 64.

28. I can find no record of any narrative which resembles this; it would seem to be no longer extant.

29. In this story Feng, courtesy name Shixing 時行, was (no date has been supplied) prefect of Wanzhou 萬州, which was situated in the Kuizhou Route 夔州 (modern Wanxian Shi 萬縣市 in eastern Sichuan). Feng had the temple of a local cult destroyed as he believed the deity to be a ghost in disguise so as to extort offerings from the local populace. After this he was haunted and even experienced a visitation whereby he entered into a conversation with the "deity." During the subsequent haunting, Feng's seven to eight year old son was said to have been tied to a tree by the "deity." The disturbances did not cease until after Feng had left the district. *Bing*: 2: 373.

30. The name Jiang Mao does not appear in Wang Xiumei's index found at the end of the 1981 and 1994 editions, suggesting that this narrative is no longer extant. Fukuda Chikashi is of the same opinion. In fact, Fukuda further suggests that "were-birds" is a title and, along with *Feng Dangke, Huang of Jianchang's Injustice,* and *Matters of Jiang Mao's Heart,* comprise the four accounts which Hong speaks about removing in the postscript at the conclusion of the preface to the *Yi zhi.* See Fukuda Chikashi 福田知可志, "*Ikenshi* jijo o meguru mondai ten," 夷堅志自序をめぐる問題てん *Chūgoku Gakushi: Osaka shiritsu daigaku chūbun gakkai* 中国学志 大阪市立大学中文学会 11 (2000): 119.

31. *Yi*: 1: 190–91.

32. Hong uses the term *haoshi junzi* 好事君子. It is derived from Gan Bao's preface to his *Soushen ji* by which he referred to his readership. It subsequently became widely used to discuss unorthodox pursuits and inferred that the reading and writing of *zhiguai* texts was motivated by personal interest. It has sometimes been translated as "the curious." See William Nienhauser Jr., 281.

33. There is a discrepancy here between Hong's stated 267 and the actual number of 355 contained in the 1981 and 1994 editions. Of these 355, the text of seven is missing and only their titles remain. There is, therefore, a discrepancy between the original *Bing* installment and that which appears in the 1981 and 1994 editions.

34. Zhang Zhuping, "Fan Chengda *Xia Furen* gushi yuanmao ji qi liubian kao," 范成大 俠夫人故事原貌及其流變考 *Wenxue yichan* 文學遺產 4 (1997): 106–109.

35. See ibid., 108. Zhang refers to Hong Mai's comments in the preface to the third (*Bing*) installment whereby Hong cites this account, among others, whose details he later found inaccurate (Hong Mai [1994], 363). Zhang suggests that Hong reedited the conclusion of this account for his 1180 Jianning edition. Zhang further points out that Hong's preface to the second (*Yi*) installment told of a later edition (published in 1172) in which selected accounts had been edited and/or replaced. Although Hong does not supply a reason, Zhang correctly argues that this and later editions included an edited version of the account. And since the 1981 Beijing edition was based on post-1172 editions, the original version never came to the attention of scholars. For further details on this aspect of textual history, see Alister Inglis, *Hong Mai's Yijian zhi and its Song Dynasty Context* (unpublished Ph.D. diss., University of Melbourne, 2002), ch. 2.

36. Hong Mai (1994), 537.

37. Charles Gardner, *Chinese Traditional Historiography* (Cambridge Mass.: Harvard University Press 1961), 64.

38. *Sanshiwan yan* 三十萬言. The actual number of extant stories in the 1981 edition is, however, 1,101 (which includes extant titles whose text is missing).

39. Sima Qian.

40. This refers to the passage in the *Analects of Confucius* which states that Confucius did not talk about "extraordinary things, feats of strength, disturbances, or spirits." See Confucius, 21: 88.

41. Yang Xiong 揚雄 (53 B.C.E.–18 C.E.) is mainly remembered as a talented *fu* poet. He was also an old text author of the *Fayan* 法言 (*Exemplary Sayings*), the *Taixuan jing* 太玄經 (*Classic of Supreme Mystery*), and the *Fangyan* 方言—a collection of

linguistic variata from the periphery of Han civilization, which—ironically, in this context—Campany links to the *zhiguai* tradition. See Campany, 138.

42. Duke Mu of Qin 秦穆公, alternative name *Qin Miao Gong* 秦繆公 (?–621 B.C.E.), was ruler of the State of Qin (r. 659–621 B.C.E.) during the Spring and Autumn period. Zhao Jianzi 趙簡子, alternate name Zhao Yang 趙鞅 (?–475 B.C.E.) was a Regular Chamberlain of the State of Jin 晉 during the Spring and Autumn period. It is recorded in the *Shiji* that both these men experienced comatose states for some days. Upon waking, they reported having experienced prophetic dreams about the political and military future of their respective states. In the case of Zhao Jianzi, he was said to have dreamed of visiting the abode of the supreme deity, Shangdi 上帝, where the deity instructed him to shoot a black and brown bear using a bow and arrow. The deity thereby rewarded him with two caskets of jewels and a Mongolian dog for his son. See Sima Qian, *Shiji* 47 (Beijing: Zhonghua shuju, 1959), 1786–87 (*Zhao shijia di shisan* 趙世家第十三). Also, see Wang Chong 王充, *Lunheng* 論衡, *Qiguai pian* (Shanghai: Shanghai renmin chuban she, 1979), 223–24.

43. According to the *Shiji*, Zhang Liang 張良 (?–180/185 B.C.E.), Marquis of Liu 留侯, met an extraordinary old man who gave him a book about government. After that, he predicted that he would reappear as a yellow stone at the foot of Mt. Gucheng. See Sima Qian, 55: 2034–35.

44. Jing Ke 荊軻 (?–227 B.C.E.) was an assassin of the Warring States period who attempted to assassinate the Qin emperor. See Sima Qian, 86: 2526–38.

45. Xia Wuju 夏無且 (dates uncertain) was an imperial physician to Qin Shihuang (r. 221–209). When Jing Ke went to assassinate the emperor, Xia delayed him and thus bought time for the emperor to draw his sword and strike the would-be assassin. Xia was thereafter rewarded with gold and accolades.

46. See Sima Qian, 55: 2049.

47. It is, in all probability, the true preface to the *Ding zhi* since it tallies with the *Guests Retire*. Perhaps only the last line, clearly originating from the *Wu zhi*, is out of place.

48. Robert Scholes, *Elements of Fiction* (New York: Oxford University Press, 1968), 6. This and the citation below are also found in John C. Y. Wang, "Early Chinese Narrative: The *Tso-chuan* as an Example," in Andrew Plaks, 22. See also Campany, 17.

49. Robert Scholes and Robert Kellogg, *The Nature of Narrative* (London and New York: Oxford University Press, 1968), 72–73.

50. Alan Sinfield, *Faultlines: Cultural Materialism and the Politics of Dissident Reading* (Oxford: Oxford University Press, 1992), 45.

51. Ye Huishu 葉晦叔; Huishu was the style name of Ye An 葉黯, who—at one time—held a position as reviser (*shandingguan* 刪定官). He was an official in Fujian during the Shaoxing period (1131–1162), which concurs with the date of this preface. See Chang Bide, et al., comp., *Index to Bibliographical Materials of Song Figures* (Taipei: Dingwen shuju, 1974), 3243. In the *Rongzhai suibi*, Hong Mai gives the text of a poem written by Ye and tells us that he was a commander (*shuaishu* 帥屬) in Fujian in 1149 (525–526).

52. Hong Mai (1978), *Sibi*: 9: 719.

53. The *Yijian lu* 夷堅錄.

54. Dangtu 當塗 was an alternative name for Taiping zhou 太平州 (modern Dangtu in Jiangsu), where Hong served as a provincial official from 1189–1190. See Wang Teh-yi, 2 (1964), 464–65.

55. Modern Jinan 濟南 in Shandong Province.

56. Modern Luoyang in Henan Province.

57. Bai Juyi 白居易 (772–846), Tang Dynasty poet. Letian 樂天 was his courtesy name.

58. Su Dongpo 蘇東坡, or Su Shi 蘇軾 (1036–1101). It is unclear to which particular stories Hong refers here. Possibly he alludes to the prolific nature of both these author's writings, and draws a comparison between himself and their literary careers.

59. Rongzhai 容齋 was the name of Hong's studio, which literally means the "tolerant studio."

60. Xiang Juyuan's 向巨源 (dates uncertain) other name was Xiang Fan. His native place was Kaifeng. He is the author of the *Guizhai zagao* 癸齋雜稿. What Hong referred to as "questions and answers" is, unfortunately, unclear.

61. I have followed Carrie Reed's translation. See "Motivation and Meaning of a 'Hodge-Podge': Duan Chengshi's *Youyang zazu*," *Journal of the American Oriental Society* 123, no. 1 (2003): especially 1–2.

62. The traditional Chinese method of calculating age includes the foetus's gesticulation period. Furthermore, if a baby was born shortly before the lunar New Year, it would then gain an additional year with the advent of the festival. Hence, a new born could be considered two years old by traditional reckoning. By Western reckoning, Hong would have been seventy, which fits available biographical information.

63. 櫰復 Alternatively pronounced "Guifu." This is the first mention of Hong's youngest son in the *Record* prefaces. His name appears several times in later prefaces and also in the preface to the fourth installment of the *Rongzhai suibi* 容齋隨筆 (2: 613). Furthermore, in the first installment of the same work, Hong discusses having conferred on him official status under his *yin* privileges (1: 121). Wang Teh-yi, Hong's biographer, dates this to 1179. Hence, it can be inferred that Huaifu was born in this year, since Hong told us that he was one *sui* at the time. See Wang Teh-yi, 450. For a discussion on *yin* privileges, whereby officials could confer official status to their offspring and relatives, see Winston Lo, *An Introduction to the Civil Service of Sung China* (Honolulu: University of Hawaii Press, 1987), 102–9.

64. See Wang Teh-yi, 450.

65. This phrase is derived from the *Tangwen* chapter of the *Book of Liezi*. See *Liezi duben* (Taipei: Sanmin shuju, 1979), 153. A. C. Graham translates it as: "But also there is nothing limitless outside what is limitless, and nothing inexhaustible within what is inexhaustible." See Graham, 95. Note that Hong Mai has modified the phrase slightly to better suit the new context.

66. The translation is Wing-tsit Chan's. See *Sources of Chinese Tradition* (New York: Columbia University Press, 1960), 1: 69 and 73 respectively.

67. Ke Gu 軻古 is the style name of Duan Chengshi 段程式 (c. 800–863), author of the *Miscellaneous Morsels from Youyang* (*Youyang zazu* 酉陽雜俎); the title's translation is Carrie Reed's. See Carrie Reed, *A Tang Miscellany: An Introduction to the Youyang*

zazu (New York: Peter Lang, 2003). Duan's father, Duan Wenchang 段文昌 (772–835), the one-time great government minister, procured a position for his son in the imperial library where Chengshi gained access to rare books and secrets which he incorporated into the *Miscellaneous Morsels.*

68. Thirty chapters (including the continuation). This work contains many *zhiguai* motifs and a prominent cosmological focus. According to Schafer, Duan—not unlike Hong Mai—took measures to ascertain the accuracy of reports he received and, at times, expressed doubt about the reliability of some. Hong Mai often mentioned both Duan and his work in both this and other prefaces, suggesting that he was influenced by Duan. More will be said about this below. See Edward Schafer in William Nienhauser Jr., 940–941.

69. For studies on recently recovered stories, see Barend ter Haar. Also Otagi Matsuo, "Kō Mai *Ikenshi* itsubun shui," 洪邁夷堅志逸文拾遺 *Bunka* 文化 29, no. 3 (1965): 472–79.

70. Wing-tsit Chan, *Sources of Chinese Tradition*, ed. Theodore de Bary (New York: Columbia University Press, 1960), 68.

71. A. C. Graham, *Chuang Tzu: The Inner Chapters and Other Writings from the Book of Chuang-Tzu* (London: Allen & Unwin, 1981), 29.

72. Fung Yu Lan, *A History of Chinese Philosophy*, ed. Dirk Bodde (New York: McMillan, 1956), 231.

73. *Chuang tzu: Basic Writings*, trans. Burton Watson (New York: Columbia University Press, 1964).

74. "The Writings of Kwang-3ze," trans. James Legge, in *The Sacred Books of the East*, ed. Max Müller (London: Oxford University Press, reprinted 1927), v. 39.

75. Jack Goody, 170.

76. The *La* Festival was held in the twelfth (lunar) month during this period.

77. Hong Mai took up a posting as prefect in Kuaiji in the second lunar month of this year (1190). His purpose would seem to be a journey home for the *La* Festival. His comments about being too old to read books are supported in the preface he wrote for his anthology of Tang poems, the *Tangren jueju baijuan* 唐人絕句百卷 which was dated the eleventh month of that year. See Wang Teh-yi (1964), 466.

78. Judging from this translation, there seems to have been three installments published concurrently. This, however, is not the case when we look closer at the original text. The verb used here, *xucheng* 緒成, means to complete the unfinished work of others. In this case, I would understand "others" as relatives who brought him stories.

79. Hong Bing 洪炳 (dates uncertain). As noted in chapter 1, he was posthumously awarded the rank of junior guardian 少保 and his wife, Madame He, received the title of Lady Jiguo 紀國夫人.

80. As discussed above, here Hong refers to Duan Chengshi.

81. *Baiguan xiaoshuo jia* 稗官小說家. During the Song, this phrase referred to writers whose works had been traditionally classified as *xiaoshuo*. Originally this term referred to the minor officials of antiquity who collected unofficial, and otherwise unobtainable, information throughout the back-alleys and byways of the empire.

82. Hui Shi 惠施, mentioned in the *Zhuangzi*, was a famous book collector whose collection was supposed to have comprised five cartloads.

83. 庚桑楚 A follower of Zhuangzi; he later became a recluse.

84. This refers to a story from the *Zhiding zhi* in which a scholar from a philanthropic family passes the imperial exams with the help of another scholar. Yet when later checked, no record of the helper could be found. Hong Mai notes his being unable to verify the story in an end commentary at the conclusion of the narrative. See *Zhiding*: 2: 977.

85. This refers to the narrative entitled "Education Officer Liu Gaizhi." See *Zhiding*: 6: 1015–1016.

86. The *Dengke ji* 登科記. Only the records for three years are extant.

87. This refers to a narrative entitled "The Extraordinary Bamboo of Ocean Mountain." It tells of a merchant who brings back an unusual species of bamboo from abroad and sells it for an exorbitant price. The buyers then inform him that it can be used to produce precious stones. In an end-commentary, Hong Mai expresses disbelief. See *Zhiding*: 3: 986–87.

88. This story is no longer extant.

89. Hong Mai (1994), *Zhiding*: 6: 1014–15.

90. The county seat of Qizhou 蕲州 was near the modern city of Qichun 蕲春 in Hubei Province. The account to which Hong refers, entitled "The Four Ancestor's Pagoda" 四祖塔, is found in the *Zhiding zhi* (*Zhiding*: 7: 1020). In this story, an official named Zhang visits the site of the Four Ancestor's Pagoda which had been previously destroyed by marauding troops. During a visit to the Buddha statue which had been housed in a makeshift-type area, the abbot told him about the discovery of a tablet attributed to Guo Pu 郭璞 (276–324). This was thought to foretell of one named Zhang who would visit and rebuild the temple. After this Zhang went and raised money which resulted in the temple's rebuilding (not without anomalous manifestations). In a metatextual comment at the conclusion of the narrative, Hong expresses his disbelief as to the stele's authenticity based on his knowledge of Guo Pu's biography.

91. Guo Jingchun 郭景純 is Guo Pu's courtesy name. Guo was an editor and commentator on the *Classic of Mountains and Seas*.

92. On this principle, see Charles Gardner, *Chinese Traditional Historiography* (Cambridge, MA: Harvard University Press, 1961), 64.

93. This refers to one of the "digest" (*lan* 覽) sections in the *Lüshi chunqiu*. See Lü Buwei 呂不韋, *Lüshi chunqiu* 呂氏春秋 (Taipei: Taiwan zhonghua shuju, 1965), 19: 3b.

94. There were two Duke Zhuangs of Qi 齊莊公. One, named Gou 購, was the son of Duke Cheng 成公 and acceded to the throne in 794 B.C.E. He reigned for sixty-four years and was accorded the posthumous title of Zhuang. The other, to whom Hong refers, was named Guang 光 and was the son of Duke Ling 靈公. He acceded to the throne in 553 B.C.E., taking over from Cui Zhu 崔杼 who was regent. In 548 B.C.E., after six years on the throne, he was assassinated by Cui Zhu after having seduced the latter's wife. Since the Bin Beizhong story follows discourse on Duke Ling, we can be sure that he was the duke in question here.

95. Rania Huntington, "The Supernatural," in *The Columbia History of Chinese Literature*, ed. Victor Mair (New York: Columbia University Press, 2001), 6: 110–11.

96. 蓬萊山. This refers to Mt. Penglai—a mythical mountain thought to be the domain of gods.

97. This refers to the traditional method of counting days according to the system of earthly branches and heavenly stems. As noted in chapter 1, *gengwu* refers to the seventh day in the (sixty-day) cycle, while *guichou* refers to the fiftieth. Of all Hong Mai's statements regarding his speed of production, this is by far the most accurate.

98. The character "liao" 潦 in this name—as it appears in the 1981 edition of the text—is incorrect and should be "zhen" 溱. Wu Zhen 吳溱, courtesy name Wu Boqin 吳伯秦 (dates uncertain), was from Poyang 鄱陽. His father was Wu Liangshi 吳良史 (dates uncertain). For a brief biographical account, see Wang Nianshuang, 258–59. Lü Deqing 呂德卿, courtesy name Lü Danian 呂大年, was grandson of the early Shaoxing period grand councilor, Lü Yihao 呂頤浩 (1071–1139) and was himself an active official. For a brief biographical account, see Wang Nianshuang, 261.

99. Wu Zhen provided the material for chapters 7, 8, and 9 of the *Zhigeng zhi* (see Hong Mai [1994], 1211), in addition to a story in chapter 6 of the same installment (see Hong Mai [1994], 1180). Lü Deqing provided the initial ten accounts for chapter 5 of the *Zhigeng zhi* (Hong Mai [1994], 1173), as well as material for the whole of chapter 3 of the same installment (Hong Mai [1994], 1161). In addition to this, he provided numerous other accounts for other installments.

100. 東坡志林. A work of *biji* literature by Su Shi, this is a collection of Su's thoughts and jottings written over an extended period of time. It is considered important not only for reasons of literary style, but also because of the diverse nature of its motifs. Apart from strange and anomalous events (some of which Hong professed to have replicated in the *Record*—see Appendix 1), it talks about the deeds of famous personalities, politics, and travels.

101. The *Shiyou tanji* 師友談記, one chapter. Written in *biji* format by Li Jian 李廌 (dates uncertain), it records the discussions held between famous Song personalities, such as poet, painter, calligrapher, and author Su Shi, as well as poet and painter Huang Tingjian 黃庭堅 (1045–1105), lyric poet Qin Guan 秦觀 (1049–1100) and so on. While it discusses philosophical and historiographical matters, it also contains several narratives which display *zhiguai* motifs not unlike those contained in the *Record*. Unfortunately there is no internal evidence, such as names of informants or personal names, which could link it to extant *Record* accounts.

102. 錢丕 *Xingnian zaji* 行年雜記. This work is no longer extant.

103. Yu Chu 虞初 (dates uncertain) was a Han Dynasty *xiaoshuo* author to whom the 943 chapter (commonly referred to as 900 chapters) *Zhoushuo* 周說 was attributed, according to the *Bibliographic Treatise of the History of the Han*. The original commentary to this tells us that he held the rank of attendant gentleman and was referred to as a justiciar of the yellow chariot (*huangche shizhe* 黃車使者). Then there was the *xiaoshuo* work entitled *Yu Chu zhi* 虞初志 by an anonymous author of the Tang period. Given the number of chapters mentioned by Hong Mai in this preface, it would seem that he was referring to the Han author's *Zhoushuo* rather than the Tang work.

104. The *Kuiche zhi* is sometimes translated as *A Cartload* (or chariotload) *of Ghosts.* It derives it title from the *kui* 暌 hexagram (no. 38) of the *Book of Change* whose exegesis mentions a cartload of ghosts. See Chang Fu-jui in *A Sung Bibliography*, 346. For a translation of the Hexagram, see Legge, *The I Ching* (New York: Dover Publications, 1963), 139–40. The extant work comprises six chapters. Its motifs are predominantly *zhiguai* and the narratological structure of its accounts is similar to that of the *Record.* It was published not many years after the publication of the *Record*'s first installment. See the *Gui'er sanji* 貴耳三集 by Zhang Duanyi 張端義 (1179–1250). The relevant section is quoted in Djang Chu et al., 92.

105. Hong Mai, *Zhiding*: 8: 1027–28.

106. Valerie Hansen, 19.

107. The *Qilüe* 七略 (*Seven Epitomes*) was jointly authored by Liu Xiang 劉向 (c. 79–c. 6 B.C.E.) and his son, Liu Xin 劉歆 (c. 50 B.C.E.–23 C.E.). It is a bibliographic catalogue which was included in the *Bibliographic Treatise of the History of the Han.*

108. Liu Xiang was a poet, compiler of anecdotal literature, and a bibliographer. Liu became an official and was responsible for the collection and collating of canonical, philosophical, and poetical texts under Emperor Cheng 成 (r. 32–7 B.C.E.) of the Han Dynasty. Although he was attributed as a coauthor of the *Qi Lüe* with his son, the latter completed the text.

109. Ban Gu (32–92) 班固. Although he died before completing his *History of the Han*, the *Bibliographic Treatise* was completed by his sister, Ban Zhao 班昭 (32–102).

110. Completed by Ban Zhao, this is the bibliographical catalogue incorporated into the *History of the Han.*

111. *The Sayings of Yi Yin* (*Yiyin shuo*) 伊尹說 in fifty-one chapters is no longer extant. Another of the same title comprising twenty-seven chapters is also no longer extant. Lu Xun postulates that it was probably written during the Warring States Period (403–227 B.C.E.). It is thought to have been a Taoist philosophical work. *The Sayings of Yuzi* 鬻子說 originally comprised twenty-one chapters of which only one has survived. Thought by some to have been a Taoist work, quotes attributed by Lu Xun to an unknown Tang scholar suggest that this was not the case. The "Green-clad Official" (Qing Shizi 青史子) was an early historian whose work, although no longer extant, was classified as *xiaoshuo* by the famous historian, Liu Zhiji 劉知機 (661–721). For further information on these works, see Lu Xun (1973), 167–71. The translations of the titles are by Yang Hsien-yi and Gladys Yang in Lu Xun, *A Brief History of Chinese Fiction* (Peking: Foreign Languages Press, 1959), 23.

112. *Zhou shuo* 周說. As observed above, this was said to have contained 943 stories according the *Bibliographic Treatise of the History of the Han.* See the Ban Gu, *Han shu* (Beijing: Zhonghua shuju, 1962), 30: 1745.

113. The surviving fragments from the *Records of Zhou* (*Zhou shuo*) are not unlike the *Classic of Mountains and Seas* (*Shanhai jing*) and the *Biography of King Mu* (*Mu Tianzi zhuan*). The only information Lu Xun offers about its author, Yu Chu, is that he jointly placed curses on the Huns and the men of Ferghana (*op cit.*).

114. The phrase "Gentlemen of the Yellow Chariot" refers to officials who collected intelligence from the common people and other such sources which, although considered trivial, was not without a certain degree of political significance, given that such

material could indicate the mood of the people. The phrase later came to mean writers of works considered as *xiaoshuo*.

115. The authorship is attributed to Zhang Heng 張衡 (78–139 A.D.), courtesy name Ziping 子平, Han Dynasty mathematician and astronomer. In his commentary to this work, Li Shan tells us that Yu Chu was referred to as officer of the yellow chariot because he rode a horse dressed in yellow garments. See Xiao Tong, comp., *Wen xuan*, (Beijing: Zhonghua shuju, 1977), 2: 45.

116. *Xu xuanguai lu* 續宣怪錄, alternatively entitled the *Sougu yilu* 搜古異錄 and the *Xu youguai lu* 續幽怪錄. Its narratives were originally arranged in three categories. The *Xin Tang shu* has a listing for five chapters, whereas the *Junzhai dushu zhi* contains one for ten. It contains many *zhiguai* motifs and, as suggested by the title, is a continuation of Niu Sengru's *Xuanguai lu*. Uncertainty exists as to the author's identity. One possibility is that he unsuccessfully sat for the *juren* exam in 840 and came from Longxi 隴西. Another possibility is that he was Li Liang 李諒 (775–833), style name Fuyan 復言, who attained the doctoral degree in 800. See Hou Zhongyi, *Sui, Tang, Wudai xiaoshuo shi*, (Zhejiang: Zhejiang guji chuban she, 1997), 112.

117. The *Yiwen ji* (*Record of Strange Things Heard*) 異聞記. It is now no longer extant, but Lu Xun recovered two accounts in his *Gu xiaoshuo gouchen* 古小說鉤沈. From the title and extant content, it is likely to have contained many *zhiguai* stories, yet there was an element of the scientific: for example, there is an anecdote about driving fish out of a pond by using mirrors. In chapter 3 of his *Zhongguo xiaoshuo shilüe*, Lu Xun postulates that this was not the work of Chen Han, but rather a fabrication on the part of Ge Hong 葛洪 (283–343), in whose *Baopuzi* we find the first extant quote from this work. Lu's reason is that the language approximates that of a *fangshi* 方士. Liu Zhaoyun, however, does not believe this to be the case since another quote can also be found by the Tang scholar, Duan Gonglu 段公路, in his *Beihu lu* 北戶錄, where the source is obviously different from Ge Hong. Hong Mai's above quote would support this, although it is unclear where Hong derived his information. See Liu Zhaoyun in the *Zhongguo wenxue da cidian*, 2400. Liu gives the author's name as Chen Han 陳漢 or Chen Shi 陳寔, which differs somewhat from Hong Mai's Chen Han 陳翰.

118. *Tanbin* 談賓, ten chapters. The original is no longer extant, but a portion has been preserved in the *Extensive Records*. It contains anecdotes about Tang officials and the Tang Imperial Court gleaned from the author's conversation with his guests. It also contains anecdotes about painting, calligraphy, and music.

119. Qian Sunzi, three chapters. The author, Wen Tingyun 溫庭筠 (812–870) was an official descended from Wen Yanbo 溫彥博 (574/75–637), grand councilor during the reign of Tang Taizong (r. 627–649). Because of his predilection to satirize the powerful, he was often criticized and attacked. He wrote many other works, including poetry.

120. The *Yishi* 逸史, three chapters. Eclectic in content, this work contains numerous *zhiguai* stories, yet many of the figures are historical. The author Lu Zi, style name Zifa, passed the imperial exams as a *zhuangyuan* 狀元 in 843.

121. *Xiao xiang lu* 瀟湘錄. Originally comprising ten chapters, this work contains many *zhiguai* stories. There are also numerous anecdotes about the Tang Imperial Court.

122. Chen Zhensun, in his *Zhizhai shulu jieti*, has a listing for Li Yin's *Fantastic Stories of the Great Tang Dynasty* (*Da Tang qi shi*) 大唐奇事. The *Bibliographic Treatise of the History of the Tang* (*Tang Yiwenzhi*), however, gives Liu Xiang as the author. The *Bibliographic Treatise of the History of the Song* indicates that they are the same, although it lists both works separately. See Hou Zhongyi, 187–88.

123. The *Bibliographic Treatise of the History of the Tang* (*Tang Yiwenzhi* 唐藝文志).

124. See Schafer's article on the *Miscellaneous Morsels from Youyang* (*Youyang zazu*) in Nienhauser (1986), 940–41.

125. Hong Yan 洪偃 (dates uncertain) was the second son of Hong Mai's third son, Hong Zi 洪梓 (dates uncertain).

126. Dingchen 鼎臣 was Xu Xuan's style name, author of the *Examining Spirits* (*Jishen lu*).

127. Posthumous title awarded to Zhang Qixian 張齊賢 (943–1014), whose style name was Shiliang 師亮. He was moved to Luoyang at the age of three in the wake of the turmoil surrounding the fall of the Later Jin Dynasty (936–946). He attained the doctoral degree (*jinshi*) in 977 and became an official. His *Luoyang jiuwen ji* 洛陽舊聞記 is a five-chapter *biji* work containing many anecdotes about historical figures, particularly those of the Five Dynasties. An alternative title is the *Old Stories from the Gentlemen of Luoyang* (*Luoyang jinshen jiuwen ji*) 洛陽搢紳舊聞記. As inferred by the title, a significant proportion of the stories were from oral sources. According to the *Four Libraries* catalogue, the contents are not, however, without historical inaccuracies and embellishments. This was, according to Xiao Xiangkai, the author's deliberate intention. For further reading, see Xiao Xiangkai, 232–35.

128. Xibai 希白 was the style name of Qian Yi 錢易 (c. 968–1026), author of the *Record of Humble Words* (*Dongwei zhi* 洞微志). Qian became an official after passing the doctoral exam in 999. Of all the works he wrote, only the *Record of Humble Words*—mentioned here—and the *Nanbu xinshu* 南部新書 survive, apart from a couple of stories which were included in Liu Fu's 劉斧 (c. 1040–c. 1113) *High-Minded Conversations beneath the Green Lattice Window* (*Qingsuo gaoyi* 青瑣高議). Although the original of the *Record of Humble Words* is no longer extant, over thirty stories are preserved in other works (see Xiao Xiangkai, 175). The *Junzhai dushu zhi* has an entry of ten chapters for this title, but the *Zhizhai shulu jieti* and the *Bibliographic Treatise of the History of the Song*; both record only three chapters. These remaining stories display many *zhiguai* motifs.

129. Zhang Junfang 張君房 (style name of Yunfang 允方 or Yinfang 尹方, *jinshi* 1005). Due to his extensive knowledge of Buddhism and Taoism, Zhang worked as a state editor of Taoist works during the reign of the Zhenzong (r. 997–1022) emperor. His *Examining Anomalies*, or *Chengyi ji* 乘異記, contained many *zhiguai* motifs. Although the original is no longer extant, some stories have been preserved in other works (see Xiao Xiangkai, 173–74). The *Junzhai dushu zhi* contains an entry of three chapters for this title, while the *Zhizhai shulu jieti* gives a date of 1003 as its completion, supposedly based on the original preface.

130. Zhang Shizheng 張師正, (or Sizheng 思正), was known to have been a magistrate in Yizhou 宜州 in 1059. Disaffected in his career, he is thought to have later turned his attention to writing. He is the author of the Song Dynasty *Record of*

Expanding Anomalies (*Kuoyi zhi* 括異志), in ten chapters. The title given here, however, is *Shuyi zhi* 述異志; yet this was a Six Dynasty work by Ren Fang 任昉 (460–506) which also contained many *zhiguai* motifs. The title given in this preface would appear to be a typographical error. The *Record of Expanding Anomalies* contains mainly *zhiguai* motifs, including Taoist themes and retribution. Its author, like Hong Mai, gives reference to his sources. On its author, see Xiao Xiangkai, 179.

131. Campany, 132–33.

132. Gardner, 67.

133. There were, however, rare exceptions to this. See, for example, the story entitled 'Sun Devil's Face," *Bing*: 4: 393, in which Hong claims to have seen the protagonist.

134. Hong Mai (1978), *Suibi*: 4: 52–53. The translation is mine.

135. Xu Qian 徐謙 (dates unknown) contributed a considerable amount of material that can be found in the 1981 edition which are as follows: *Zhigui*: 8: 1282, *Sanji*: 2: 1319 (originally the entire chapter), *Sanji*: 4: 1334, *Sanji*: 9: 1376, *Sanxin*: 2: 1401 (entire chapter), *Sanxin*: 9: 1458, *Sanxin*: 10: 1466. Given Hong Mai's comments in this preface, the question then arises as to whether these extant accounts were originally located in the *Sanzhi yi* installment, or whether they represent more than what Hong mentions in this preface. Unfortunately, given the lack of an original text, there is no way to verify this.

136. 徐仲車. Nothing seems to be known of this person, apart from what Hong Mai mentions here.

137. Wang Hsiu-huei rediscovered many previously lost accounts in the following local gazetteers: the *Xianchun Lin'an zhi* 咸淳臨安志, the *Jiading zhenjiang zhi* 嘉定鎮江志 and the *Kuaiji zhi* 會稽志. See Wang Hsiu-huei, (1989b), 165–66, and (1989a), 204–6.

138. Shen Qizhan, preface to the Zhou edition of the *Record*, in Hong Mai (1994), 1835.

139. The Chinese phrase is *sansheng jieyuan* 三生結願. This is a Buddhist term linked to reincarnation whereby one expresses a wish to be married to one's spouse for three incarnations.

140. Known in Chinese as the *xiongjing chigu* 熊經鴟顧法 method, it involved meditating in a position resembling a bear climbing a tree that was combined with the look of an owl that glances around without moving the rest of its body. It was thought to be beneficial for attaining long life and good health.

141. The Master referred to here is Confucius, known for his reluctance to engage in discourse on otherworldly matters. This fueled the literati's prejudice throughout the imperial period against literary works focusing on *zhiguai* motifs.

142. One of the commentaries to the *Annals of Spring and Autumn*, considered by Chinese traditional scholars as a masterpiece of official historiography, which employs narrative techniques.

143. Teng Yanzhi 膝彥智 (dates uncertain). Apart from the account which I cite in the next note, Teng also provided one now found in the supplementary section of the 1981 edition; *Bu*: 9: 1629.

144. Lu Dangke 路當可, style name of Lu Shizhong 路時中 (dates uncertain).

145. The narrative referred to here, entitled "Lu Dangke," is located in the *Dingzhi*. Lu is the storyteller. He tells of a nearly unsuccessful attempt to exorcise a girl possessed by an earth god. Due to powerful resistance at the girl's house, Lu was forced to conduct his operations at a local Taoist temple. The spirit was exorcised after fire consumed the temple which was near the girl's home (*Ding*: 18: 684–85). This account comes after another featuring the same topic and protagonist (Lu Dangke) in the *Bing zhi*. In the introduction to the *Ding zhi* version, Hong told us that the *Bing zhi* version was inaccurate. Here is another example of him rectifying inaccuracies already recorded *ipso facto*. We can be certain that these two accounts were originally located in the *Bing* and *Ding* installments respectively since Hong mentions the location of the *Bing* account in the introduction of the *Ding* version. For the original account, see *Bing*: 13: 479.

146. Huang Yongfu 黃雍父 is the style name of Huang Tang 黃唐 (dates uncertain) from Changle 長樂 in Fujian. He enjoyed the career of an eminent official and once served in Poyang, Hong's native place. He Zhuo's 1981 edition tells us that the character *zhi* in the sentence "*Huang Yongfu zai zhi guan shi*" 黃雍父在之館時 is suspect. I have, therefore, translated this part as "protegé" according to Wang Nianshuang's interpretation. See Wang Nianshuang, 309.

147. This account is no longer extant in the 1981 edition.

149. Kuai Liang 蒯亮 was said to have been over ninety years old. He became Xu Xuan's servant and was, according to Jiang Shaoyu's 江少虞 (*jinshi* ca. 1115–d. after 1145) *A Collection of Famous Words and Deeds in the Northern Song Dynasty* (*Shishi leiyuan* 事實類苑 , a *biji* work of 778 chapters), the source of most stories in the *Jishen lu*. See Djang's Chu translation, 144.

149. Yang Wengong is the posthumous title awarded to Yang Yi 楊億, style name Danian 大年 (974–1020). He was said to have been a child prodigy, able to compose essays at the age of seven. At the age of eleven, his poetry came to the attention of the Taizong emperor (r. 976–997) and he was granted an official posting as a proofreader. When the Zhenzong (r. 997–1022) emperor came to the throne, Yang worked on the editing of Taizong's veritable records. Unfortunately, he later became involved in the machinations which occurred over the succession of Zhenzong in 1020 and died in the twelfth lunar month of that year. His work, now known as the *Yang Wengong tan yuan* 楊文公談苑, was originally written in fifteen chapters. Only one hundred excerpts are extant, now preserved in the *Comprehensive Record of Imperial Reigns* (*Lidai quanzheng yaolüe* 歷代詮政要錄).

150. Xu Xuan 徐鉉 (917–992) gained renown for his literary prowess at a young age. He served in the administration of the later Tang and came to be particularly trusted by its last ruler, Li Yu 李煜 (937–978). The latter sent him to negotiate peace with the besieging Song army, a mission which, nevertheless, led to Li's surrender. After Xu went with his former sovereign to the Song capital, he was appointed to advisory and literary posts. For example, he participated in the editing of the encyclopedic *Extensive Records*, the *Taiping yülan* 太平御覽, and the *Wenyuan yinghua* 文苑英華. He coauthored an edition of the etymological dictionary, the *Shuowen jiezi* 說文解字, with his brother, Xu Kai (920–974) and he himself was author of the above-mentioned *Examining Spirits* (*Jishen lu*). Many of the stories in the *Examining Spirits* were said to be the inventions of his retainer, Kuai Liang (dates uncertain).

151. Chen Zhensun, *Zhizhai Shulu Jieti*, chapter 11, in Hong Mai (1994), 1821–22.

152. The translation is Djang Chu and Jane Djang's, 144. For a transcription of the original, see Ting Chuan-ching, 127–28.

153. The account mentioned here is now found in the *Bing* installment, 4: 393. Whether or not it was originally elsewhere is not possible to determine, although the first four installments are the best preserved of all.

154. *Youming lu* 幽明錄.

155. The *Taiping yülan* (hereafter *Imperial Digest*) was compiled concurrently with the *Extensive Records* nominally by the famous historian, Li Fang 李肪 (925–996). Li had many scholars working under him on both projects, which were completed in a relatively short time. The *Imperial Digest* derives its name from having been read by the emperor Taizu (r. 960–976) and contains what was considered to be more or less factual and respectable material on a variety of topics. Many *zhiguai* motifs were, however, included.

156. The account entitled "Dreaming of the Son of Heaven" (*Meng tianzi*), located in the third supplementary section (*Sanbu*, 1805), however, corresponds almost verbatim to an account from chapter 136 of the *Extensive Records*, entitled "The Gaozu Emperor of the Jin Dynasty" (*Jin Gaozu*). This, to my knowledge, is the only *Record* account wholly derived from the *Extensive Records*. It was redacted from the *Great Encyclopedia of the Yongle Period* (*Yongle dadian*), which cited the *Record* ("*Yijian zhi*") as its source (135/13135/12B). Wang Hsiu-huei, however, argued that it was wrongly attributed to the *Record*, presumably because of the text's existence in the *Extensive Records*, which cites the *Yutang xianhun* from The Five Dynasties as its source. This, to me, is scant reason for a false attribution. See Wang Hsiu-huei (1989a), 204.

157. Han Yu (768–824). Changli gong 昌黎公 was Han Yu's sobriquet.

158. This is a quote from the essay in question. See Han Yu, "Yuan gui" 原鬼, in *Han Yu quanji jiaozhu* 韓愈全集校註, ed. Qu Shouyuan et al. (Chengdu: Sichuan daxue chuban she, 1996), 1701–1704. The translation is mine.

159. Another direct quote from Han Yu: *You guai er yu minwu jiezhe* 有怪而與民物接者. The following sentence also borrows heavily from the original.

160. This phrase comes from the *Analects of Confucius*, the *Bayou* 八佾 chapter (Book 3). See Confucius, trans. D. C. Lau, 69.

161. *Ming Gui* 明鬼. This is a treatise in which Mozi argued for the existence of ghosts. See Mozi, "Ming gui," in *Mozi: Basheng xianshu* 八聖賢書 (Chongqing: Xinan shifan daxue chubanshe, 1995), 188–205.

162. *Xieshuo yinci* 邪說淫辭. This refers to a tract from Book 3: b of the *Mencius* whereby Mencius explains *xieshuo yinci* as various phenomena accompanying the fall of a dynasty which indicate social and moral collapse. To quote the D. C. Lau translation: "The Duke of Chou wanted to punish those who ignored father and prince. I, too, wish to follow in the footsteps of the three sages in rectifying the hearts of men, *laying heresies to rest*, opposing extreme action, and *banishing excessive views*" (emphasis added). See *Mencius*, trans. D. C. Lau, Book 3, Part b, 113. I have followed Lau's wording here, changing the order slightly to better fit the context.

163. Soon after Zhao Kuangyin 趙匡胤 (the Song Taizu emperor) established the Song Dynasty, the compiling of both the *Extensive Records* and the *Imperial Digest* was ordered by imperial decree. The main editor, as already noted, was Li Fang. The *Extensive Records* comprised five hundred chapters and was completed in 978. It contained narratives displaying *zhiguai* motifs arranged according to a classification system based on motif. The material ranges from the Han to the Tang. Initially it was not widely circulated, yet, judging from Hong Mai's comments in several of his prefaces, it would seem to have been in some form of circulation by Hong's time.

164. The *Leiju*. This is an abbreviated title of the *Topicalized Compedium of Bibliographical Treatises* (*Yiwen leiju* 藝文類聚), a Tang Dynasty encyclopedia compiled around 620 by Ou-yang Xun (557–641).

165. Gao Yao 皋陶 was a legendary justiciar of the legendary Emperor Shun. His style name, according to the *Zuozhuan* commentary, was Tingjian 庭堅. See Wang Nianshuang, 104.

166. The initial brashness of Hong's tone is not lost on Fukuda Chikashi, who observes how rare it was when compared to the prefaces of similar works such as the *Miscellaneous Morsels* and Gan Bao's *Soushen ji*. See Fukuda Chikashi, 133–34. Anne McLaren also remarked on Hong's "brashness" during our discussions on Hong Mai and the *Record*.

167. See the *Guier sanji* by Zhang Duanyi (1179–1250). The relevant section is quoted in Djang Chu et al., 92.

168. Chen Chun, "Beixi ziyi," in Wing-tsit Chan, *Neo-Confucian Terms Explained* (*The Pei-hsi tzu-i*) *by Chen Chun, 1159–1223* (New York: Columbia University Press, 1986), 162–63. For the *Record* account, see *Jia*: 14: 126. For a translation of the account in question, see pages 111–12 chapter 3 of this volume.

169. That is, Hong Mai.

170. Wang Shipeng 王十朋, *Meixi Wang xiansheng wenji* 梅溪先生文集, *hou ji*, 9.3, in the *Sibu congkan* edition, 4: 110.

171. Campany, 49–52. For Zhang's biography in the *Jin shu*, see Yang Jialuo et al., *Jin shu* (Taipei: Dingwen shuju, 1979), 36: 1068–79.

172. Wang Jingwen, "Yijian biezhi," in Hu Yinglin's *Shaoshi shanfang bicong* in Hong Mai (1994), 1825–26. See also Ma Duanlin's, *Wenxian tongkao* (Taipei: Xinxing shuju, 1962), 217: 1770–72.

173. This refers to chapters 14 and 15 of Duan Chengshi's (c. 800–863) *Miscellaneous Morsels from Youyang*, entitled the *nuogao ji* 諾皋記, *shang*, and *xia* respectively. In the sequel *Xuji* 續集, chapters 1, 2, and 3 are entitled the *Zhi nuogao* 支諾皋, *shang*, *zhong*, and *xia* respectively. As discussed below, narratives containing *zhiguai* motifs in the *Miscellaneous Morsels* tend to be concentrated in these chapters. Hong's frequent references to Duan suggest that he was influenced by him and held his work in high esteem. Although the overall corpus of the *Miscellaneous Morsels* is quite different from the *Record* in terms of breadth of subject matter, form, and so forth, these particular chapters are so similar that they could be described as a blueprint for the *Record* in terms of form, motif, narrative structure, presence of temporal and spatial markers, and the citation of informants.

174. The original Chinese term used is *shibu* 史補, literally "a supplement to history."

175. According to Chinese traditional folklore, a turtle has long been a symbol of longevity which, in turn, was a much sought-after and discussed state-of-being since ancient times.

176. Lu You, "Ti Yijian zhi hou" 提夷堅志後, in the *Historical Studies from the jianyan Period* (*Jianyan shikao* 建炎史考), 37. Quoted from Katherine Kerr's thesis, 29.

177. Zhao Yushi, *Guests Retire* (Shanghai Guji Chubanshe, 1983), 97.

178. Chen Zhensun, *Zhizhai Shulu Jieti*, chapter 11, in Hong Mai (1994), 1821–22.

179. William H. Nienhauser Jr., "Creativity and Storytelling in the *Ch'uan-ch'i*: Shen Ya-chih's T'ang Tales," *Chinese Literature: Essays, Articles and Reviews* 20 (1998): 31–70.

180. Zhou Mi, *Guixin zashi*, in the *Siku quanshu zhenben* series, ed. Wang Yunwu (Taipei: Taiwan shangwu yinshu guan, 1980), 1040–43.

181. This was a private bibliographic catalogue listed in the philosophers section of the *Four Libraries* catalogue as "miscellaneous authors" (*zajia lei* 雜家類).

182. Chen Li, *Qinyou tang suilu*, in Hong Mai (1994), 1822.

183. Hu Yinglin 胡應麟, *Shaoshi shanfang bicong* 少室山房筆叢 (*Collected Essays from the Shaoshi Shanfang Studio*) and the *Shaoshi shanfang leigao* 少室山房類稿 (*Notes from the Shaoshi Shanfang Studio*), in Hong Mai (1994), 1823–26.

184. The editor, Zhou Xinchuan 周信傳, published a *jinxiang* 巾箱 edition under the imprint of the *Gengyan cao tang* 耕煙草堂.

185. The *Shanhai jing* 山海經.

186. Shen Qizhan, preface to the Zhou edition of the *Yijian zhi*, in Hong Mai (1994), 1835.

187. He Qi, preface to the above-mentioned Zhou edition of the *Record*, in Hong Mai (1994), 1835–36.

188. See Lu Xinyuan's preface to the *Record* in Hong Mai (1994), 1838–39.

189. This differs from what Chen actually wrote. See my translation on 60.

190. Ji Yun 紀昀 et al., *Siku quanshu zongmu* 四庫全書總目, ch. 142. Cited in Hong Mai (1994), 1826–27.

191. For a detailed discussion of the didactic nature of Ji Yun's *Close Scrutiny*, see Leo Tak-hung Chan, 187–243.

192. Lu Xun, *Zhongguo xiaoshuo shilüe* (Beijing: 1973), 242–43. The translation is mine.

193. Tuo Tuo et al., *Songshi* (Beijing: Zhonghua shuju, 1977), 11573–74.

194. Wang, Teh-yi. (1964), 2: 405–74.

195. "Les themes dans le *Yi-kien Tche*," *Cina* 8 (1964): 51–55.

196. "Le *Yi-kien Tche* et la société des Song," *Journal Asiatique* 256 (1968): 55–93.

197. "L'influence du *Yi-kien Tche* sur les oeuvres literaires," in *Etudes d'histoire et de littérature Chinoises offertes au Professeur Jaroslav Prusek*, ed. Yves Hervouet (Paris: 1976), 51–61.

198. *I Chien Chih T'ung chien* 夷堅志通檢 (Taipei: Taiwan xuesheng shuju, 1976).

199. For the former see Yves Hervouet, *A Sung Bibliography*, 344–45; for the latter see Herbert Franke, *Sung Biographies*, 464–78.

200. "Vingt-sept Recits Retrouves du *Yijian Zhi*," *T'oung Pao* (1989a): 191–202; "Yijian zhi yishi jibu" 夷堅志佚事輯補, in *Hanxue yanjiu* 漢學研究 7:1 (June 1989b): 163–83.

201. "Guji yu dian'nao fenxi yunyong—yi *Yijian Zhi* wei li" 古籍與電腦分析運用—以"夷堅志"為例, in *Hanxue yanjiu tongxun* 漢學研究通訊, 14:2, no. 54 (June 1995): 83–87.

202. "*Yijianzhi*: A Didactic Diversion," *Papers on Far Eastern History* 35 (1987): 79–88.

203. "Fenlei Yijian Zhi yanjiu," 分類夷堅志 研究 *Huadong Shifan Daxue xuebao; zhexue shehui kexue ban* 華東師範大學學報: 哲學社會科學版 3 (1997): 80–86; "Wenyan xiaoshuo pingdiande yaoji; timing Zhong Xing ping 'Xinding zengbu *Yijian zhi*' pingyi," 文言小說評點的要籍: 題名鐘惺評 "新訂增補夷堅志" 評議 *Nantong shizhuan xuebao (shehui kexue ban)* 南通師專學報 (社會科學版), Journal of Nantong Teachers College (Social Sciences) 13, no. 3 (1997): 25.

204. "Kō Mai to *Ikenshi*—rekishi to genjitsu no hazama nite," 洪邁と夷堅志—歷史と現實の狹間にて (Hong Mai and His I-chien chih—Between History and Actuality) *Tōdai chutetsubun gakkaihō* 當代中哲文学会報 5 (1980): 75–96.

205. "Kō Kō to Kō Mai," 洪皓と洪邁 *Hosei daigaku kyoyōbu kiyō jimbun kagakuhen* 法制大学教養部紀要人文科学篇 74 (1990): 1–17.

206. "*Yikenshi* kōshi nijū ken no seiritsu katei ni tsuite," 夷堅志甲志二十卷の成立課題について *Okayama Daigaku bungakubu kiyō*, 岡山大学文学部紀要 21 (1994): 43–52.

207. "*Ikenshi* jijo o meguru mondai ten," 夷堅志自序をめぐる問題てん *Chūgoku Gakushi: Osaka shiritsu daigaku chūbun gakkai* 中国学志 大阪市立大学中文学会 11 (2000): 113–38.

CHAPTER THREE

1. *Yi*: 1: 188. "Mountain of Crabs," *Jia*: 1: 3–4

2. *Jia*: 1: 3–4.

3. See, for example, *Jia*: 8: 65, "Saved by the Buddha from Past Enmity;" *Bing*: 7: 420–21, "An's Injustice;" *Zhijia*: 5: 9: 749, "Liu the scholar;" *Zhigui*: 6: 1262, "Yi Da."

4. *Zhiyi*: 7: 847–48.

5. *Zhijing*: 8: 946.

6. *Jia*: 13: 112. For other examples, see *Ding*: 9: 611, "Zheng the Butcher of Hedong;" *Zhijing*: 5: 916, "Tong Qi the Butcher."

7. Lu Xun, *Zhongguo xiaoshuo shilüe* in *Lu Xun quanji* 9 (Beijing: Renmin wenxue chuban she, 1981), 70.

8. Cai You (1077–1126) was a son of Cai Jing (1046–1126). Cai Jing was a long-standing grand councilor under the Huizong emperor upon whom traditional Chinese historians accorded much of the blame for the fall of the Northern Song. The office of supply mentioned here was probably one used to store precious rocks and flowers

collected by Huizong's infamous "rocks and flower network." The aim of this was to provide a source of rare specimens to fill the emperor's Northeastern Marchmount.

9. *Jia*: 2: 14. The translation is Katherine Kerr's; reproduced with permission of Dr. Kerr. See her unpublished Ph.D. dissertation entitled *The Yijian zhi: An Alternate Perspective*, (University of Sydney, 1998), 90–91.

10. *Yi*: 15: 308.

11. *Yi*: 3: 203.

12. *Jia*: 7: 58.

13. See the narrative entitled "Madame Ouyang" in chapter 395. In this an orphan woman's father reappears after having been separated from her during her childhood. As the father is poor, the woman neither recognizes him nor allows him to sleep on her doorstep. She is consequently struck dead by lightning after the father lodges a writ at a nearby lightning god temple. See Gao Guang et. al., eds., *Taiping guangji* (Tianjin: Tianjin guji chuban she, 1994), 395: 1520–21.

14. See, for example, *Ding*: 12: 638, "Chen Fourteen and his Son;" *Zhijia*: 3: 732, "Xiong Er is Unfilial."

15. *Jia*: 20: 180. Translated by Katherine Kerr (1998), 112–13; reproduced with permission of Dr. Kerr.

16. For a similar example, see *Ding*: 15: 667, "Wu Er's Filial Gesture."

17. See Yang Lien-sheng, "The Concept of *pao* as a Basis for Social Relations in China," in *Chinese Thought and Institutions*, ed. John K. Fairbank (Chicago: University of Chicago Press, 1957), 291–309; also Livia Kohn, "Counting Good Deeds and Days of Life: The Quantification of Fate in Medieval China," *Asiatische Studien* 52 (1998), 833–70.

18. See, for example, *Zhijia*: 10: 792.

19. See, for example, *Zhijia*: 2: 724–25, "Hu Huang's Servant;" *Zhijia*: 4: 737–38, "Lord Gongxiang;" *Zhiyi*: 5: 834–35, "The Goh-Playing Monk of Xiu Prefecture."

20. *Jia*: 14: 126.

21. *Jia*: 5: 40.

22. *Zhijia*: 8: 777.

23. *Jia*: 7: 62

24. *Jia*: 8: 65

25. *Zhijia*: 5: 749–50

26. *Zhijia*: 1: 717–18

27. *Zhiyi*: 8: 857–58.

28. *Zhiding*: 1: 973.

29. See the case of Jiang Jian, for example, who was called into the netherworld for eating beef. In this instance, however, Jiang narrowly escaped death by considering the fate of his elderly mother while being interrogated by one of the kings of hell. See *Jia*: 10: 788–790.

30. *Ding*: 5: 578–79

31. *Sanzhi xin*: 3: 1404.

32. *Zhijia*: 10: 792–93.

33. *Jia*: 7: 58–59.

34. *Jia*: 2: 14. The translation is mine. First published in *Renditions*, 57 (Spring 2002): 30–31; reprinted by permission of the Research Centre for Translation, The Chinese University of Hong Kong.

35. *Ding*: 3: 556, "Jiang Zhiping."

36. See, for example, *Ding*: 2: 550–51; also *Jia*: 4: 33–34.

37. *Ding*: 2: 550–51.

38. For a discussion of Lu You's patriotic poetry, see Michael Duke, *Lu You* (Boston: Twayne Publishers, 1977), 65–80. For a translation and exegesis of Lu You's poem *Autumn Sentiments*, written in 1177, see Yoshikawa Kōjirō, *Five Hundred Years of Chinese Poetry 1150–1650* (Princeton, NJ: Princeton University Press, 1989), 18.

39. For Hong's relationship with both Lu You and Xin Qiji, see Wang Teh-yi, "Hung Jung-chai Hsien-sheng nien-p'u," in *Songshi yanjiu ji* 2 (Taipei: Zhonghua congshu weiyuanhui, 1964), 405–74 (originally appeared in *Yu-shih hsüeh-pao* 3.2 [April 1961]: 1–63), especially 409 and 413.

40. For a discussion of Fan's relationship with Hong Gua, see J. D. Schmidt, *Stone Lake: The Poetry of Fan Chengda (1126–1193)* (Cambridge and New York: Cambridge University Press, 1992), 8–9.

41. See Yu Beishan, *Fan Chengda nianpu* (Shanghai: Shanghai guji chubanshe, 1987), 85, n. 2. Schmidt, however, contradicts this by asserting that Hong Mai was the recipient of the poem. See Fan Chengda, *Fan shi hu ji* (Shanghai, 1962, repr. Hong Kong 1974), 119, cited from Schmidt, 9.

42. *Yi*: 1: 191; *Bing*: 17: 511.

43. Chen Guocan and Fang Rujin, *Song Xiaozong* (Changchun Shi: Jilin wen shi chu ban she, 1997), 177–78 and 243–44. For Jiang's account, see Hong Mai (1994), *Yi*: 2: 197.

44. Ibid. Also see Hong Mai, *Jia*: 17: 151; *Yi*: 14: 302.

45. Chen Junqing 陳俊卿 (1113–1186), cognomen Yingqiu 應求, was once banished to a lowly teaching post in the south by Qin Gui (for information on Chen's appointment to the court of Xiaozong as an anti-Jurchen official, see Chen Guocan and Fang Rujin, 87. For his account in the *Record*, see *Jia*: 15: 135); Liu Gong (1122–1178) was banished from the court by Qin Gui during the Shaoxing 紹興 period. Wang Gangzhong 王剛中 (1103–1165) from Leping 樂平 in Raozhou 饒州 (in modern Zhejiang, Raozhou), cognomen Shiheng 時亨, received his *jinshi* degree in 1155. Yet it was not long before he was dispatched to a lowly teaching position after having offended Qin Gui. Wang provided three accounts appearing in the second installment (ibid., 166; also see Hong Mai [1994], *Yi*: 5: 223); Wang Ju 王柜 (d. 1173) was a well-known official and member of the war party in the late Shaoxing and early Qiandao 乾道 periods (ibid., 87; also see Hong Mai [1994], *Jia*: 14: 126, *Jia*: 19: 172, *Jia*: 20: 182, *Yi*: 1: 189, *Yi*: 3: 210, *Yi*: 5: 222, *Yi*: 7: 244, *Yi*: 13: 298, *Yi*: 14: 307, *Yi*: 15: 315, *Yi*: 19: 347 & 348, *Bing*: 15: 495, *Bing*: 16: 505, *Bing*: 20: 533). Wang Shipeng 王十朋 (1112–1171), outspoken critic of peace initiatives and high-ranking minister early in Xiaozong's reign, was a close associate of Hong Mai and provided the latter with at least one account appearing

in the second installment (ibid. See also Hong Mai [1994], *Yi*: 4: 218); Zhang Chan 張 闡 (1091–1164) was dismissed from office after having offended Qin Gui (ibid., See also Hong Mai [1994], *Bing*: 9: 441); an anonymous friend of Zhang Jun gave an account appearing in the third installment. Zhang Jun's son, Zhang Shi (1133–1180), provided two accounts appearing in the second and third installments [for Zhang Jun's friend's account, see Hong Mai [1994], *Bing*: 4: 400. For his son's accounts, see *Yi*: 4: 215, *Bing*: 15: 495); Zhou Cao 周 操 (1135 *jinshi*) enjoyed an illustrious career which concluded as an academician in the Longtu Ge 龍 圖 閣 (*op cit.*, 124).

46. This refers to the Jurchen.

47. *Zhigeng*: 7: 1192.

48. These two famous generals were supposed to have died at this time. Yet, Zhang Jun was still alive. Here is another example of erratic dates sometimes found in the *Record*, which I will discuss further in chapter 6. For the account itself, see Hong Mai (1994), *Bing*: 16: 4: 500.

49. See Zhang Kuo 張 擴, *Dong chuang ji* (Taipei: Shangwu yinshu guan, 1983), 12: 15 *xia*.

50. See Erving Goffman, *Frame Analysis: An Essay on the Organization of Experience* (Cambridge, MA: Harvard University Press, 1974).

51. *Yi*: 17, 331

CHAPTER FOUR

1. See Paul Katz, *Images of the Imortal: The Cult of Lü Dongbin at the Palace of Eternal Joy* (Honolulu: Hawaii University Press, 1999), 10–12.

2. Valerie Hansen, 17.

3. Robert Campany, 24. For further reading on Bakhtin-influenced genre theory, see Michael Bakhtin, *Speech Genres and Other Late Essays*, trans. Vern W. McGee (Austin: University of Texas Press, 1986); Bakhtin and Medvedev, *The Formal Method in Literary Scholarship; A Critical Introduction to Sociological Poetics*, trans. Albert J. Werle (Baltimore: John Hopkins University Press, 1978); William F. Hanks, "Discourse Genres in a Theory of Practice," *American Ethnologist* 14 (1987): 668–92; Charles L. Briggs and Richard Baumann, "Genre, Intertextuality and Social Power," *Journal of Linguistic Anthropology* 2 (1992): 131–72; Douglas L. Medin and Scott Atran, *Folkbiology*, (Boston: MIT Press, 1999); William H. Foley, "Genre, Poetics, Ritual Languages and Verbal Art," *Anthropological Linguistics: An Introduction* (Oxford: Blackwell, 1997), 359–78.

4. See Benjamin Penny, *Early Daoist Biography: A Study of the Shenxian Zhuan* (unpublished Ph.D. diss., Australian National University: 1993).

5. For further reading on this subject, see Nie Chongqi's detailed analysis in Hong Ye et al., *Yiwenzhi ershizhong zonghe yinde* (Beiping: Yanjing University Library, 1933), 22–39.

6. For example, Ji Yun et al., *Siku quanshu zongmu*, 142: 2803; Ma Duanlin's *Wenxian tongkao*, 217: 1770; *Song shi*, 5227; Chen Zhensun, 11: 22–24.

7. *Collected Essays*, 371.

8. Ibid., 374.

9. Valerie Hansen, 17.

10. This can be found in the *Cailüe* section. See Liu Xie, Huang Shulin et al., eds., *Zengding wenxin diaolong jiaozhu* (Beijing: zhonghua shuju, 2000), 1: 576.

11. Herbert Franke, "Some Aspects of Chinese Private Historiography," in Beasley and Pullyblank, *Historians of China and Japan* (London: Oxford University Press, 1961), 116.

12. Y. W. Ma, "Pi-chi," in Nienhauser, 650–51.

13. Ibid., 650. For a further—albeit brief—discussion of *biji*, see also Joseph S. M. Lau and Y. W. Ma, eds., *Traditional Chinese Stories: Themes and Variations* (New York: Columbia University Press, 1978), xxii.

14. See, for example, Karl S. Y. Kao, ed., *Classical Chinese Tales of the Supernatural and the Fantastic* (Bloomington, IN: Indiana University Press, 1985). On page 4, Kao asserts that Hu was the first to use the term to refer to a literary genre. DeWoskin was also under this impression. See Kenneth DeWoskin, 22. Campany, however, has pointed out that it was the poet, painter, calligrapher, and Taoist Gu Kuang 顧況 (c. 725–c. 814) who first used the term in his preface to Dai Fu's *Guangyi ji*. See Robert Ford Campany, 29.

15. Chen Zhensun in Hong Mai (1994), 1821–22.

16. When referring to *Record* accounts at the time of the second installment's completion, he wrote: "Together they embody the cream of strange and uncanny (*guaiguai qiqi* 怪怪奇奇) stories found throughout the world." (preface to the *Yi zhi*, 185); when referring to his choice of material, he wrote: "When I first began compiling the book of *Yi Jian*, I was solely concerned with the extraordinary and the adoration of the strange." (*jiu yi chong guai* 鳩異崇怪) (preface to the *Bing zhi*, 363); through the words of an interlocutor when defending the authenticity of his stories, he wrote: "You accept whatever strange story (*yiwen* 異聞) is to be had." (preface to the *Ding zhi*, 537); when talking about growing old and losing his interest in certain pursuits, except for strange stories, he writes: "My love for the strange (*qi qi* 奇氣) is still very strong." (preface to the *Zhiyi zhi*, 795); when discussing the reliability of his stories, he writes: "I took several stories in order to test their strangeness." (*yi* 異) (preface to the *Zhiding zhi*, 967); when talking of the almost obsessive nature of his collecting and recording strange stories in relation to the possible inadvertent inclusion of spurious material, he confesses: "such is the curse of loving the strange." (*qi* 奇) (preface to the *Zhiwu zhi*, 1051); when evaluating the authenticity of the stories of others, he ventures: "Yet none surpass that of Lü Lan for its strangeness." (*ke guai zhe* 可怪者) (Ibid.); when lamenting accounts which escaped his collection, he writes: "When Huang Yong's father was an official, he spoke of the strange business of the Purple Maiden (*zigu zhi yi* 紫姑之異) and the traveler named Guo from Dongyang, but I did not write of it immediately." (preface to the *Sanzhi Ji*, 1303); when referring to a parallel text which had found its way into the *Record*, he argues: "I have said all along how I have considered that, among stories of deities and strange happenings (*shen qi zhi shi* 神奇之事)—past and present—there are no two alike." (preface to the *Sanzhi Xin*, 1385).

17. Kenneth DeWoskin, 22.

18. Campany, 28.

19. Ibid., 22.

20. Ibid., 24–25.

21. Confucius, *The Analects*, trans. D. C. Lau, VII: 21, 88.

22. Confucius, *The Analects*, trans. Arthur Waley (London: reprinted 1971), XII: 20, 127.

23. Ibid.

24. Confucius, "The Analects," in *The Chinese Classics*, 6, trans. James Legge, (Hong Kong: Hong Kong University Press, 1960), XII: 201.

25. Ibid.

26. *Lunyu zhu shu*, ed. He Yan (Taipei: Taiwan Zhonghua shuju, 1965), 7: 5a.

27. *The Analects*, 6: 20, 8: 21, 11: 11.

28. The *jifa* 祭法 section of the *Liji* 禮記. See the *Sibu beiyao* edition, 14: 2a.

29. "Spirits" here refers to animistic spirits, as opposed to the anthropomorphic notion of a "god" which humans might transform into after death.

30. *Hanyu da cidian*: 7: 486.

31. There are several examples of *guai* in the *Guoyu* 國語: "*Guai* of rocks and plants are called *Kui* 夔 and *Wangliang* 蝄蜽, *guai* of waterways are called dragons and *wangxiang* 蝄象, *guai* of soil are called *fenyang* 羵羊 (*Guoyu*, Sibu beiyao edition, 5: 7b). The *wangliang* were, according to the Wei Zhao 韋昭 commentary to the *Guoyu*, mountain sprites (*shanjing* 山精) capable of mimicking human voices for the purpose of entrapment (Ibid.). The *Shuowen* defines them as animistic spirits (*jingwu* 精物) of the waterways and mountains (*Shuowen jiezi*, 282). The *Huainan wang* 淮南 王 describes a creature it calls a *wangliang* as being shaped like three-year-old children with warm black bodies and red eyes, long ears, and handsome whiskers (see the *Hanyu da cidian*, 8: 916). The category of *guai* pertaining to waterways, according to the *Guoyu*, encompasses both dragons and *wangxiang* (ibid.). Since dragons are well known in Chinese folklore, I will refrain from discussing them here. *Wangxiang* were thought to be a type of sea deity and are mentioned in the "sea Rhapsody" 海賦 of the *Wenxuan* 文選 (Ibid., 8: 915–16). Another passage in the *Luyu* 魯語 section of the *Guoyu* talks of a goat (spirit) found in a jar in the ground which was identified as a *fenyang*, or a *fen* goat. This would seem to refer to a special type of animistic spirit. The finder is told by his informant that *guai* of rocks and plants are called *kui* and *wangliang* (*Guoyu*, Sibu beiyao edition, 5: 7b). There is also a reference to *kui* in the *Shanhai jing* where we are told that it was a one-legged beast, dark in color and without horns. It had a body similar to that of an ox and could bring about wind and rain when it emerged. Such creatures could be found at a legendary mountain in the Eastern Ocean (Guo Pu, *Shanhai jing*, Sibu beiyao edition, 14: 7a). The *Zhuangzi* has a reference to a one-legged creature called a *kui* (*Zhuangzi*, *Basheng xianshu* [Chongqing: Xinan shifan daxue chubanshe, 1995, the *qiushui* 秋水 chapter, 214]). The *Shuowen jiezi* defines it as a one-legged, financially-destructive ghost—*shenxu* 神魖 (*Shuowen jiezi*, ch. 5 [*xia*], 112). Thus, for this one term there are several explanations covering different phenomena. From its context in the *Guoyu*, it would appear to be what postmodern Western scholars might understand as a type of animistic spirit. According to the *Shanhai jing* it was a legendary creature, while the *Shuowen* defines it as a type of

ghost notorious for wreaking financial ruination. The animistic spirits of the ground were, according to the *Guoyu*, defined as *fenyang*.

32. Xu Shen, *Shuowen jiezi*; Duan *zhu*, ed. Wang Yunwu (*Sibu boiyao* ed.), 81·10: b: 27.

33. Chen Zhensun, in Hong Mai (1994), 1821–22.

34. See Ban Gu, *Han shu* (Taipei: Dingwen shuju, 1986), 56: 2498.

35. See Robert Ford Campany, 102–26.

36. Ibid., 105.

37. See, for example, the *Record* account of a wife who devoutly prays and serves her husband's ancestral temple. When she succumbs to an illness caused by ghosts, she is saved by ancestral spirits. While the account is set in a background of ancestral spirit worship, and this motif plays an integral thematic part in the subsequent narrative, it is not the focus of the plot. Rather, it is the three-way encounter between the sick woman, the ghosts, and the ancestral spirits that constitutes the element of *guai*. See Hong Mai (1994), *Jia*: 12: 107–8.

38. Yuan Ke, ed., *Shanhai jing* (Shanghai, Shanghai guji chubanshe, 1980), 478. The translation is mine.

39. In another part of the text where Guo discusses "extraordinary beasts" (*guaishou* 怪獸) and "extraordinary fish" (*guaiyu* 怪魚), he defines the term "extraordinary" (*guai*) as something which has unusual features (*maozhuang quqi* 貌狀屈奇) which are not normal (*buchang* 不常). Ibid, 3.

40. For a detailed elucidation of this subject, see Hans Robert Jauss, *Aesthetic Experience and Literary Hermeneutics* (Minneapolis: University of Minnesota Press, 1982).

41. Feng Menglong, preamble to the "Guaidan" section to his *Gujin tan'gai* 1: 2.1, cited in Judith Zeitlin, *Historian of the Strange—Pu Songling and the Chinese Classical Tale* (Stanford, CA: Stanford University Press, 1993), 6. The translation is Zeitlin's.

42. In his paper on ghosts, for example, Anthony Yu postulated that, in what he refers to as "traditional prose fiction": "though its focus (i.e. the focus of traditional prose fiction) concentrates on the dead and dying, the values and concerns of the living predominate." See Anthony C. Yu, "'Rest, Rest, Perturbed Spirit!' Ghosts in Traditional Chinese Fiction," *Harvard Journal of Asiatic Studies* 47, no. 2 (Dec. 1987): 434.

43. Campany, 210.

44. 東方朔 (154–93 B.C.E.)

45. *Op cit.*, 145–46. The translation is Campany's.

46. *Siku quanshu zongmu* in Hong Mai (1994), 1826–27.

47. Jacques Attali, *Noise: The Political Economy of Music*, trans. Brian Massumi (Minneapolis: University of Minnesota Press, 1987), 87.

48. I am grateful to David Holm for this perceptive observation.

49. For a detailed survey of the awarding of official titles to popular deities and the destruction of what were seen as "pernicious" deities, see Valerie Hansen.

50. In chapter 1 of *The Religious System of China*, De Groot observes how gods are associated with the *yang* principle while ghosts are associated with *yin*. He then discusses how the *yang* gods exert order over the *yin* ghosts in "an eternal struggle."

See J. J. M. De Groot, *The Religious System of China* (Taipei: Literature House, 1964), 6: 929–33 (see especially 930).

51. Campany, 22.

52. For reader-respose literary theory, the work of Wolfgang Iser and Hans Robert Jauss has been groundbreaking. For Iser, see *The Implied Reader: Patterns of Communication in Prose Fiction from Bunyan to Beckett* (Baltimore: John Hopkins University Press, 1974); *The Act of Reading: A Theory of Aesthetic Response* (Baltimore: John Hopkins University Press, 1978); *Prospecting: From Reader Response to Literary Anthropology* (Baltimore: John Hopkins University Press, 1989). For Jauss, see *Aesthetic Experience and Literary Hermeneutics* (Minneapolis: University of Minnesota Press, 1982).

53. *Op. cit.*, 24–32.

54. *Op. cit.*, 21–32.

55. Shen Qizhan, preface to the Zhou edition of the *Yijian zhi*, in Hong Mai (1994), 1835.

56. Jan Vansina, 13.

57. For example, "Li Jinren's Attracting Attention" (*Zhiding*: 5: 1009) is about an official who remonstrates with a superior over a local drought during the Zhenghe (1111–1118) or Xuanhe period (1119–1126) when it was prohibited to do so by the court. While this could be construed as thematically linked with the preservation of order (good government) over disorder (drought), no overt *guai* element is discernible. Also, in "Han Shiwang's Bow and Arrow," a boastful official loses a bet with Han Shiwang, brother of the famous general Han Shizhong, over a private archery competition. There is no element of the strange throughout the narrative, nor is there any struggle between order and disorder. "Khitans Recite Poetry" briefly documented the manner in which Khitan children learned and recited poetry, and is more concerned with linguistics, ethnography, and literary conventions than *guai* phenomena.

CHAPTER FIVE

1. Hong Mai, (1978), *Sibi*: 9: 719.

2. This is summarized in Zhao Yushi. See Hong Mai (1994), 1818.

3. This is reproduced in Hong Mai (1994), 1825–26. See also Ma Duanlin's, *Wenxian tongkao* (Taipei: Xinxing shuju, 1962), 217: 1770–72.

4. For an account of historical personae featured in the accounts, see Chang Fu-jui, (1968): 55–93. For a biographical data about Hong's informants, see Wang Nian-shuang, 231–340. For indexes of people and places mentioned in the text, see Chang, Fu-jui's *I Chien Chih T'ung chien* (Taipei: Taiwan xuesheng shuju, 1976). For an index of people mentioned in the text, whether they be recognizably historical or not, see Wang Xiumei's index at the back of the 1981 Beijing Zhonghua shuju edition.

5. Han was awarded the title Han Xian'an by the Gaozong emperor in 1143 as recognition for service to the state. See Tuo Tuo et al., 11367. For Han's biography in the *History of the Song*, see ibid., 11355–368. Also Herbert Franke, 373–76. For details about the property, see the *Canglang ting xin zhi* 滄浪亭新志 (*New Record of the Blue Wave Pavilion*) by Jiang Jinghuan 蔣鏡寰 (Suzhou: Suzhou meishuguan, 1929). The transmission of ownership is given in the postscript.

6. Hong Mai, *Jia*: 17: 150–51.

7. Ou-Yang Xiu, *Xin Wudai shi* (Taipei: Zhonghua shuju, 1965), 63: 791.

8. Jinmingchi was a famous lake surrounded by extensive gardens, located to the northwest of the Xizhengmen Gate area in the Northern Song capital. See Hong Mai (1994), *Jia*: 4: 29.

9. A garden constructed by order of Song Huizong in the vicinity of the Northern Song capital, in which rare and exotic birds were collected. See Hong Mai (1994), *Bing*: 13: 478.

10. A famous garden in which the Ningzong emperor's minister, Han Tuozhou, was assassinated supposedly under the orders of Empress Yang. See Hong Mai, *Jia*: 2: 14.

11. For the *Jinming chi*, see Tuo Tuo et al., 297. For the Northeastern Marchmount, see Ding Chuanjing, 62. For the Jade Ford Garden, see ibid., 108.

12. Tuo Tuo et al., 1089.

13. Hong Mai (1994), *Zaibu*: 10: 1780.

14. For both spatial and temporal setting, see Chang Bide et al., 3180.

15. Ibid., 825.

16. Hong Mai (1994), *Jia*: 2: 16. For Kerr's discussion of this point, see "*Yijianzhi*: A Didactic Diversion," *Papers on Far Eastern History* 35 (1987): 80.

17. Glen Dudbridge, 143.

18. Huang Gongdu was, according to Wang Teh-yi, a friend of Hong's. See Wang Teh-yi, 2 (1964): 408

19. Hong Mai, *Zhiding*: 4: 1000.

20. Xu Song, ed., *Important Collected Documents of the Song* [*Song huiyao jigao*] (Taipei: Xinwenfeng chuban gongsi, 1976), 3945/3; 4224/2; 4239/3–4; 4362/3; 4604/1.

21. Valerie Hansen discusses these two versions in her *Changing Gods in Medieval China.*

22. *Song huiyao jigao*, 3959/4.

23. The translation is Valerie Hansen's. See 173–74. For Hong Mai's version, see *Jia*: 20: 182–83.

24. Valerie Hansen, 23.

25. *Tiaoxi ji*: 22: 7b–8a, *Wuxing jinshi*: 8: 21a. Quoted from Hansen, 22–23.

26. Hong Mai, *Jia*: 10: 88. The translation is Hansen's, 22. Reproduced by permission of Princeton University Press.

27. Hansen, 22. Reproduced by permission of Princeton University Press.

28. *Sanji*: 9: 1371.

29. See Chang Bide et al., 1086.

30. *Bing*: 18: 518.

31. Zhou Hui 周煇, *Qingbo zazhi* 清波雜志 in *Biji xiaoshuo daguan* (Jiangsu: Guangling guji keyin chuban, 1983), v. 2, 3: 326. The translation is Djang Chu's, 757.

32. Hong Mai (1994), 494. Hong gives reference to Wu Huchen as the storyteller of this and a second story at the conclusion of the account following this one. Huchen is the courtesy name of Wu Zeng.

33. Ibid.

34. Huizong's Northeastern Marchmount, or the Genyue 艮 嶽 (alternatively written as 艮岳).

35. The translation is Djang Chu's, 756–57. For the original, see Wu Zeng 吳曾, *Nenggai zhai manlu* 能改齋漫錄, Biji xiaoshuo daguan edition (1983), v. 8, 18: 301.

36. Hong Mai, *Bing*: 14: 483. For the *Chunzhu jiwen* account, see He Wei, 24–25.

37. *Jia*: 17: 151.

38. He Wei, *Chunzhu jiwen*, 22.

39. Fang Hao, *Song shi* (Taipei: Huagang chuban youxian gongsi, 1975), 1: 74.

40. *Bing*: 4: 393.

41. *Jia*: 5: 42.

42. Huangfu Mei 皇甫枚, *Sanshui xiaodu* 三水小牘 (Shanghai: Zhonghua shuji, 1960), 5. According to Carl S. Kao, however, he was known to have been a superintendent of records in Lushan County, Henan, around 873 (386). This work contains many stories of a *zhiguai* nature and, according to Kao, was written in 910 when Huangfu was staying in the Shaanxi area.

43. For further reading, see Hou Zhongyi, 235–40.

44. *Huan* 鍰, a unit of currency, evidently a considerable sum judging from this account.

45. Huangfu Mei, 5.

46. Gardner, 64.

47. He Wei, 21–22.

48. 靈響 *lingxiang*. An ambiguous term which meant that either the deity was reliable in answering prayers, or that the deity actually emited a sound.

49. Hong Mai, *Jia*: 8: 65.

50. This possibly refers to the Jurchen invasion which ended the Northern Song Dynasty (960–1127).

51. Hong Mai, *Jia*, 17: 148–50. This piece was translated by me. It was first published in *Renditions* 57 (Spring 2002), 32–34; reprinted by permission of the Research Centre for Translation, The Chinese University of Hong Kong. It has been modified slightly here.

52. Liu Fu 劉斧, *Qingsuo gaoyi* 青瑣高議 (Shanghai, 1959), 9.

53. 謝紅蓮.

54. *Op cit.*

55. Not only do the personal names in each account bear semantic similarities (i.e., "lotus"), but the surnames are also pronounced the same—strongly suggesting that oral retelling played a part in its transmission.

56. Interestingly enough, a version closely akin to the *Record* version later found its way into the Song *biji* work, the *Leshan lu* 樂善錄. See the *Biji xiaoshuo daguan* edition (Taipei: Xinxing shuju, 1981), 2: *juan shang*, 14b–15b (1309 10).

57. See Patricia Buckley Ebrey, *The Inner Quarters: Marriage and the Lives of Chinese Women in the Sung Period* (Berkeley and Los Angeles: University of California Press, 1993), 225.

58. Since this corresponds to the location of the ghost story, it is likely that Guan heard the story during his incumbency there.

59. See Wang Nianshuang, 335.

60. These are as follows: *Yi*: 8: 247, *Bing*: 4: 392, and *Bing*: 19: 530.

61. See Wang Nianshuang, 315–16. The Battle of Caishi (modern Ma'an Shan 馬鞍山 City in Anhui) led to a strategic defeat of the invading Jurchen army, which saw their retreat from Song territory. Yu played a pivotal role in the Song victory when he organized both civil and military resistance and rallied flagging morale after the previous general, Wang Quan (dates uncertain), was recalled due to lack of initiative, and before his replacement, Li Xianzhong, (1110–1178) was able to arrive. See the *Song shi*, (Beijing: Zhonghua shuju, 1977), 32: 608–11.

62. *Yi*: 14: 302.

63. *Jia*: 17: 147–48.

64. See T. Tsiperovitch's article about the *Qingsuo gaoyi*, in Yves Hervouet, ed., *A Sung Bibliography* (Hong Kong: Chinese University Press, 1978), 342.

65. There are, of course, well-known examples in Tang *chuanqi* whereby historical figures are the subject of "fictionalized" accounts (at least in the finer details), such as Tang Xuanzong (r. 712–756) and Yang Guifei in the *Changhen zhuan* 長恨傳. Yet we are dealing with a murder never brought to justice in the *Record* account. This is quite different from the well-known events in the *Changhen zhuan* which could loosely be described as "historical fiction."

66. Zhou Mi in Wang Yunwu, ed., 1040–3.

Appendix 1

Chart Showing Accounts from the *Record* and Antecedents from other Earlier Literary Sources

YI JIAN ZHI STORY	PARALLEL TEXT	REFERENCE GIVEN BY HONG MAI Y/N
Bing gui, *Jia*: 1: 9: 6	Hong Hao 洪皓, *Songmo jiwen* 松漠記聞, 12–14.	N
Ah Baoji Shoots a Dragon, *Jia*: 1: 10: 6	Ibid.	N
The Dragon of Cold Mountain, *Jia*: 1: 11: 6	Ibid.	N
The Dragon of Xizhou, *Jia*: 1: 12: 7	Ibid.	N
Sun Juyuan's Career, *Jia*: 4: 12: 33–34	*Nanyou Jijiu* in Ding Chuanjing, *Compilation of Anecdotes on Song Personae*, 429–30	N
The Villager from Jiangyin, *Jia*: 5: 14: 42	Huangfu Mei 皇甫枚, *Sanshui xiaodu* 三水小牘, 5	Y
Saved by Buddha from Past Enmity, *Jia*: 8: 3: 65	He Wei 何薳, *Chunzhu jiwen* 春渚紀聞, 21–22	N

(continued)

YI JIAN ZHI STORY	PARALLEL TEXT	REFERENCE GIVEN BY HONG MAI Y/N
Meng Wenshu, *Jia*: 10: 10: 87	Guo Sanyi 郭三益, *Wenshu muzhi* 溫舒墓誌	Y
Third Sister Xie, *Jia* 17: 5: 1148–50	Liu Fu 劉斧, *Qingsuo gaoyi* 青瑣高議, 9	N
Xu Guohua, *Jia* 17: 9: 151	He Wei, *Chunzhu Jiwen*, 22	N
Yang Daming, *Yi*: 3: 11: 208–9	Veritable Records	Y
Mr. Wang, *Yi*: 10: 6: 267	*Guoshi houbu* 國史後補	Y
The Lufu Ghost, *Yi*: 20: 9: 358–59	Zhang Shizheng 張師正, *Kuoyi zhi.* 括異志	Y
Nie Congzhi, *Bing*: 2: 10: 379–81	Wang Minchong 王敏仲, *Quanshan lu* 勸善錄	Y
Sun Ghost's Face, *Bing*: 4: 4: 393	*Taiping Yülan* 太平御覽, 1676, also the *Taiping guangji* 太平廣記 ch. 276	Y
The Xuanhe Dragon, *Bing*: 9: 4: 439–40	Cai Tiao 蔡條, *Houshi bu* 後史補	Y
Liu Jingwen, *Bing*: 10: 10: 453	Zhou Zizhi 周紫芝, *Zhupo shihua* 竹坡詩話	Y
The Woman of Yongxi's Lyric, *Bing*: 10: 11: 474	Ibid.	Y
Lan Jie, *Bing*: 13: 1: 473–74	*Zhang Chang zhuan* 張敞傳, (Han Dynasty)	Y
The Person from Changxi, *Bing*: 13: 2: 474	*Mingsi baoying* 冥司報應	Y
The Strange Pig of Fuzhou, *Bing*: 13: 3: 474	Ibid.	Y
The Fuzhou Butcher's Son, *Bing*: 13: 4: 475	Ibid.	Y

(continued)

YI JIAN ZHI STORY	PARALLEL TEXT	REFERENCE GIVEN BY HONG MAI Y/N
Lin wengyao, *Bing*: 13: 5: 475	Ibid.	Y
Zhang Guizi, *Bing*: 13: 10: 478	Chen Zhengmin 陳正敏, *Dunzhai xianlan* 遯齋閑覽	Y
Ice Flowers on a Tin Tray, *Bing*: 14: 4: 487–88	He Wei, *Chunzhu Jiwen*, 24–25	Y
The Taoist who planted Aniseed, *Bing*: 15: 6: 494	Wu Zeng 吳曾, *Nenggai zhai manlu* 能改齋漫錄 in *Biji xiaoshuo daguan*, 1983 ed., v. 8, ch. 18: 9, 301	Y
Taoist of Supreme Purity Temple, *Bing*: 16: 2: 499	*Zhang Wenqian ji* 張文潛集	Y
Wang Wushan, *Bing*: 16: 3: 499	Ibid.	Y
Liu Yishu, *Bing*: 17: 11: 512	*Jianyan yilai xinian yaolu* 建炎以來繫年要錄, ch. 182	N
The Dead Woman of Xuancheng, *Ding*: 2: 18: 553	*Jingshan bian* 荊山編	Y
Assistant to the Bureau of Destiny, *Ding*: 4: 2: 565	*Fuxiu ji* 浮休集	Y
Liu Shiyan, *Ding*: 4: 3: 565	Ibid.	Y
The House at Dailou Gate, *Ding*: 7: 1: 591	Zhu Shengfei 朱勝非, *Xiushui xianju lu* 秀水閒居錄	Y
Lin's Daughter-in-law's Bond Maid, *Ding*: 7: 2: 591	Ibid.	Y
Wang Hou's Carrot, *Ding*: 7: 3: 592	Ibid.	Y

(continued)

YI JIAN ZHI STORY	PARALLEL TEXT	REFERENCE GIVEN BY HONG MAI Y/N
The Jade Toad of Tiantai, *Ding*: 7: 4: 592	Ibid.	Y
The Freak Horse of Jizhou, *Ding*: 7: 5: 592	Ibid.	Y
The Tortoise and Snake of Nanjing, *Ding*: 7: 6: 592–93	Ibid.	Y
The Gentleman of Bingguo, *Ding*: 7: 7: 593	Ibid.	Y
Zhu Shengsi's Seal, *Ding*: 7: 8: 593	Ibid.	Y
The Limp Tiger of Mt. Dahong, *Ding*: 10: 9: 622	*Handong zhi* 漢東志	Y
Liu Yaoju, *Ding*: 9: 17: 683	Guo Tuan 郭彖, *Kuiche zhi* 睽車志	Y
Wei Shihui, *Zhijia*: 2: 12: 726–27	*Wenshan lu* 聞善錄	N
The Old Monk of Qiantang, *Zhijia*: 4: 13: 742	Gong Tingjun 龔廷筠, *Ciren zhi* 慈仁志	Y
The Dolphinfish of Nine Pines, *Zhijia*: 4: 13: 743	Ibid.	Y
Wang of Fuli's Silkworms, *Zhijia*: 8: 3: 771	Duan Kegu 段成式, *Youyang zazu, Zhinuo* 酉陽雜俎支諾上, first account, 199	Y
10 stories, *Zhiyi*: 2: 3–12: 806–11	*Mengzhao lu* 夢兆錄	Y
Re-writing Mr. Xu's Error, *Zhiyi*: 4: 8: 826–27	Wang Yanfu 王彥輔, *Zhushi* 麈史	Y
Luo Bogu's Head Tumor, *Zhiyi*: 6: 2: 836–37	He Wei, *Chunzhu Jiwen*	Y

(continued)

YI JIAN ZHI STORY	PARALLEL TEXT	REFERENCE GIVEN BY HONG MAI Y/N
Yang Shouzi, *Zhiyi*: 10: 14: 875–76	Tang Dynasty *xiaoshuo*	Y
True Person Zhu of Fengling, *Zhijing*: 6: 1: 924–25	Sun Shaowei 孫少魏 (1077–1123), *Donggao zalu* 東皋雜錄	Y
Ye Zuyi, *Zhijing*: 6: 2: 925	Ibid.	Y
The Magistrate of Liling, *Zhijing*: 6: 1: 925	Ibid.	Y
The Dwarfs of Daozhou, *Zhijing*: 6: 1: 926	Ibid.	Y
The Kaifu Pagoda, *Zhijing*: 6: 1: 926	Ibid.	Y
Li Sui Pacifies the Flames, *Zhijing*: 6: 1: 926–27	Ibid.	Y
Liu Fangming, *Zhijing*: 7: 10: 938	Wang Zhongxing 王中行, *Tujing* 圖經	Y
The Plum Poem of the Ninth Month, *Zhijing*: 7: 11: 938	Ibid.	Y
Zhao Sanweng, *Zhiding*: 8: 1: 1027–28.	Guo Tuan, *Guiche zhi*	Y
Girl from Ezhou's South Market, *Zhigeng*: 1: 1: 1136–37	*Qingzun lu* 清尊錄	Y
Xu Wen the True Taoist, *Zhigeng*: 6: 8: 1184	*Dongpo zhilin* 東坡志林	Y
Zhigeng: 7: all: 1168–93	Wu Liangshi 吳良史, *Shixuan jushi biji* 時軒居士筆記	Y
Zhigeng: 8: all: 1194–1201	Ibid.	Y
Zhigeng: 9: all: 1203–10	Ibid.	Y

(continued)

YI JIAN ZHI STORY	PARALLEL TEXT	REFERENCE GIVEN BY HONG MAI Y/N
Zhao Chengzhi Travels to Daiyue, *Zhigui*: 1: 8: 1228	Zhao Chengzhi 趙承之, *Zhuyin jishi ji* 竹隱畸士集	Y
Mu Zipei and Cock Fighting, *Zhigui*: 2: 7: 1234–35	Mu Zipei 穆次裴, *Yi meng lu* 異夢錄	Y
The Stone Buddha of Linzhi, *Zhigui*: 4: 12: 1253	*Shuyi zhi*	Y
Su Dongpo Dreams of Visiting Immortals, *Zhigui*: 7: 1: 1270–71	Ma Yongqing, *Mengxian ji* 夢仙記 (游仙記?)	Y
The Plaque on the Chunhua Pavilion, *Zhigui*: 10: 2: 1294–95	Ma Yongqing 馬永卿, *Lan zhenren lu* 懶真人錄	Y
Cai Que Dreams of Attaining Power, *Zhigui*: 10: 3: 1295	Ibid.	Y
Master of the Old Pagoda, *Zhigui*: 10: 4: 1295	Ibid.	Y
The Fair Maiden of Mt. Shiliu, *Sanzhi ji*: 1: 1: 1304–5	*Shuoyi* 說異 (not extant by Southern Song)	Y
The Stone Fish of Xiaogan Temple, *Sanzhi ji*: 1: 2: 1305	Ibid.	Y
Qin Zhong is Branded, *Sanzhi ji*: 1: 3: 1305–6	Ibid.	Y
Ying Ying, *Sanzhi ji*: 1: 4: 1306–9	Wang Shan 王山, *Bilian lu* 筆奩錄	Y
Li Mei of Chang'an, *Sanzhi ji*: 1: 5: 1309–10	Ibid.	Y
Sanzhi ji: 8: all: 1360–67	Li Ziyong 李子永, *Lanze yeyu* 蘭澤野語	Y

(continued)

YI JIAN ZHI STORY	PARALLEL TEXT	REFERENCE GIVEN BY HONG MAI Y/N
The Rich Man of Kuaiji, *Sanzhi ji*: 9: 1: 1369	Ibid.	Y
Chen Yingzhong's Dream, *Sanzhi ji*: 9: 2: 1369	Ibid.	Y
The Puzhao Statue of Zhizhou, *Sanzhi ji*: 9: 3: 1369	Ibid.	Y
The Cave of Wuzhou, *Sanzhi ji*: 9: 4: 1370	Ibid.	Y
The Beauty of Mt. Pojin, *Sanzhi ji*: 9: 5: 1370	Ibid.	Y
The Toad of Sweet Water Lane, *Sanzhi ji*: 9: 6: 1371	Ibid.	Y
stories 3–15, *Sanzhi xin*: 4: 1411–17	Chen Xinshu 陳莘叔, *Songxi jushi jingxing lu* 松溪居士徑行錄	Y
Book Twenty seven, *Sanzhi xin*: 9: 6: 1444	Guo Tuan, *Kuiche zhi*	Y
The Temple of Zhang Yide, *Sanzhi ren*: 7: 1: 1516	Wang Minshu 王敏叔, *Yitang ji* 頤堂集	Y
Mr. Wang Daocheng, *Sanzhi ren*: 7: 2: 1517	Ibid.	Y
The Bronze Horse of Pi County, *Sanzhi ren*: 7: 3: 1518	Ibid.	Y
The Longevity Snail, *Sanzhi ren*: 7: 4: 1518–19	Ibid.	Y
Shu's Lyric, *Sanzhi ren*: 7: 5: 1519	Ibid.	Y
Hui Zong's Plate Stone, *Sanzhi ren*: 7: 6: 1519–20	Ibid.	Y

(continued)

YI JIAN ZHI STORY	PARALLEL TEXT	REFERENCE GIVEN BY HONG MAI Y/N
Six Lyrics in the *Qingping Yue, Sanzhi ren*: 7: 7: 1520–21	Ibid.	Y
The Purple Maiden's Lyrics, *Sanzhi ren*: 7: 8: 1521	Ibid.	Y
Zhou Meicheng's Lyric, *Sanzhi ren*: 7: 9: 1521–22	Ibid.	Y
Hui Rou the Servant Boy, *Sanzhi ren*: 7: 10: 1522	Ibid.	Y
Mo Shaoxu's Lyric, *Sanzhi ren*: 7: 11: 1522	Ibid.	Y
Wang Lan, *Bu*: 6: 3: 1604–5	*Yishi* 逸史 and *Xu Xuanguai lu* 續玄怪錄	Y
Liu, Master of the Cave, *Bu*: 7: 7: 1615	*Lishi huanhun lu* 李氏還魂錄	Y
The Temple of Ancestral Sacrifice, *Bu*: 9: 2: 1627–28	Ma Chun 馬純, *Taozhu xinlu* 陶朱新錄 (1 ch., 1142)	N
The Monk of Kaiyuan Temple, *Bu*: 13: 6: 1669	Su Che 蘇徹, *Longchuan lüezhi* 龍川略志	N
Master Zhao of Gao'an, *Bu*: 13: 11: 1673–74	Ibid.	Y

The above chart is based on my own research into the *Record* and other literary texts.

Source: The references are derived from Hong's own citations throughout the corpus of the *Record*. Those which he did not cite a reference for have been uncovered myself.

Appendix 2

The First Installment—Locations, Dates, and Informants

REFERENCE	NAME OF INFORMANT	INFORMANT'S BIRTHPLACE	LOCATION OF EVENT	EVENT DATE
1: 1	孫久鼎	山東沂州	汴河北岸	1113
1: 2	孫久鼎	山東沂州	江西饒州	?
1: 3	孫久鼎	山東沂州		1133
1: 4	張維	燕山三河縣	燕山三河村	1125
1: 5			河北蔚州	
1: 6				
1: 7			金國興中府	1140
1: 8			濟州	1137
1: 9	洪皓	江西饒州	汴梁太康縣	
1: 10	洪皓	江西饒州		
1: 11	洪皓	江西饒州	冷山	1135
1: 12	洪皓,趙伯璘	江西饒州,?	甘肅熙州	
1: 13			汴梁	徽宗朝
1: 14				
1: 15			燕京	1137

(continued)

REFERENCE	NAME OF INFORMANT	INFORMANT'S BIRTHPLACE	LOCATION OF EVENT	EVENT DATE
1: 16	趙伯璘		汴梁	
1: 17	趙伯璘		汴梁	元豐年間
1: 18			汾陰	紹興年間
1: 19				紹興年間
2: 1			汴梁	
2: 2			濰州	**1158**
2: 3			江陰	**1190**
2: 4	朱新仲	安徽舒州	蔡州,徐州	政和年間
2: 5			浙江秀州	宣和年間
2: 6	胡條然	江西饒州	汴梁	大觀年間
2: 7	胡條然		江西饒州	
2: 8	胡條然	江西饒州		1134
2: 9	胡條然	江西饒州		1134
2: 10	趙令衿		湖北蘄州	1123
2: 11	黃襲	江西建昌	江西建昌	
2: 12				元祐年間
2: 13			浙江台州寧海縣	1117
2: 14	崔祖武			
3: 1	董猷	江西徽州	江西徽州	
3: 2	洪端	江西饒州	江西饒州	宣和末
3: 3	陳燻	浙江台州臨海縣	浙江會稽	
3: 4			浙江會稽	1141
3: 5	何叔達,程資忠	浙江浦江縣,?	浙江婺州浦江縣	

(continued)

REFERENCE	NAME OF INFORMANT	INFORMANT'S BIRTHPLACE	LOCATION OF EVENT	EVENT DATE
3:6	桂繡	江西信州貴溪	江西信州貴溪	1140
3:7	桂繡	江西信州貴溪		
3:8	桂繡	江西信州貴溪	江西信州貴溪	
3:9			臨安	1122
4:1			江東	1144
4:2	江續之		汴梁	
4:3	希賜(僧)		廣南嶺南	1147
4:4	余因		安徽池州	政和年間
4:5	馬登	江西饒州樂平縣	江西饒州	
4:6	李鏞	江西徽州婺源	江西徽州婺源	
4:7	李鏞	江西徽州婺源	江西徽州婺源	
4:8	王堯臣		江西饒州德興	1147
4:9			浙江秀州	
4:10				
4:11	高思道		山東密州	1085
4:12	李益謙	山東太安縣		
4:13	林熙載		浙江溫州	1140
4:14	林熙載		浙江溫州	宣和年間
4:15	林熙載		浙江溫州	1146
5:1	林熙載		福建南劍	1149

(continued)

REFERENCE	NAME OF INFORMANT	INFORMANT'S BIRTHPLACE	LOCATION OF EVENT	EVENT DATE
5: 2	陳爟, 林熙載	浙江台州臨海縣, ?	福建平陽	1146
5: 3	陳爟	浙江台州臨海縣	浙江台州	
5: 4	陳爟	浙江台州臨海縣	浙江台州	
5: 5	陳爟	浙江台州臨海縣	江蘇真州	
5: 6	陳爟	浙江台州臨海縣	浙江婺州	
5: 7				1147
5: 8				1140
5: 9	薛允功		福建福州	1149
5: 10	嚴康以		汴梁	政和年間
5: 11	錢符		浙江台州	1143
5: 12	葉若谷	江西洪州	江西虔州	1144
5: 13	高介卿		福建福州	
5: 14	林明甫		江西江陰	1146
5: 15				
5: 16				
5: 17	陳寅		江西撫州	
5: 18				紹興初
6: 1				**1178**
6: 2			荊南	**1192**
6: 3	蘇粹中		汴梁	1108
6: 4	葉平甫		江蘇蘇州	

(continued)

REFERENCE	NAME OF INFORMANT	INFORMANT'S BIRTHPLACE	LOCATION OF EVENT	EVENT DATE
6: 5			福建福州永福縣	
6: 6	陳爟	浙江台州臨海縣	福建福州	1150
6: 7	林亮功	浙江溫州		
6: 8	劉翔	福建福州	福建福州	宣和年間
6: 9				
6: 10	鄭東卿	福建福州閩縣	福建福州閩縣	熙寧年間
6: 11	鄭東卿	福建福州閩縣	福建福州吉田	崇寧初
6: 12	鄭東卿	福建福州閩縣	福建福州	
6: 13	劉翔	福建福州		元祐初
7: 1	李郁	福建邵武軍	明州	
7: 2	林亮功	浙江溫州	江西建康	
7: 3	日智(僧)	安徽宣州	湖南岳州平江	1136
7: 4			浙江台州	1132
7: 5			湖南岳州平江	1138
7: 6			江西常州	1134
7: 7				
7: 8				靖康年間
7: 9				
7: 10	曹績		汴梁	大觀年間
7: 11	李舒長	福建寧德縣	汴梁	

(continued)

REFERENCE	NAME OF INFORMANT	INFORMANT'S BIRTHPLACE	LOCATION OF EVENT	EVENT DATE
7: 12				
7: 13	本衲			
7: 14			常德府	**1195**
7: 15			仁和縣	乾道年間
7: 16			江西鄱陽	慶元初
7: 17	朱亨叟		浙江溫州	
7: 18	戴宏中	浙江溫州瑞安縣		
7: 19			福建漳州漳浦縣	
8: 1	陳彌作	福建閩縣	江蘇興化	
8: 2	陳彌作	福建閩縣	福建福州	
8: 3	陳彌作	福建閩縣	臨安	建炎年間
8: 4	林亮功	浙江溫州	汴梁	宣和年間
8: 5	惟學 (福州永福縣僧)		福建福州	
8: 6	黃仍		江蘇壽春府	
8: 7	黃仍		河南鄧州南陽縣	靖康年間
8: 8	黃仍			
8: 9	梁宏夫			汴梁
8: 10	吳則禮	廣西富川縣		
8: 11	黃仍			
8: 12			江西饒州	1141
8: 13			江西饒州	1135
8: 14			江西鄱陽	

(continued)

REFERENCE	NAME OF INFORMANT	INFORMANT'S BIRTHPLACE	LOCATION OF EVENT	EVENT DATE
8: 15			江西饒州東湖	1150
8: 16	山僧某		廣南昭州恭城	皇祐年間
8: 17			廣州西海	1138
9: 1				
9: 2			江西崇仁縣	
9: 3	余執度		安徽池州建德縣	1151
9: 4	余執度			1124
9: 5	余執度		浙江睦州建德	1098
9: 6	黃文薦	福建邵武軍	福建邵武泰寧	
9: 7	黃文薦	福建邵武軍	福建邵武	1119–1146
9: 8	黃文薦	福建邵武軍	福建邵武泰寧	1134
9: 9	黃文薦	福建邵武軍	福建邵武泰寧	1123
9: 10			安徽池州建德縣	1149?
9: 11	鄭東卿	福建福州閩縣	福建福州閩縣	宣和年間
9: 12	鄭東卿	福建福州閩縣	福建福州閩縣	1149
9: 13	鄭東卿	福建福州閩縣	福建福州	
10: 1	朱翌		安徽舒州桐城縣	

(continued)

REFERENCE	NAME OF INFORMANT	INFORMANT'S BIRTHPLACE	LOCATION OF EVENT	EVENT DATE
10: 2	朱翌		安徽舒州桐城縣	
10: 3	董廷	江西廬陵縣		1132
10: 4	希賜 (英州僧)		廣南英州真陽縣	1135
10: 5	希賜 (英州僧)		廣南英州	1149
10: 6	希賜 (英州僧)			
10: 7	傅雱	浙江浦江縣	江西吉州	
10: 8	張昭			宣和年間
10: 9	郭三益	江蘇常州	山東濮州	
10: 10	黃文驀		廣南惠州, 潮州	1132, 1133
10: 11	黃文驀		福建建州浦城	
10: 12	黃文驀		廣南惠州	紹興年間
10: 13	鄭焦	福建莆田縣		
10: 14	吳价	湖州	江蘇湖州	
10: 15	邊知白	江蘇平江府	浙江秀州魏塘鎮	1117
10: 16	李鯹		湖南岳州平江	
10: 17	李鯹		湖南岳州平江	
10: 18	李鯹		江蘇湖州	
11: 1	洪興祖	江蘇丹陽縣	江西鄱陽	1150
11: 2	洪興祖	江蘇丹陽縣		

(continued)

REFERENCE	NAME OF INFORMANT	INFORMANT'S BIRTHPLACE	LOCATION OF EVENT	EVENT DATE
11: 3	洪興祖	江蘇丹陽縣	江西江陰	
11: 4	洪興祖	江蘇丹陽縣	江蘇湖州	
11: 5	洪興祖	江蘇丹陽縣	浙江秀州	
11: 6	洪興祖	江蘇丹陽縣		
11: 7	強行父	浙江錢塘縣	江蘇海州	熙寧年間
11: 8			二相公廟	1118
11: 9	南安軍僧某		南安軍東嘉祐寺	紹興初
11: 10	連潛			1151
11: 11	張端愨	浙江處州	福建泉州	
11: 12	鄭資之	江蘇徐州		宣和年間
11: 13			浙江錢塘	
11: 14	黃文薦		湖北黃州	崇寧
11: 15				
11: 16			浙江處州縉雲	
11: 17	李彌正	江蘇平江府	江蘇常州	宣和年間
12: 1			河南蔡州	
12: 2			故蘇	
12: 3	甚老 (僧)		江蘇鎮江	1146
12: 4			湖南岳州平江	1148
12: 5	呂丘寧孫		浙江處州縉雲	建炎年間
12: 6	強行父	浙江錢塘縣	汴梁	宣和年間
12: 7	強行父	浙江錢塘縣	汴梁	

(continued)

REFERENCE	NAME OF INFORMANT	INFORMANT'S BIRTHPLACE	LOCATION OF EVENT	EVENT DATE
12: 8	聞人滋	江蘇秀州	江蘇秀州	
12: 9				
12: 10	崔		江蘇真州六合縣	
12: 11	晁公遡		儋耳	
12: 12	黃文鷹		福建邵武泰寧縣	
12: 13	陳彌作	福建閩縣		
12: 14	祖璠		江西洪州	1153
12: 15	周汸			
13: 1	郟次南			
13: 2	傅世修	浙江會稽縣	浙江天台	1138
13: 3	傅世修,?	浙江會稽縣	浙江會稽縣	1150
13: 4	樊國均	浙江衢州		1130
13: 5	傅世修	浙江會稽縣		
13: 6			江西饒州樂平縣	1153
13: 7			江西徽州婺源縣	1153
13: 8	劉邦翰		浙江婺州武義縣	1154
13: 9	邢孝肅			
13: 10	鄭知剛	福建永福縣	福州侯官縣	
13: 11	竇思永,?	江蘇徐州	江西洪州	1153
13: 12	盧熊	福建邵武軍		1151
13: 13				1135
13: 14	唐信道		拱州	

(continued)

REFERENCE	NAME OF INFORMANT	INFORMANT'S BIRTHPLACE	LOCATION OF EVENT	EVENT DATE
13: 15			甘肅秦州	
13: 16		福建邵武軍		1143
13: 17	了達(江西吉州隆慶寺僧)			
13: 18	杜莘老	四川眉州青神縣	四川蜀州新津	
14: 1	陳安國	福建潮州		
14: 2	張可久		福建漳州	
14: 3	張可久			崇寧年間
14: 4	張可久		江西吉州吉水	1152
14: 5	張可久		廣南桂陽	建炎年間
14: 6	張可久		廣東	紹興初
14: 7	董爛	江西饒州		
14: 8	李景遹			
14: 9			安徽舒州	1155
14: 10			江西婺州四明海	
14: 11				建炎年間
14: 12			羅源鸛坑	
14: 13				
14: 14			江西饒州樂平縣	
14: 15			江西鄱陽	**1196**
14: 16				
14: 17	王秬	河北中山縣		
15: 1			四川恭州	紹興初

(continued)

REFERENCE	NAME OF INFORMANT	INFORMANT'S BIRTHPLACE	LOCATION OF EVENT	EVENT DATE
15:2	劉襄		橫山寨	1153
15:3	楊朴	四川資州	四川果州	1126
15:4	張宗元	河南唐州方城縣	四川閬州	1131
15:5	張達		夔州	1147
15:6	善同(僧)		湖南衡山	
15:7	張宗一	河南唐州方城縣	河南府伊陽縣	
15:8	張宗一	河南唐州方城縣		1128
15:9	張宗一	河南唐州方城縣	河南唐州方城縣	
15:10			河南唐州方城縣	
15:11	劉襄			
15:12	劉襄		武昌	1138
15:13	馬元益	江西饒州樂平縣		1140
15:14	關注、強行父	浙江錢塘(兩)	浙江越州新昌縣	紹聖年間
15:15	鄭總	廣東英州	廣南循州龍川	
15:16			浙江衢州江山	
15:17	陳俊卿	福建莆田縣	福建莆田縣	
16:1	徐榑			
16:2	徐榑		江蘇鎮江金壇	

(continued)

REFERENCE	NAME OF INFORMANT	INFORMANT'S BIRTHPLACE	LOCATION OF EVENT	EVENT DATE
16: 3	徐榑		浙江錢塘湯村	
16: 4	徐榑		江西信州玉山	1146
16: 5	李紹祖		豫章村	1154
16: 6	李紹祖		河南光州	
16: 7	李紹祖		江西南康建昌縣	
16: 8	張宗元	河南唐州方城縣	江蘇常州無錫	
16: 9			河南唐州方城縣	
16: 10	杜莘老	四川眉州青神縣		
16: 11	洪耰	江西洪州	江西洪州	
16: 12	尚定國			
16: 13	尚定國			
16: 14			江西江州湖口	1154
16: 15	金安節		浙江錢塘縣	宣和年間
17: 1	虞允文	四川仁壽縣		
17: 2	虞允文	四川仁壽縣	四川永康軍	
17: 3	虞允文	四川仁壽縣	四川成都	
17: 4	虞允文	四川仁壽縣	四川果州南充	1157
17: 5	虞允文	四川仁壽縣	臨安	1158
17: 6	虞允文	四川仁壽縣	四川成都	1151
17: 7	虞允文	四川仁壽縣	四川資州	

(continued)

REFERENCE	NAME OF INFORMANT	INFORMANT'S BIRTHPLACE	LOCATION OF EVENT	EVENT DATE
17: 8	邵德升		汴梁	1126
17: 9			廣西昭州	建炎年間
17: 10	黃子淳	湖北德安縣	江西德安府	崇寧年間
17: 11	路彬	山西晉陽縣		
17: 12	林之奇	福州侯官縣	福州長樂縣	
17: 13	劉琪	福建崇安縣	福建建陽	
17: 14			廣州清遠縣	
18: 1	吳興拳	杭州富陽縣		花石之亂
18: 2	楊朴	四川資州	四川資州	
18: 3	楊朴	四川資州	四川資州	
18: 4	楊朴	四川資州	四川劍州梓潼縣	
18: 5	楊朴	四川資州		1117–1147
18: 6	楊朴	四川資州		1124
18: 7	楊朴	四川資州	四川資州	
18: 8	任古	湖北廣濟縣		
18: 9			安徽衢州、安徽明州	1147 etc.
18: 10	朱倬	福建閩縣	汴梁	政和初
18: 11	朱倬、李季長	福建閩縣	福建福州	
18: 12	朱倬	福建閩縣	汴梁	
18: 13	朱熙載	江蘇金壇縣	晉雲巾子山	1145
18: 14	劉琪	福建崇安縣		1154
18: 15	陳方石	福建泉州	福建泉州	

(continued)

REFERENCE	NAME OF INFORMANT	INFORMANT'S BIRTHPLACE	LOCATION OF EVENT	EVENT DATE
18:16	程大昌	安徽徽州休寧縣	臨安	1147
19:1	魏志		江蘇平江府	
19:2				1158
19:3	竇思永	江蘇徐州		1159
19:4	杜莘老	四川眉州青神縣	四川瀘州合江	
19:5	唐閱		汴梁	
19:6	王祖	河北中山縣		
19:7	王祖	河北中山縣	福建泉州	1152
19:8	王祖	河北中山縣	汴梁,?	
19:9	王祖	河北中山縣	汴梁	
19:10				1144
19:11	謝芷	福建泉州	福建泉州	1154
19:12			廣南梅州	1150
19:13				1150
19:14	韓彥直	陝西延安府		紹興初
20:1	汪叔詹	江西徽州歙縣		1148
20:2	唐閱		杭州西湖靈芝寺	1150
20:3	唐閱		浙江處州	1126
20:4			福建泉州晉江	1130
20:5	周時	四川成都	四川	1150
20:6	竇思永	江蘇徐州	江蘇鹽官縣	1159

(continued)

REFERENCE	NAME OF INFORMANT	INFORMANT'S BIRTHPLACE	LOCATION OF EVENT	EVENT DATE
20: 7	竇思永	江蘇徐州	餘杭	1159
20: 8	竇思永	江蘇徐州	江蘇秀州海鹽	1158
20: 9			福建南劍	1130
20: 10	王秬	河北中山縣	福建泉州葵山	
20: 11	王秬	河北中山縣	廣南融州天寧寺	
20: 12	王秬	河北中山縣	福建泉州	1147

Source: The dates, locations of occurrence, and informant's names have been extracted from the text itself. Boldface denotes that the account in question has been either replicated from another section (and, therefore, possibly did not originally appear in the first installment), or bears a date later than that of the latest possible year of completion for the first installment (1160 or 1161). This indicates missing sections of the original Song Dynasty text which were supplimented during the editing of a Yuan Dynasty edition. Information about the informant's birthplace, where known, has been drawn from Okamoto Fujiaki's 1994 study of *Jia zhi* informants. Since I have chosen to use the first names—as opposed to style names—of informants, in cases where Hong Mai has given the style name of the informant, I have relied on Okamoto's scholarship.

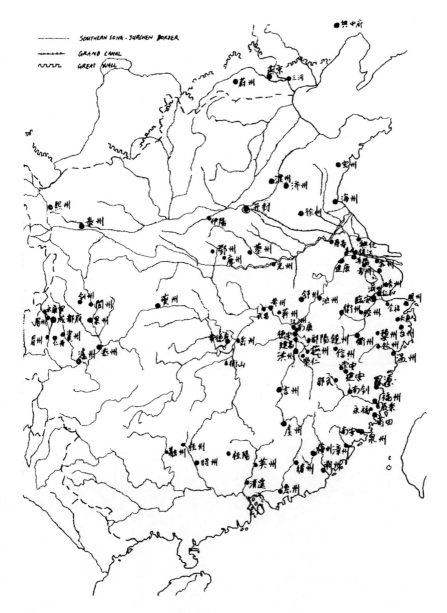

Map 1. Locations of Occurrences for Accounts from the first installment.

Selected Bibliography

The following bibliography is arranged according to language of publication. Works produced before 1920 are cited by title.

CHINESE SOURCES

Bin Tui Lu 賓退錄, Zhao Yushi 趙與時. In Hong Mai (1994), 1817–21.

Canglang ting xin zhi 滄浪亭新志, Jiang Jinghuan 蔣鏡寰. Suzhou: Suzhou meishuguan, 1929.

Cangyuan qunshu jingyan lu 藏園群書經眼錄, Fu Zengxiang 傅增湘. Beijing: Zhonghua shuju, 1983.

Chang Bide et al., comp. *Index to Biographical Materials of Song Figures*. Taipei: Dingwen shuju, 1974.

Chang Fu-jui. "Hong Mai yu *Yijian zhi*." In *'93 Zhongguo gudai xiaoshuo guoji yantaohui lunwen ji* '93 中國古代小說國際研討會論文集. Beijing: Kaiming chuban she, 1996, 134–40.

Chen Guocan and Fang Rujin. *Song Xiaozong* 宋孝宗. Changchun Shi: Jilin wen shi chuban she, 1997.

Cheng Hong 程弘. "Guanyu *Yijian Zhi* yiwen ji 'Dongchuang shifan'" 關於夷堅志佚文及東窗事犯. *Wenxian* 文獻 32 (1987): 285–86.

Chuanshi lou Song-Yuan ben shumu 傳是樓宋元本書目, Xu Qianxue 徐乾學. In Hong Mai (1994), 1828.

Chunzhu jiwen 春渚紀聞, He Wei 何薳. Beijing: Zhonghua shuju, 1983.

Dong chuang ji 東窗集, Zhang Kuo 張擴. Taipei: Shangwu yinshuguan, 1983.

Duan Xingmin. *Liu Zihou yuyan wenxue tanwei* 柳子厚寓言文學探微. Taipei: 1978.

Fang Hao 方豪. *Song shi* 宋史. Taibei: Huagang chuban youxian gongsi, 1975.

Fang Rujin and Chen Guocan. *Song Xiaozong* 宋孝宗. Changchun Shi: Jilin wen shi chuban she, 1997.

Fengyun lou shumu 縫雲樓書目, Qian Qianyi 錢謙益. In Hong Mai (1994), 1827.

Gui'er sanji 貴耳三集, Zhang Duanyi 張端義. In Ting Chuan-ching, *A Compilation of Anecdotes of Sung Personalities*. Translated by Djang Chu and Jane Djang. Jamaica, NY: St. Johns University Press, 1989.

Gujin tangai 古今譚概, Feng Menglong 馮夢龍. Shenyang Shi: Chun feng wen yi chu ban she, 1989.

Guixin zashi 癸辛雜識, Zhou Mi 周密, *Qinding siku quanshu zhenben* 四庫全書珍本 edition. Taipei: Taiwan shangwu yinshuguan, 1980.

Guixin zashi 癸辛雜識, Zhou Mi 周密. Biji xiaoshuo daguan edition. Vol. 3. Taibei: Xinxing shuju, 1981.

Guo Licheng 郭立誠. "Yijian zhi yanjiu: jiantan Songdaide minsu shiliao" 夷堅志研究兼談宋代的民俗史料. *Zhonghua Wenhua Fuxing Yuekan* 中華文化復興月刊: 10/2, 37–42.

Guo Zhenyi. *Zhongguo xiaoshuo shi* 中國小說史. Hong Kong: Taixing shuju, 1961.

Guoyu 國語. Edited by Wang Yunwu. *Sibu beiyao* edition. Vol. 282.

Han shu 漢書, Ban Gu 班固, with commentary by Yan Shigu 顏師古. Beijing: Zhonghua shuju, 1962.

Han Yu quanji jiaozhu 韓愈全集校註, Han Yu 韓愈. Edited by Qu Shouyuan et al. Chengdu: Sichuan daxue chubanshe, 1996.

Hong Ye 洪業 et. al. *Yiwenzhi ershizhong zonghe yinde* 藝文志二十種綜合引得. Beiping: Yanjing University Library, 1933.

Hou Zhongyi 侯忠義. *Sui, Tang, Wudai xiaoshuo shi* 隨唐五代小說史. Zhejiang: Zhejiang guji chubanshe, 1997.

Jin shu 晉書. Edited by Yang Jialuo et al. Taipei: Dingwen shuju, 1979.

Kang Baocheng 康保成. "*Yijian Zhi* jiyi jiuze" 夷堅志輯佚九則. *Wenxian* 29 (1986): 21–24.

Kuiche zhi 睽車志, Guo Tuan 郭彖. Biji xiaoshuo daguan edition. Vol. 7. Yangzhou: 1983.

Leshan lu 樂善錄, Li Changling 李昌齡. Biji xiaoshuo daguan edition. Vol. 2. Taibei: Xinxing shuju, 1981.

Li ji 禮記. Edited by Wang Yunwu. *Sibu beiyao* edition. Vols. 7 & 8.

Li Yumin 李裕民. "*Yijian zhi* buyi sanshi ze" 夷堅志補佚三十則. *Wenxian* 文獻 46 (1990): 172–84.

Liaozhai zhiyi huijiao, huizhu, huiping ben 聊齋志異, Pu Songling 蒲松齡. Zhang Youhe. Revised edition. Shanghai: reprinted 1986.

Lienü zhuan jiaozhu 烈女傳校注, Liu Xiang 劉向. Edited by Liang Duan. Shanghai: Zhonghua shuju, 193?.

Liezi duben 列子讀本. Taipei: Sanmin shuju, 1979.

Liu Jingzhen 劉靜貞. "Songrende mingbao guan—Hong Mai *Yijian zhi* shitan" 宋人的冥報觀—洪邁夷堅志試探. *Shihuo ban yuekan* 食貨半月刊 9:2, (February 1980): Part 2, 454–60.

Liu Langming. "Hong Mai dui zhiguai xiaoshuo lilun pipingde lishixing gongxian" 洪邁對志怪小說理論批評的歷史性貢獻. In *Wuhan daxue xuebao* 武漢大學學報 (*zhexue shehui kexue ban* 哲學社會科學版) 6 (1996): 93–98.

Liu Shouhua 劉守華. "Songdaide minjian gushi jicheng 'Yijian zhi'" 宋代的民間故事集成 "夷堅志." *Gaodeng hanshou xuebao (zhexue shehui kexue ban)* 高等函授學報 (哲學社會科學版) 2 (1999).

Liu Yeqiu. *Gudian xiaoshuo luncong* 古典小說論叢. Beijing: Zhonghua shuju, 1959.

Longchuan lüezhi 龍川略志, Su Che 蘇徹. Biji xiaoshuo daguan edition. Vol. 2. Taibei: Xinxing shuju, 1981.

Lu Xun 魯迅. *Zhongguo xiaoshuo shilüe* 中國小說史略. Beijing: 1973.

———. *Zhongguo xiaoshuo shilüe* 中國小說史略. Shanghai, Renmin wenxue chuban she, 1981.

Lunheng 論衡, Wang Chong 王充. Shanghai: Shanghai renmin chubanshe, 1974.

Lunyu zhushu 論語註疏. Edited by He Yan 何彥. Taipei: Taiwan Zhonghua shuju, 1965.

Lüshi chunqiu 呂氏春秋, Lü Buwei 呂不韋. Taipei: Taiwan zhonghua shuju, 1965.

Meixi Wang xiansheng wenji 梅溪先生文集, Wang Shipeng 王十朋. The *Sibu congkan* 四部叢刊 edition, 4: 110.

Mozi 墨子. "Ming gui" 明鬼. In *Mozi*. Basheng xianshu 八聖賢書 edition, 188–205. Chongqing: Xinan shifan daxue chubanshe, 1995.

Nenggai zhai manlu 能改齋漫錄, Wu Zeng 吳曾. Biji xiaoshuo daguan edition. Vol. 8. Jiangsu: Jiangsu guangling guji keyin chuban, 1983.

Qianqing tang shumu 千頃堂書目, Huang Yuji 黃虞稷. In Hong Mai (1994), 1827.

Qidong yeyu 齊東野語, Zhou Mi 周密. Beijing: Zhonghua shuju, 1983.

Qingbo zazhi 清波雜志, Zhou Hui 周煇. Biji xiaoshuo daguan edition. Vol. 2. Jiangsu: Guangling guji keyin chuban, 1983.

Qingsuo gaoyi 青瑣高議, Liu Fu 劉斧. Beijing: Zhonghua shuju, 1959.

Ren Chongyue 任崇岳. *Song Huizong, Song Qinzong* 宋徽宗宋欽宗. Changchun shi: Jilin wenshi chuban she, 1996.

Rongzhai Suibi 容齋隨筆, Hong Mai 洪邁. Shanghai: Shanghai guji chuban she, 1978.

Sanshui xiaodu 三水小牘, Huangfu Mei 皇甫枚. Shanghai: Zhonghua shuju, 1960.

Shanhai jing 山海經, Zhang Hua 張華. Edited by Wang Yunwu. *Sibu beiyao* edition. Vol. 284.

Shanhai jing 山海經, Zhang Hua 張華. Edited by Yuan Ke 袁珂. Shanghai: Shanghai guji chuban she, 1980.

Shaoshi shanfang bicong 少室山房筆叢, Hu Yinglin 胡應麟. In Hong Mai (1994), 1825–26.

Shaoshi shanfang leigao 少室山房類稿, Hu Yinglin 胡應麟. In Hong Mai (1994), 1823–25.

Shiji 史記, Sima Qian 司馬遷. Beijing: Zhonghua shuju, 1959.

Shuowen jiezi 說文解字, Xu Shen 許慎. Edited by Wang Yunwu. *Sibu beiyao* edition. Vol. 81.

Shuowen jiezi 說文解字, Xu Shen 許慎. Beijing: Zhonghua shuju, 1965.

Sichao wenjian lu 四朝聞見錄, Ye Shaoweng 葉紹翁. Beijing: Zhonghua shu ju, 1989.

Siku quanshu zong mu 四庫全書總目. Edited by Ji Yun 紀昀 et al. Taipei: Yiwen yinshu guan, 19--.

Song huiyao jigao 宋會要集稿. Edited by Xu Song 徐松. Taipei: Xinwenfeng chuban gongsi, 1976.

Songmo jiwen 松漠記聞, Hong Hao 洪皓. Edited by Wang Yunwu. Taipei: Shangwu yinshuguan, 1979.

Song shi 宋史. Edited by Tuo Tuo 脫脫 et al. Beijing: Zhonghua shuju, 1977.

Songshi yiwen zhi bu 宋史藝文志補, Ni Can 倪燦. In Hong Mai (1994), 1828.

Soushen ji 搜神記, Gan Bao 干寶. Beijing: Zhonghua shuju, 1979.

Taiping guangji 太平廣記. Edited by Li Fang 李昉 et al. Shanghai: Shanghai guji chuban she, 1990.

Taiping guangji 太平廣記. Edited by Li Fang 李昉 et al. Gao Guang et al. Revised edition. Tianjin: Tianjin guji chuban she, 1994.

Taiping yülan 太平御覽. Edited by Li Fang 李昉 et al. Beijing : Zhonghua shuju, 1960.

Tan Qixiang 譚其驤 et al., eds. *Zhongguo lishi ditu ji* 中國歷史地圖集. Vol. 6. Shanghai: Cartographic Publishing House, 1982.

Terachi Jun 寺地遵, Liu Jingzhen 劉靜貞 et al., trans. *Nansong chuqi zhengzhishi yanjiu* 南宋初期政治史研究. Taipei: Daohe chubanshe, 1995.

Ting Chuan-ching 丁傳靖. *Songren yishi huibian* 宋人軼事彙編. Beijing: Zhonghua Shuju, 1981.

Waiguo yuyan xueyuan 外國語言學院 et al., eds. *A Chinese-English Dictionary.* Beijing: Shangwu chubanshe, 1979.

Wang Hsiu-huei 王秀惠. "Guji yu dian'nao fenxi yunyong—yi *Yijian Zhi* wei li" 古籍與電腦分析運用—以夷堅志爲例. *Hanxue yanjiu tongxun* 漢學研究通訊 14: 2: 54 (June 1995): 83–87.

———. "Yijian Zhi yishi jibu" 夷堅志佚事輯補. *Hanxue yanjiu* 漢學研究 7: 1 (June 1989b): 163–83.

Wang Nianshuang 王年雙. *Hong Mai shengping ji qi Yijian zhi zhi yanjiu* 洪邁生平及其夷堅志之研究. Unpublished Ph.D. dissertation. Taipei: Chengche University, 1988.

Wang Teh-yi 王德毅. "Hung Jung-chai hsien-sheng nien-p'u" 洪容齋先生年譜. In *Songshi yanjiu ji.* Vol. 2, 405–74. Taipei: Zhonghua congshu weiyuanhui, 1964. First appeared *Yu-shih hsüeh-pao* 3.2 (April 1961): 1–63.

Wang Zhizhong 王枝忠, Okamoto Fujiaki 岡本不二明, trans. "Kuiche zhi yu Yijian zhi: kexue yu zhiguai zhiyi" 暌車志與夷堅志—科學與志怪之一. *Gansu shehui kexue* 甘肅社會科學 6 (1995): 86–90.

Wenxian tongkao 文獻通考, Ma Duanlin 馬端臨. Taibei: Xinxing shuju faxing, 1962.

Wenxian tongkao 文獻通考. In Hong Mai (1994), 1822.

Wenxin diaolong 文心雕龍. Edited by Liu Xie, Huang Shulin et al. *Zengding wenxin diaolong jiaozhu.* Beijing: zhonghua shuju, 2000.

Xiao Tong, ed. *Wen xuan.* Beijing: Zhonghua shuju, 1977.

Xiao Xiangkai 蕭相愷. *Song Yuan xiaoshuo shi* 宋元小說史. Zhejiang: Zhejiang guji chubanshe, 1997.

Shenxian zhuan 神仙傳, Ge Hong 葛洪. Taibei: Yiwen, 1967.

Xinbian zuiweng tanlu 新編醉翁談錄, Luo Ye 羅燁. In *Zhongguo wenxue cankao ziliao congshu* 中國文學參考資料叢書. Shanghai: Gudian wenxue, 1957.

Xin Wudai shi 新五代史, Ou-Yang Xiu 歐陽修. Taibei: Taiwan Zhonghua shuju, 1965.

Yi Jian Zhi 夷堅志, Hong Mai 洪邁. Edited by He Zhuo. Taipei: Mingwen shuju, 1994.

Yi Jian Zhi 夷堅志, Hong Mai 洪邁. *Wanwei biecang ben* 宛委別藏本. Edited by Ruan Yuan. Manuscript, Qing (1644–1911). In the collection of the Imperial Palace Museum Library, Taipei.

Yi Jian Zhi 夷堅志, Hong Mai 洪邁. Edited by Shen Tianyou. Yuan Dynasty (year uncertain). In the Seikadō Bunkō collection, Tokyo.

Yi Jian Zhi 夷堅志, Hong Mai 洪邁. Edited by Yan Yuanzhao. Manuscript, 1804. In the collection of the National Library, Taipei.

Yiyun shushe Songben Shumu 藝芸書舍宋本目錄, Wang Shizhong 汪士鐘. In Hong Mai (1994), 1830.

Yongle dadian. Beijing: Zhonghua shuju, 1986.

Yongzhuang Xiaopin 湧幢小品, Zhu Guozhen 朱國楨. In Hong Mai (1994), 1826.

Youming lu 幽明錄, Liu Yiqing 劉義卿. Beijing: Wenhua yishu chuban she, 1988.

Youyang zazu, 幽陽雜俎, Duan Chengshi 段成式. Beijing: Zhonghua shuju, 1981.

Yu Beishan 于北山. *Fan Chengda nianpu* 范成大年譜. Shanghai: Shanghai guji chubanshe, 1987.

Zhang Zhuping 張祝平. "Wenyan xiaoshuo pingdiande yaoji; timing Zhong Xing ping *Xinding zengbu Yijian zhi* pingyi" 文言小說評點的要籍: 題名鐘惺評 "新訂增補夷堅志" 評議 *Nantong shizhuan xuebao (shehui kexu ban)* 南通師專學報 (社會科學版). 13 (1997): 3 25.

———. "Fenlei *Yijian Zhi* yanjiu" 分類夷堅志研究. *Huadong Shifan Daxue xuebao; zhexue shehui kexue ban* 華東師範大學學報: 哲學社會科學版, 3 (1997): 80–86.

———. "Fan Chengda *Xia Furen* gushi yuanmao ji qi liubian kao" 范成大俠夫人故事原貌及其流變考. *Wenxue yichan* 文學遺產 4 (1997): 106–9.

———. "Zhu Yunming chaoben *Yijian ding zhi* dui jinben *Yijian yi zhi* de jiaobu 祝允明抄本夷堅丁志對今本夷堅乙志的較补," *Wenxian* 文獻 3 (2003): 140–50.

Zhaode xiansheng junzhai dushu zhi 昭德先生郡齋讀書志, Chao Gongwu 晁公武. *Siku quanshu* electronic version.

Zhizhai Shulu Jieti 直齋書錄解題, Chen Zhensun 陳振孫. Edited by Wang Yunwu. *Siku quanshu zhenben* edition. Taipei: Taiwan shangwu yinshuguan, 1980.

"Zhizhai shulu jieti" 直齋書錄解題, Chen Zhensun 陳振孫. In Hong Mai (1994), 1821–22.

Zhuangzi 莊子, Basheng xianshu 八聖賢書 edition. Chongqing: Xinan shifan daxue chubanshe, 1995.

Zhuangzi jinzhu jinyi 庄子今注今譯. Edited by Chen Guying. Beijing: Zhonghua shuju, 1983.

Zhuzi yulei 朱子語類, Zhu Xi 朱熹. Edited by Li Jingde. Taipei: Zhengzhong shuju, reprinted 1973.

JAPANESE SOURCES

Fukuda Chikashi 福田知可志. *"Ikenshi* jijo o meguru mondai ten" 夷堅志自序をめぐる問題てん. *Chūgoku Gakushi: Osaka shiritsu daigaku chūbun gakkai* 中国学志 大阪市立大学中文学会 11 (2000): 113–38.

Okamoto Fujiaki 岡本不二明. "Kuiche zhi yu Yijian Zhi; kexue yu zhiguai zhiyi" 睽車志" 與 "夷堅志"—"科學與志怪" 之一. Translated by Wang Zhizhong and Lu Zhonghui. *Gansu shehui kexue* 甘肅省社會科學 6 (1995): 88–90. First appeared in Kagoshima Kenritsu Tanki Daigaku jinbun gakkai lonshu *Jinbun* 鹿兒島縣立短期大學人文学会論集 "人文" 13 (June 1989).

———. *"Yikenshi* kōshi nijū ken no seiritsu katei ni tsuite" 夷堅志甲志二十卷の成立課題について. *Okayama Daigaku bungakubu kiyō* 岡山大学文学部紀要 21 (1994): 43–52.

Ōtsuka Hidetaka 大塚高秀. "Kō Mai to *Ikenshi*—rekishi to genjitsu no hazama nite" 洪邁と夷堅志—歷史と現實の狹閒にて *Tōdai chutetsubun gakkaihō* 當代中哲文学会報 5 (1980): 75–96.

Ōtagi Matsuo 愛宕松男. "Kō Mai *Ikenshi* itsubun shui" 洪邁夷堅志逸文拾遺. *Bunka* 文化 29, no. 3 (1965): 472–79.

Shimura Ryoji 志村良治. "Shōsetsu no hatsusei" 小說の發生. In *Chūgoku bunka sōsho* 中国文化叢書 5: *Bungakushi* 文学史. Edited by Suzuki Shōji 鈴木修次, Takagi Masakazu 高木正一, and Maeno Naoaki 前野直彬, 97–107. Tokyo: Taishūkan shoten, 1967.

Suzuki Kiyoshi 鈴木靖. "Kō Kō to Kō Mai" 洪皓と洪邁. *Hosei daigaku kyoyōbu kiyō jimbun kagakuhen* 法制大学教養部紀要人文科学篇 74 (1990), 1–17.

Takeda Akira 竹田晃. "Shikai, denki" 志怪，傳奇. *Chūgoku bunka sōsho* 中國文化叢書 4: *Bungaku gairon* 文学概論. Edited by Suzuki Shōji 鈴木修次, Takagi Masakazu 高木正一, and Maeno Naoaki 前野直彬, 215–28. Tokyo: Taishūkan shoten, 1967.

———. *Chūgoku no setsuwa to koshōsetsu* 中国の說話と古小說. Tokyo: Daizō shōin, 1992.

WESTERN SOURCES

Analects of Confucius. Translated by D. C. Lau. Harmondsworth, United Kingdom: Penguin, 1979.

"The Analects." In *The Chinese Classics*. Vol. 1. Translated by James Legge. Oxford: Oxford University Press, 1935. Reprinted edition, Taipei: Southern Materials Center, 1972.

The Analects. Translated by Arthur Waley. London: Unwin & Allen, 1938. Reprinted 1971.

Attali, Jacques. *Noise: The Political Economy of Music*. Translated by Brian Massumi. Minneapolis: University of Minnesota Press, 1987.

Auerbach, Erich. "Figura." In *Scenes from the Drama of European Literature*. Gloucester, MA: Peter Smith, 1973.

Bakhtin, M. M. *Speech Genres and Other Late Essays*. Translated by Vern W. McGee. Austin: University of Texas Press, 1986.

———, Bakhtin, M. M., and N. Medvedev. *The Formal Method in Literary Scholarship; A Critical Introduction to Sociological Poetics*. Translated by Albert J. Werle. Baltimore: John Hopkins University Press, 1978.

Beasley, W.G., and E.G. Pulleyblank. *Historians of China and Japan*. London: Oxford University Press, 1961.

Birch, Cyril. *Studies in Chinese Literary Genres*. Berkley: University of California Press, 1974.

Boltz, Judith M. "Not by the Seal of Office Alone: New Weapons in Battle with the Supernatural." Edited by Patricia Buckley Ebrey and Peter N. Gregory. *Religion and Society in T'ang and Sung China*, 241–305. Honolulu: University of Hawaii Press, 1993.

Book of Lieh-tzu. Translated by A. C. Graham. London: J. Murray, 1960.

Briggs, Charles L., and Richard Baumann. "Genre, Intertextuality and Social Power." In *Journal of Linguistic Anthropology* 2 (1992): 131–72.

Campany, Robert Ford. *Strange Writing; Anomaly Accounts in Early Medieval China*. Albany: State University of New York Press, 1996.

Chan, Leo Tak-hung. *The Discourse on Foxes and Ghosts: Ji Yun and Eighteenth-Century Literati Storytelling*. Honolulu: University of Hawaii Press, 1998.

Chan, Wing-tsit. *Neo-Confucian Terms Explained (Pei-hsi tzu-i) by Chen Chun 1159–1223*. New York: Columbia University Press, 1986.

Chang Fu-jui 張復蕊. *I-chien chih t'ung chien* 夷堅志通檢. Taipei: Taiwan xuesheng shuju, 1976.

———. "Hong Hao;" "Hong Gua;" "Hong Mai" (biographies of). In Herbert Franke, ed. *Sung Biographies*, 464–78.

———. "I-chien chih." In Yves Hervouet. *A Sung Bibliography*, 344–45.

———. "Les themes dans le *Yi-kien–tche*." *Cina* 8 (1964): 51–55.

———. "Le *Yi-kien–tche* et la société des Song." *Journal Asiatique* 256 (1968): 55–93.

———. "L'influence du *Yi-kien–tche* sur les oeuvres literaires." In *Études d'histoire et de littérature Chinoises offertes au Professeur Jaroslav Prusek*. Edited by Yves Hervouet. Paris: 1976, 51–61.

———. *La vie et L'oeuvre de Hung Mai (1123–1202)*. Unpublished Ph.D. dissertation, University of Paris V11: 1971.

Chang, Han-liang. "Towards a Structural Generic Theory of Tang *Ch'uan-chi*." In John J. Deeney. *Chinese-Western Comparative Literature Theory and Strategy*. Hong Kong: Chinese University Press, 1980.

Chia, Lucille. *Printing for Profit: The Commercial Publishers of Jianyang, Fujian 11ᵗʰ–17ᵗʰ Centuries*. Cambridge, MA: Harvard-Yenching, 2002.

Chuang tzu: Basic Writings. Translated by Burton Watson. New York: Columbia University Press, 1964.

Chuang tzu: The Inner Chapters and Other Writings from the Book of Chuang-tzu. Translated by A. C. Graham. London: Allen and Unwin, 1981.

Dawson, Raymond. *The Legacy of China*. Oxford: Clarendon University Press, 1964.

de Bary, Theodore, ed. *Sources of Chinese Tradition*. New York: Columbia University Press, 1960.

de Groot, J. J. M. *The Religious System of China*. Taipei: Literature House, 1964.

DeWoskin, Kenneth. "The Six Dynasties *Zhiguai* and the Birth of Fiction." In Andrew Plaks, ed. *Chinese Narrative: Critical and Theoretical Essays*. Princeton: Princeton University Press, 1977.

Davis, Edward. *Society and the Supernatural in Song China*. Honolulu: University of Hawaii Press, 2001.

Dudbridge, Glen. *Religious Experience and Lay Society in Tang China; a Reading of Dai Fu's Kuang-i chi*. Cambridge: Cambridge University Press, 1995.

Duke, Michael. *Lu You*. Boston: Twayne, 1977.

Ebrey, Patricia Buckley. *The Inner Quarters: Marriage and the Lives of Chinese Women in the Sung Period*. Berkley: University of California Press, 1993.

Ebrey, Patricia Buckley and Peter N. Gregory, eds. *Religion and Society in Tang and Sung China*. Hawaii: University of Hawaii Press, 1993.

Elvin, Mark. "The Man Who Saw Dragons: Science and Styles of Thinking in Xie Zhaozhe's Fivefold Miscellany." *Journal of the Oriental Society of Australia* (Sydney) 25–26 (1993–1994): 1–41.

Emerson, Caryl, and Michael Holquist. Introduction to Bakhtin's *Speech Genres and Other Late Essays*. Austin: University of Texas Press, 1986.

Eugene Eoyang. "A Taste for Apricots." In Andrew Plaks, ed. *Chinese Narrative: Critical and Theoretical Essays*. Princeton: Princeton University Press, 1977.

Fairbank, John K. *Chinese Thought and Institutions*. Chicago: University of Chicago Press, 1957.

Fletcher, Angus. *Allegory, the Theory of a Symbolic Mode*. Ithaca, NY: Cornell University Press, 1964.

Foley, William H. *Anthropological Linguistics: An Introduction*. Oxford: Blackwell Publishers, 1997.

Fong, Wen C. *Beyond Representation: Chinese Painting and Calligraphy 8th–14th Century*. New York: Metropolitan Museum of Art; New Haven: Yale University Press, 1992.

Fung Yu Lan. *A History of Chinese Philosophy*. Edited by Derk Bodde. New York: Mac-Millan, 1956.

Franke, Herbert. "Some Remarks on the Interpretation of Chinese Dynastic Histories." *Oriens* 3 (1950): 113–122.

———. "Some Aspects of Chinese Private Historiography." In Beasley and Pullyblank, *Historians of China and Japan*. London: Oxford University Press, 1961.

———, ed. *Sung Biographies*. Wiesbaden: Steiner, 1976.

Gardner, Charles S. *Chinese Traditional Historiography*. Cambridge, MA: Harvard University Press, 1961.

Gernet, Jacques. *Daily Life in China on the Eve of the Mongol Invasion 1250–1276*. Translated by H. M. Wright. Stanford: Stanford University Press, 1962.

Goffman, Erving. *Frame Analysis: An Essay on the Organization of Experience*. Cambridge, MA: Harvard University Press, 1974.

Goody, Jack. *The Interface between the Written and the Oral*. Cambridge: Cambridge University Press, 1987.

Graham, A. C. *Chuang Tzu: The Inner Chapters and Other Writings from the Book of Chuang-Tzu*. London: Allen & Unwin, 1981.

Hanan, Patrick. *The Chinese Vernacular Story*. Cambridge, MA: Harvard University Press, 1981.

Hanks, William F. "Discourse Genres in a Theory of Practice." *American Ethnologist* (1987) 14: 668–92

Hansen, Valerie. *Changing Gods in Medieval China 1127–1276*. Princeton, NJ: Princeton University Press, 1990.

Hartman, Charles. "Allegory." In William Nienhauser Jr. *The Indiana Companion to Chinese Literature*, 946–49. Bloomington, IN: Indiana University Press, 1986.

Hervouet, Yves, ed. *A Sung Bibliography*. Hong Kong: Chinese University Press, 1978.

Huntington, Rania. "The Supernatural." In Victor Mair, ed. *The Columbia History of Chinese Literature*, 110–11. New York: Columbia University Press, 2001.

———. *Alien Kind: Foxes and Late Imperial Chinese Narrative*. Cambridge, MA: Harvard University Asia Center, 2003.

Hymes, Robert. *Way and Byway: Taoism, Local Religion, and Models of Diversity in Sung and Modern China*. Berkeley and Los Angeles: University of California Press, 2002.

Inglis, Alister. *Hong Mai's Yijian zhi and its Song Dynasty Context*. Unpublished Ph.D. dissertation. University of Melbourne, 2002.

———. "Informants of the *Yijian zhi*." *Journal of Sung-Yuan Studies* (2002): 83–125.

———. "Two Stories from *Yijian zhi*." *Renditions* 57 (2002): 28–34.

Iser, Wolfgang. *The Implied Reader: Patterns of Communication in Prose Fiction from Bunyan to Beckett*. Baltimore: John Hopkins University Press, 1974.

———. *The Act of Reading: A Theory of Aesthetic Response*. Baltimore: John Hopkins University Press, 1978.

———. *Prospecting: From Reader Response to Literary Anthropology*. Baltimore: John Hopkins University Press, 1989.

Jauss, Hans Robert. *Aesthetic Experience and Literary Hermeneutics*. Minneapolis: University of Minnesota Press, 1982.

Jung, Carl Gustav. "The Psychological Foundations of Belief in Spirits." In *Collected Works*, Vol. 8, 301–18. New York: Pantheon, 1960. Translated from "Die psychologischen Grundlagen des Geisterglaubens." In *Über psychische Energetik und das Wesender der Träume*. Zurich: Rascher, 1948.

Kao, Karl S. Y., ed. *Classical Chinese Tales of the Supernatural and the Fantastic*. Bloomington, IN: Indiana University Press, 1985.

———. "Aspects of Derivation in Chinese Narrative." *Chinese Literature: Essays, Articles and Reviews* 7 (1985): 1–36.

Katz, Paul. *Images of the Imortal: The Cult of Lü Dongbin at the Palace of Eternal Joy.* Honolulu: Hawaii University Press, 1999.

Kerr, Katherine. "*Yijianzhi*: A Didactic Diversion." *Papers on Far Eastern History* 35 (1987): 79–88.

———. *The* Yijian Zhi: *An Alternate Perspective.* Unpublished Ph.D. dissertation. University of Sydney: 1998.

Lau, Joseph S. M., and S. M. Ma. *Traditional Chinese Stories: Themes and Variations.* New York: Columbia University Press, 1978.

Liu, James T. C. *China Turning Inwards: Intellectual-Political Changes in the Early Twelfth Century.* Cambridge, MA: Council on East Asian Studies, 1988.

Lo, Winston. *An Introduction to the Civil Service of Sung China.* Honolulu: University of Hawaii Press, 1987.

Lu, Sheldon. *From Historicity to Fictionality; the Chinese Poetics of Narrative.* Stanford, CA: Stanford University Press, 1994.

Lu Xun. *A Brief History of Chinese Fiction.* Translated by Yang Hsien-yi and Gladys Yang. Peking: Foreign Languages Press, 1959.

Ma, Y. M. "Pi-chi." In William Nienhauser Jr. *The Indiana Companion to Traditional Chinese Literature.* Second revised edition. Taipei: SMC Publishing, 1986.

Ma, Y. M., and Joseph S. M. Lau. *Traditional Chinese Stories: Themes and Variations.* New York: Columbia University Press, 1978.

Mair, Victor, ed. *The Columbia History of Chinese Literature.* New York: Columbia University Press, 2001.

Medin, Douglas L., and Scott Atran. *Folkbiology.* Cambridge, MA: MIT Press, 1999.

Mengzi. Translated by D. C. Lau. Harmondsworth, UK: Penguin, 1970.

Müller, Max. *The Sacred Books of the East.* Vol. 39. London: Oxford University Press, reprinted 1927.

Nienhauser, William H. Jr. *The Indiana Companion to Traditional Chinese Literature.* Second revised edition. Taipei: SMC Publishing, 1986.

———. "Creativity and Storytelling in the *Ch'uan-ch'i*: Shen Ya-chih's T'ang Tales." *Chinese Literature: Essays, Articles and Reviews* (1998): 31–70.

Penny, Benjamin. *Early Daoist Biography: A Study of the Shenxian Zhuan.* Unpublished Ph.D. dissertation. Australian National University, 1993.

Plaks, Andrew, ed. *Chinese Narrative: Critical and Theoretical Essays.* Princeton: Princeton University Press, 1977.

———. *Archetype and Allegory in the* Dream of the Red Chamber. Princeton: Princeton University Press, 1976.

Propp, V. *Morphology of the Folktale.* Translated by Laurence Scott. Austin: University of Texas Press, 1968.

Prusek, Jaroslav. "Urban Centers: Cradle of Popular Fiction." In Cyril Birch, ed. *Studies in Chinese Literary Genres,* 259–98. Berkley: University of California Press, 1974.

Rawski, Evelyn. *Education and Popular Literacy in Ch'ing China.* Ann Arbor, MI: University of Michigan Press, 1979.

Reed, Carrie. "Motivation and Meaning of a 'Hodge-Podge': Duan Chengshi's *Youyang Zazu*." *Journal of the American Oriental Society* 123.1 (2003): 121–45.

———. *A Tang Miscellany: An Introduction to the Youyang zazu*. New York: Peter Lang, 2003.

Rolston, David. *Traditional Chinese Fiction and Fiction Commentary: Reading and Writing between the Lines*. Stanford, CA: Stanford University Press, 1997.

Schmidt, J. D. *Stone Lake: The Poetry of Fan Chengda (1126–1193)*. Cambridge and New York: Cambridge University Press, 1992.

Scholes, Robert. *Elements of Fiction*. New York: Oxford University Press, 1968.

Scholes, Robert, and Kellogg. *The Nature of Narrative*. New York: Oxford University Press, 1968.

Sinfield, Alan. *Faultlines: Cultural Materialism and the Politics of Dissident Reading*. Oxford: Oxford University Press, 1992.

ter Haar, Barend. "Newly Recovered Anecdotes from Hong Mai's (1123–1202) *Yijian Zhi*." *Journal of Sung-Yuan Studies* 23 (1993): 19–41.

Ting Chuan-ching. *A Compilation of Anecdotes of Sung Personalities*. Translated by Djang Chu and Jane Djang. Jamaica, NY: St. John's University Press, 1989.

Tsiperovitch, Tzetan. "Qingsuo gaoyi." In Yves Hervouet, ed. *A Sung Bibliography*. Hong Kong: Chinese University Press, 1978.

Twitchett, D. C. "Chinese Biographical Writing." In Beasley and Pulleyblank. *Historians of China and Japan*. Oxford: 1961.

Vansina, Jan. *Oral Tradition as History*. Madison, WI: University of Wisconsin Press, 1985.

Wang Hsiu-huei 王秀惠. "Vingt-sept Recits Retrouves du *Yijian Zhi*." *T'oung Pao* 75 (1989a): 191–207.

Wang, John C. Y. "Early Chinese Narrative: The *Tso-chuan* as an Example." In Andrew Plaks, ed. *Chinese Narrative: Critical and Theoretical Essays*, 3–20. Princeton: Princeton University Press, 1977.

Watson, Burton. *Su Tung-p'o: Selections from a Sung Dynasty Poet*. New York, Columbia University Press, 1965.

Wilkinson, Endymion. *The History of Imperial China; a Research Guide*. Cambridge, MA: 1974.

Yang Lien-sheng. "The Concept of *Pao* as a Basis for Social Relations in China." In *Chinese Thought and Institutions*, 291–309. Edited by John K. Fairbank. Chicago: University of Chicago Press, 1957.

Yoshikawa, Kōjirō. *Five Hundred Years of Chinese Poetry 1150–1650*. Princeton, NJ: Princeton University Press, 1989.

Yu, Anthony C. "'Rest, Rest, Perturbed Spirit!' Ghosts in Traditional Chinese Fiction." *Harvard Journal of Asiatic Studies* 47, no. 2 (Dec. 1987): 397–434.

Yu, Pauline. *The Reading of Imagery in the Chinese Poetic Tradition*. Princeton, NJ: Princeton University Press, 1987.

Zeitlin, Judith T. *Historian of the Strange—Pu Songling and the Chinese Classical Tale*. Stanford, CA: Stanford University Press, 1993.

Index